To MAT
BEST WISHES!

CONQUERING THE POLITICAL DIVIDE

How the Constitution Can Heal
Our Polarized Nation

Eric A. Beck (signature)

ERIC A. BECK

AUTHOR ACADEMY elite

Conquering the Political Divide
How the Constitution Can Heal Our Polarized Nation

Copyright © 2019 by Eric A. Beck
All rights reserved.
Printed in the United States of America
Published by Author Academy Elite
P.O. Box 43, Powell, OH 43035
www.AuthorAcademyElite.com

Paperback: 978-1-64085-106-1
Hardback: 978-1-64085-107-8
E-book: 978-1-64085-108-5

Library of Congress Control Number: 2017952725

Cover Design by:
Beth Carroll Leoni
JBCL2006@yahoo.com

First Edition

To Mom and Dad.
You gave me everything.

CONTENTS

PART ONE
Competing Visions of the American Dream

PART TWO
Arguments on Economic Policy

PART THREE
Arguments on Health-Care Policy

PART FOUR
Arguments on Social Policy

FOREWORD

For American students of political science and public affairs, an understanding of the United States Constitution sits front and center as a foundational element of their education. But the Constitution is not just for students. Every American should acquire an understanding of the ideas and ideals embodied in the Constitution to fully and competently participate as citizens of the United States. That is because U.S. citizenship is not just a badge of honor; citizenship is a political office with obligations and responsibilities.[1] As such, every citizen has a responsibility to learn about what the Constitution is, the role it defines for the federal and state governments, and the balance it creates between individual freedom and equality.

In *Conquering the Political Divide*, I have tried to make the case for why all Americans (including those serving in the judiciary) should interpret the Constitution based on the original intent of its Framers. This intent is reflected in constitutional principles inherent in our unique form of representative government, principles that have formed a basis for national unity since our country's founding. I contrast these principles with those advocated by the progressive Left to explain why their point of view is undermining both the Constitution and the Founders' vision of the American Dream. Such contrast will allow the reader to gain a deeper understanding of what makes America exceptional, even when compared to other democracies around the world.

Whether you agree or disagree with my personal view of constitutional jurisprudence, I believe *Conquering the Political Divide* will make the reader question his or her own assumptions about the morality and effectiveness of public policy. I have encouraged such questioning by including narratives on the economy, health care, and social issues that are fact-based and sometimes provocative, but they are always focused on defending public policies that are constitutionally consistent. Therefore, this text creates an opportunity for the reader to consider how "originalists" think about public policy in deference to what the Constitution deems permissible and what is also economically realistic. It is this type of critical thinking about public policy that our nation needs more of today, not less.

Thomas Jefferson once wrote about the importance of educating the average citizen on civic affairs to protect our unique form of representative government. He wrote, "I know no safe depository of the ultimate powers of the society but the people themselves; and if we think them not enlightened enough to exercise their control with a wholesome discretion, the remedy is not to take it from them but to inform their discretion by education. This is the true corrective of abuses of constitutional power."[2] In *Conquering the Political Divide*, I have tried to take Jefferson's admonition to heart by presenting a defense of the Constitution and its founding principles as a basis for rallying our nation toward political unity. I expect that any student of the Constitution will find my defense both challenging and rewarding. Likewise, for those citizens simply looking for an informed perspective on how a commitment to the Constitution can overcome the political divide we face in America today, I believe this book is an important and valuable read. Enjoy.

Eric A. Beck
Editor-In-Chief
Free Nation Media LLC

Greenville, South Carolina
January 2019

INTRODUCTION

WHY AMERICA IS A DIVIDED NATION

America is once again a divided nation.

At several points in our nation's history, just as we are today, America has found itself at a crossroads divided by our core values and political interests. We first came to such a point in 1787 when the American colonies had to decide whether to remain a loosely affiliated group of independent states under the Articles of Confederation, or to become a single republic under a constitution. This decision split the colonies and its citizens into two camps—the Federalists and Anti-Federalists. Each camp engaged in a tough and sometimes strident campaign to press their case for America's future form of government. The Anti-Federalists were opposed to creating an empowered federal government, fearing that it would usurp state sovereignty. The Federalists ultimately prevailed because they were better organized, they articulately defended their ideas by publishing the Federalist Papers, and they presented a work product in a draft Constitution around which they could rally public support for a single republic.[3]

Ultimately, it was ratification of the U.S. Constitution in 1788, including the ideas and ideals it embodied, that became the basis for consensus that overcame the political divide of that day. Although the issue of slavery had yet to be resolved, this consensus was expanded three years later in 1791 as part of the Massachusetts Compromise through final ratification of the Bill of Rights. The foundation for a United States of America was then set, thereby establishing a nation that guaranteed individual rights (albeit at the time to white men only) while limiting the powers of the federal government.

Yet during the subsequent seventy years leading up to the election of 1860, our nation remained bitterly divided over the issue of slavery, an institution that would later become one of several major catalysts for the American Civil War. With the benefit of hindsight, we can now see with greater clarity that the institution of slavery did not live up to the ideas and ideals expressed in the Declaration of Independence, the Constitution, or the Bill of Rights: otherwise known as America's "Founding Documents."

However, in the aftermath of the Civil War, one might ask what was the motivating force that allowed our nation to heal from the detriment of slavery, eventually leading to the strengthening of our nation's character through its abolition. Some might suggest that it was the end of the war itself, and specifically victory by the Union that opposed slavery, that helped heal the nation during Reconstruction. However, the war's end did little to deliver social and economic justice for newly enfranchised black Americans. In fact, one might say it simply changed the nature of enslavement for blacks with the rise of groups like the Ku Klux Klan dedicated to maintaining their second-class citizenship.

Ultimately it was an appeal to the ideas and ideals embodied in our Founding Documents that became the authentic basis for healing our nation, even before the Civil War had ended. President Lincoln himself set the tone for this healing process during his Gettysburg Address, reminding us with his brief but impassioned words about the ideals reflected in the both the Declaration of Independence and preamble to the Constitution:

> Four score and seven years ago our fathers brought forth on this continent a new nation, conceived in liberty and dedicated to the proposition that all men are created equal. . . It is rather for us to be here dedicated to the great task remaining before us—that from these honored dead we take increased devotion to that cause for which they gave the last full measure of devotion—that we here highly resolve that these dead shall

not have died in vain—that this nation, under God, shall have a new birth of freedom—and that government of the people, by the people, for the people, shall not perish from the earth.

—President Abraham Lincoln, the Gettysburg Address, 1863.

This call for recommitment to all men being "equal" and a "new birth of freedom" was no less than a call for a renewed pledge to the ideals not yet achieved by our constitutional republic. Lincoln knew that recommitment to these ideals was ultimately the only true basis for binding up the nation's wounds. He also knew that attempts to subvert individual freedom through slavery were inconsistent with the "Laws of Nature and Nature's God."[4]

The Reverend Dr. Martin Luther King Jr. would express similar sentiments during the 1950s and 1960s as he pressed for black civil rights, working to fulfill the objectives of the abolitionist movement that began during the pre-Civil War era. Dr. King's most eloquent expression of these sentiments came during his August 1963 "I Have a Dream" speech in Washington DC. King spoke metaphorically about a promised inheritance of inalienable rights granted by the Founding Documents, rights inherited by people of all colors and creeds. He clearly understood that the moral underpinning of our constitutional republic, founded on Judeo-Christian ethics, was the key to awakening the American consciousness about the evils of segregation and the prejudicial attitudes many whites held at that time toward blacks. And awaken the American public he did, as Dr. King's speech became a key catalyst in building public support for passage of the Civil Rights Act of 1964 and Voting Rights Act of 1965. These watershed pieces of legislation expanded the promise of equal rights to all citizens, thereby advancing the ability of minorities to share more fully in the American Dream.

At each of these three pivotal junctures in American history our nation was deeply divided in terms of its core values and political interests. However, at each juncture there was also a call by national leaders of the day to return to the ideas and ideals embodied in the Founding Documents to reunite our nation politically, economically and culturally.

America is now at another pivotal juncture where we must once again turn to the Founding Documents to serve as the basis for healing our divided nation. However, the divide we face today is not about race, gender, or voting rights, but rather it is about the Constitution itself and what it represents about the role of government in our lives.

The pivotal event that best underscores America's modern-day political divide was the election of Barack Obama as president of the United States in 2008. Then Senator Obama, a liberal progressive, offered the American people a candidacy of "hope and change" that was little defined in terms of concrete policy. One might ask why Americans would be so willing to elect a presidential candidate whose prior qualifications included no executive experience, an undistinguished voting record in the U.S. Senate, and a network of supporters and associates that included many whose political philosophy could be fairly described as radical and economically socialist. Senator Obama gave us a clue to the answer in his autobiography called *The Audacity of Hope* where he said, "I serve as a blank screen on which people of vastly different political stripes project their own views."[5] If this is true, then this is a clear sign that the Center-Right American electorate did not fully grasp the nature of Mr. Obama's progressive ideology, or its political and economic implications.

What the presidential candidacy of Barack Obama did offer the electorate was an opportunity to change political direction away from two unpopular wars in Iraq and Afghanistan, and from an economic crisis whose root cause the American people did not fully understand. More importantly, his election offered the average citizen a way to make a personal statement about how far our nation had come in terms of race relations by electing America's first black president. Such a statement should be a cause for celebration given our nation's history. However, making this statement came at the price of ignoring Mr. Obama's progressive values and his stated intention to "fundamentally transform America" in ways that sought to undermine the Constitution.

As we have seen during his eight years in office, President Obama's vision for America did little to close our nation's political divide. This was not an accident. As a subscriber to modern-day progressive ideology, Mr. Obama viewed the Constitution as a frivolous annoyance, something that impeded his ability to transform our nation in ways that are consistent with his radical brand of liberalism. While the Constitution embodies a standard of individual rights and limited government, Mr. Obama preferred to speak of "collective salvation."[6] While he periodically reminded us that America does not guarantee equal outcomes, he worked to undermine private property rights through a plethora of wealth transfer initiatives that included his signature health-care reform program: The Patient Protection and Affordable Care Act (aka the "Affordable Care Act or "Obamacare"). He chose to distract Americans from the ideas and ideals of the Constitution as a basis for healing, and instead preferred to preach middle-class victimiza-tion.[7] He decried the "rugged individualism"[8] of entrepreneurs, who are the only real hope for middle-class advancement, suggesting that business owners owed their success to government.[9] He also mocked the concerns of traditional Americans by saying that they "they cling to guns or religion or antipathy toward people who aren't like them, or anti-immigrant sentiment, or anti-trade sentiment as a way to explain their frustrations."[10] It is for these reasons, and others reflected in his progressive thinking, that President Obama left office with America remaining a divided nation.

This book was written to empower Americans with a deeper understanding of the failings and dangers of progressive ide-ology. Likewise, this book was written to remind the reader about the unique benefits of America's constitutional republic that has sustained and advanced our nation for more than two hundred years. As such, it will not present a lengthy history of the Progressive movement, as other authors have covered such material in separate texts. This book will focus primarily on how modern-day progressive ideology has influenced current political debate. It will also show how progressive ideology lacks respect for the Constitution as the standard by which we restrain the federal government and secure individual rights.

Further, this book will arm the reader with a series of cred-ible arguments that refute the core ideology of modern-day progressivism; that ideology being that a bigger and more intrusive government is required to advance social and economic justice. It will also identify five strategies progressives use to build their political base and discuss why their interventionist solutions are inefficient, produce undesirable consequences, or simply do not work. In doing so, the reader will be better prepared to defend the Constitution from progressive influence in their public and private lives, this while gaining a renewed appreciation for limited government. The reader will also develop a deeper understanding of why building public support, respect, and appreciation for the ideas and ideals embodied in the Constitution and our other Founding Documents is ultimately the key to healing America's current political divide.

For those who call themselves conservatives or who lean that way politically, this book will become your playbook for argument when defending the Constitution and traditional American values from progressive influence. Therefore, you will be able to use the ideas and arguments contained herein in your daily conversation with friends, relatives and coworkers who do not yet fully understand the implications to our country of the modern-day progressive agenda.

For political independents and thoughtful liberals who claim the mantle of informed citizen and voter, this book will be one that expands your understanding and perspective on the benefits of individual freedom, free markets and limited government, and the threat that progressive ideology poses to each.

Finally, for progressives and others on the far Left whose ideas and ideals this book is challenging, here is your opportunity to demonstrate your credentials as a "thoughtful liberal." If you are already turned off and choose to ignore my direct challenge to read further, I am reminded of that wise old saying: "none are so blind than those who will not see." The fact is, true liberals who proclaim their open mindedness probably have the most to gain from this read. Therefore, read on if you dare and don't be afraid. This book only reflects a set of logically organized ideas that just may give you a new perspective on our nation's political future, and maybe even your own.

PART ONE

COMPETING VISIONS OF THE AMERICAN DREAM

1

THE FOUNDERS' VISION OF THE AMERICAN DREAM

The powers delegated by the proposed Constitution to the federal government are few and defined. Those which are to remain in the State government are numerous and indefinite. The former will be exercised principally on external objects, as war, peace, negotiation and foreign commerce. . . . The powers reserved to the several States will extend to all the objects which in the ordinary course of affairs, concern the lives and liberties, and properties of the people, and the internal order, improvement and prosperity of the State.[11]

—James Madison

America's promise for the future has always been that the current generation will leave a more prosperous nation and higher standard of living for the next generation. Every American parent wants to fulfill this promise for their own children because it is central to the American Dream. This same promise was on the forefront of the minds of the Framers[12] when they drafted the Preamble to the Constitution.

We the People of the United States, in Order to form a more perfect Union, establish Justice, insure domestic Tranquility, provide for the common defence, promote the general Welfare, and secure the Blessings of Liberty to ourselves and our Posterity, do ordain and establish this Constitution for the United States of America.

The Framers of the Constitution believed that for America to survive and prosper, it would need to form a government that delivered on the promises of the Preamble by protecting natural rights. Their commitment to natural rights was evidenced by the Declaration of Independence, a declaration to King George III describing how he had violated such rights in the American colonies. However, there was also wide consensus among the nation's Founders that government should also be accountable for protecting economic rights that included private ownership of property, participation in a free market, and sound monetary policy.[13]

The Founders were also cognizant of classical antiquity. As such, they were intent on designing a form of government that would build upon the political lessons of history to ensure our country's success and viability over time. For example, in Federalist No. 63, James Madison argued in favor of a representative form of government that would improve upon the direct democracy of ancient Greece and the Roman republican model.

It is clear that the principle of representation was neither unknown to the ancients nor wholly overlooked in their political constitutions. The true distinction between these and the American governments, lies in the total exclusion of the people, in their collective capacity. The distinction, however, thus qualified, must be admitted to leave a most advantageous superiority in favor of the United States.[14]

—James Madison (as Publius).

Madison and the other Founders wanted to design an innovative republic that would outlast the Roman Empire, which stood

4

for approximately five hundred years. They also wanted the new republic to avoid any connotation of a monarchy and to be organized in a manner such that it could be applied practically and workably across a geography as large as the thirteen colonies.[15]

Because of the Founders' design, Americans have inherited a unique form of representative government that is unlike any previously known throughout human history. Our government carries with it a unique tradition of individual freedom guaranteeing specific political and economic rights to the average citizen. As the Declaration of Independence outlines, these rights are not derived from government but rather from "the Laws of Nature and of Natures God." In other words, a citizen inherits certain fundamental and inalienable rights as part of human nature granted by our Creator—God or nature as the individual may see fit. Few countries on earth today declare the source of certain fundamental "human rights" in this manner. Herein lies the core of what has been described as "American exceptionalism," a critical distinction that makes the United States unique, even among many modern-day democracies.

Sustaining the benefits of individual and economic freedom under republican government has been historically difficult. History tells us that all previous attempts to establish a republic have failed over time, for one reason or another, even dating back to the time of Moses and the ancient Israelites.[16] Each of these previous attempts has collapsed either into tyranny or anarchy, the two extremes of the political spectrum.

Knowing this, the Founders believed that only by cultivating civic virtue within the people would the United States overcome the same fate.[17] The word *virtue*, coming from the original Greek, means "moral excellence." As such, the concept of civic virtue implies achieving excellence by each citizen living out the principles, ethics, character traits and behaviors that are embodied in a civil and successful society. Today, we might refer to the academic discipline that embodies these principles as simply *civics*.

To avoid devolving into political decay and anarchy, the Founders believed that all citizens in a republic needed to learn and rally around a common set of civic principals as a basis for healing political divisions. These "first principles," many of which are explicitly embodied in the Declaration of Independence and the Constitution, reflect both civic and economic ideas that provide a foundation for our fundamental and inalienable rights. These principles include but are not limited to:

- All people (men and women) are created equal;

- The people are endowed by their Creator (or God) with certain inalienable rights;

- The people institute governments to protect these inalienable rights;

- Governments derive their authority only from the consent of the people;

- The people retain the right to abolish a government should that government threaten their inalienable rights;

- Government authority is limited to specific powers enumerated in a Constitution;

- Government enforcement of the rule of law must be applied equally to all people;

- Government is the protector of private property rights and a free market economy; and

- Government is accountable for preserving the sound value of money.

These first principles are the central foundation upon which the Framers of our Constitution designed America's republican government. Our fundamental rights spring from and are protected by these principles, rights that are explicitly enumerated in the Constitution, the Bill of Rights, and subsequent amendments. Additionally, the Ninth Amendment to the Constitution says, "*The enumeration in the Constitution, of certain rights, shall not be construed to deny or disparage others retained by the people.*" Likewise, the Tenth Amendment to the Constitution says, "*The powers not delegated to the United States by the Constitution, nor prohibited by it to the States, are reserved to the States respectively, or to the people.*" These two Amendments assure us that the States or we the people may retain certain fundamental rights and/or powers that are not explicitly enumerated in the Constitution or its amendments.

The Founders also knew that educating all citizens in civics and basic economic principles was key to maintaining public support for our Constitution. George Washington well understood the importance of such education in preserving the nation under our Constitution and spoke about this in his Eighth annual message to Congress.

> The more homogenous our citizens can be made in these [civic] particulars the greater will be our prospect of permanent union; and a primary object of such a national institution should be the education of our youth in the science of government. In a republic what species of knowledge can be equally important and what duty more pressing on its legislature than to patronize a plan for communicating it to those who are to be the future guardians of the liberties of the country?
> —President George Washington, Eighth Annual Message, December 7, 1796

Our nation's first principles frame the common ideas and ideals of America's unique representative democracy. These principles have also provided the framework around which great American leaders have rallied support to reunify our country at times when we were socially and politically divided. Our leaders have done this because a collective understanding of, and commitment to, these principles has led historically to broad-based prosperity for ourselves and future generations.

THE DECLINE IN CIVIC LITERACY

A primary reason that we are today a divided nation is that we have raised at least one generation of Americans that do not have a competent education in civics. This claim is not without independent support. For example, in March 2012 Xavier University's Center for the Study of the American Dream in Cincinnati, Ohio, released the findings from its National Civic Literacy Survey that asked native born U.S. citizens the same questions that naturalized citizens are asked on the U.S. Citizenship and Immigration Services exam. Survey findings showed that "one in three native-born citizens failed the civic literacy test"[18] compared to the 97.5 percent pass rate [for first-time test takers] among immigrants applying for citizenship.

Similarly, in 2011, the Intercollegiate Studies Institute's (ISI) research shows that American college students remain poorly trained in civics. ISI reported that past results from their National Civic Literacy studies showed that undergraduates scored just 54 percent (an F) on their sixty-question civic literacy exam.[19] ISI concluded that "the successful study of America's history and [its] institutions [is] the key to informed and responsible citizenship . . . since republics empower the public with sovereignty, the only way for the public to exercise that power wisely is for them to understand the unique kind of self-governing society America has founded."[20]

However, one bright spot from ISI's research showed that "acquiring more and more civic knowledge encouraged greater support for America's Founding Documents, the Judeo-Christian dictates of the Ten Commandments, and the workings of the free market."[21] Effectively, ISI research showed that formal education in civics results in a stronger appreciation for the Founders' vision for America.

CHALLENGES IN ACHIEVING ECONOMIC LITERACY

Arthur Levitt, the former chairman of the American Stock Exchange, once noted that "the American economy is the eighth wonder of the world; the ninth wonder is the economic ignorance of the American people."[22] If this is true, then our nation has raised at least one generation of Americans who are ill prepared for citizenship because they lack anything near a competent understanding of how our country can achieve economic prosperity. Available research supporting Levitt's claim suggests that a primary reason is the lack of formal education in economics, including a requirement to complete a basic economics course as part of a high school curriculum.[23]

A 2005 Harris Poll conducted by the National Council on Economic Education concluded that only 50 percent of high school students had ever received any formal training in economics.[24] Extrapolating this finding to the American population, it means that a sizable percentage of the voting public may not have a credible understanding of how to assess economic policies proposed by public officials. That means the public (including Millennials) is more susceptible to being exploited by misguided populist politicians that would seek to implement policies that negatively affect our collective standard of living and that of future generations. It would seem this truth would be self-evident to anyone who has lived through the 2008 financial crisis or a previous generation of Americans who lived through the Great Depression.

Unfortunately, as with civics, economic literacy rates are inadequate to properly prepare Americans to act as fiscally responsible citizens. For example, on April 24, 2013, the U.S. Department of Education's Institute of Education Sciences released a report entitled *The Nation's Report Card: Economics 2012, Grade 12* that was conducted by the National Assessment of Education Progress (NAEP) project.[25] This report presented measured economics literacy rates for high school seniors across America and contrasted its results with a similar study that NAEP had conducted in 2006. The results were uninspiring. While the study showed that some lower performing student demographic groups improved their literacy rates between 2006 and 2012, there was no overall change in the average literacy score. NAEP's National Assessment Governing Board (NAGB) news release commented on the results saying, "on average, the nation's 12th graders have not shown improvement in their knowledge of economics since 2006."[26] Between 2006 and 2012, the percentage of students measuring "proficient" in economics rose from 42 percent to 43 percent. Another way of saying this is that 57 percent of high school seniors graduating in 2012 did not have a proficient understanding of how our economy works. David P. Driscoll, chair of the NAGB, went on to comment on these results.

> It is astonishing that high school seniors do not know more about how economics affects their wallets, their country, and the world at a pivotal time in their lives, whether they choose to enter the workforce or pursue higher education . . . We need to do more to educate all students in economics so they can make informed decisions, whether they are negotiating a car loan, voting, or reading financial news.[27]
> —David P. Driscoll, Chair, NAGB

The NAEP's findings are consistent with the 2005 NCEE Harris Poll. The poll showed that adults scored 70 percent correct (a C grade) and high school students scored 53 percent correct (an F grade) in terms of their understanding of economics and personal finance.[28] These studies reflect the fact that a sizeable percentage of Americans remain ill prepared to assess the economic implications of public policy.

And what about our elected officials in Congress and their own understanding of how the economy works. In August 2011, the Employment Policies Institute (EMI) released a study showing that nearly eight out of 10 members of Congress had no academic training in economics or business.[29] This means that just over 20 percent of the members of the 112th United States Congress had any formal training in how the economy works. This may explain why public policies led to the financial crisis in 2008, and why Washington is predisposed to place burdens on job creators that contribute directly to a sluggish economy and lackluster job growth.

Americans who have acquired a competent education in civics are better prepared to be citizens because they understand the proper balance between freedom and equality and are more likely to support public policies consistent with the ideas and ideals embodied in our Founding Documents. Likewise, a competent education in economics helps one develop a more pragmatic view of what government can realistically accomplish through public policy, and what is better left to the private sector and individual initiative. To the extent that we can encourage citizens to become better educated in both civics and economics, we help build a more a prosperous society that is better able to unify around the Founders' view of the American Dream.

PROTECTING THE AMERICAN DREAM

If America is to protect its mainstream Center-Right heritage and the Founders' vision for republican government, our nation must reject progressive political influence and unify around the Constitution. There are specific steps we can take as a nation to encourage such unity. The first and most important is to better prepare the average American to fulfill their responsibilities of citizenship. We can do this by preparing each generation of America's children with a competent education that includes both civics and economics. This education cannot wait until after high school because many children will not be college bound and most higher educational institutions no longer require a Western civilization curriculum. Therefore, America's public-school systems must fill this educational void and provide our children with a better understanding of the Constitution and its application to our daily lives.

Second, we need to arm all Americans with better economic and civic arguments they can use to counter progressive influence. These arguments must educate the public as to why progressive efforts to fundamentally transform America pose a threat to our economic prosperity and individual freedoms. Beginning in Chapter 3, this book will present the reader with constitutionally grounded arguments on economic policy, health-care policy and social policy that counter the agenda that progressives are seeking to implement. Therefore, conservative activists should find these chapters an important reference when preparing to engage the progressive Left in any public policy debate.

George Washington once reminded us that "Government is not reason, it is not eloquence—it is force. Like fire, it is a dangerous servant and fearful master." Progressive ideology that is bent on expanding the federal government's influence in our lives reflects the kind of force Washington describes. The progressive Left is intent on exchanging the individual freedoms guaranteed to all of us by the Constitution for a statist's view of social and economic equality. And the force progressives intend to use often does not come at us like a wolf at the door, but rather like termites in the basement, gradually eroding the foundation of our most basic freedoms. If we are not on guard and know what to look for, and if progressives are successful, our most basic freedoms may be lost forever.

2

PROGRESSIVE TRANSFORMATION OF THE AMERICAN DREAM

[T]he Progressives detested the bedrock principles of American government. They detested the Declaration of Independence, which enshrines the protection of individual natural rights (like property) as the unchangeable purpose of government; and they detested the Constitution, which places permanent limits on the scope of government and is structured in a way that makes the extension of national power beyond its original purpose very difficult. "Progressivism" was, for them, all about progressing, or moving beyond, the principles of our founders.[30]

—Ronald J. Pestritto, Shipley Professor of the American Constitution, Hillsdale College

A merica is socially and politically divided, possibly more so than we have seen in over fifty years. We see examples of this divide reflected in the public debate of our time, and in what has been termed "gridlock" in our nation's political system in Washington, DC. The average American may see this divide as simply political: a debate between Republicans and

Democrats or, more likely, liberals versus conservatives. But for those who view the divide in these terms, they would be wrong. Our current political divide is even more fundamental than this.

Going back as far as the 1980s and even into the early 1990s, no matter what political rhetoric came out of Washington, members of Congress and those serving in the executive branch still considered collegial relationships important. Unfortunately, this is not always the case today, and it begs the question "what has changed?" During the Reagan Era and through most of the Clinton Era, Republicans and Democrats held a common objective in that both parties sought to achieve equal opportunity for all Americans. It did not matter whether you were rich or poor, young or old, white or black, male or female. The national leadership of both major political parties held to this common objective. They had different strategies and methods of achieving this objective, strategic differences that would often generate raucous political debate. However, at least Republicans and Democrats were working toward a common end, something that formed a basis for compromise.

Today things are different.

Since the early 2000s, the Republican Party, despite whatever political flaws it may have, has remained committed to the social and economic objective of equal opportunity for all Americans. This objective seeks to enable individual Americans with the skills and capabilities they need to work their way up the economic ladder while also providing a viable social safety net that includes basic health care. This is virtually a universally accepted principle among Republicans, and for all conservatives on the political Right.

Unfortunately, at some point during the past two decades, there has been a change in political philosophy within the national leadership of the Democratic Party, and among those with influence on the political Left. This new philosophy has been driven by the influence of the modern-day "Progressive movement" that reflects a radical departure from traditional liberalism, one that goes beyond simply advocating bigger government. Progressives have established a new objective for America, that being to achieve equal social and economic outcomes for all citizens. This new objective is rooted in the progressive idea that Americans in the lower-to-middle of the economic scale are victims that do not control their own destiny. Therefore, progressives believe that government must intervene to control our economy and to allocate resources through coercive government wealth redistribution policies to achieve their vision of equality. This is not a "free market" philosophy consistent with America's first principles, but rather one that aligns with socialism and leads to "crony capitalism."

America's political division between the conservative Right and progressive Left centers on two very different visions of equality: equal opportunity versus equal outcomes. Unlike a generation ago when the political Right and Left could come together around a common objective, equal opportunity and equal outcomes are conflicting objectives that cannot be reconciled. George Will, the syndicated columnist, once spoke at the 2010 Conservative Political Action Conference (CPAC) where he commented on how the Left and Right view equality and see it as a trade-off against the level of individual freedom we enjoy. Mr. Will noted a conservative as someone willing to trade equality for freedom, and a liberal (including progressives) as someone willing to trade freedom for equality.[31] Progressives seek to decrease freedom by increasing dependency on government programs that encourage social commitment. This is their strategy for national unity and is why progressives in the Democratic Party fought so hard to pass Obamacare. This program was designed to extend government control over one of the most intimate aspects of American life, our personal health, thereby becoming a critical tool for progressives to enable equal economic outcomes.

PROGRESSIVE STRATEGIES THAT UNDERMINE THE AMERICAN DREAM

To better understand why progressivism has come to dominate the modern-day Democratic Party, we must examine the five strategies that they use to undermine the Constitution and the traditional foundations of our republican government. These five progressive strategies will be discussed in more detail throughout this book and include the following: (1) promoting victimization; (2) redistributing wealth; (3) weakening constitutionalism; (4) diluting religious liberty; and (5) subordinating the rights of children. These strategies, summarized in Figure A below, are designed to change both public opinion and American culture so that they align with the modern-day progressive vision of the American Dream. And their vision is a very different one than that of the Founders.

The Progressive Left's Desired Impact on the American Dream

The modern day Progressive Left wants to fundamentally transform the Founder's vision of the America Dream to one that aligns with radical statism and economic socialism.

The Founder's View of the American Dream	Progressive Strategy for Transforming America	Progressive End-State For a New American Dream
Promote "equal opportunity" by recognizing that all citizens can improve their lives through hard work and individual initiative.	Promote Victimization	Expand the idea of "equality" beyond that which the Founding Fathers intended and redefine it as "equal economic outcomes."
Invest in education and jobs skills to enable individuals to live independently and work their way up the economic ladder.	Redistribute Wealth	Increase citizen dependency on government programs in order to attain political control and promote social unity.
Establish a Federal government with limited enumerated powers, delegating remaining powers to the states and to the people.	Weaken Constitutionalism	Promote a "Living Constitution" where unelected judges are unconstrained in their power to expand rights and make the law.
Recognize that citizens inherit certain inalienable rights from a Creator, including the right to freely practice their religion.	Dilute Religious Liberty	Establish a secular state that restricts religious practice and makes government the final arbiter of rights and morality.
Affirm that children are our most important asset and public policy must give equal weight to the rights of children and adults.	Subordinate the Rights of Children	Depreciate the rights and value of children, both born and unborn, by giving more weight to the rights of adults who can vote.

Figure A. Progressive Strategies to Transform the American Dream

PROGRESSIVE STRATEGY NO. 1: PROMOTING VICTIMIZATION

In the mind of a progressive leftist, the current state of economic and social affairs in America is decidedly unfair and unequal. They have this halfway correct. America is both socially and economically unequal. It has always been this way, and the truth is it will always be this way. In any society that values individual rights, permits ownership of private property, and allows a free market, there will always be social and economic inequality. This is just a fact of life that progressives cannot change, at least within the bounds of the Founders' interpretation of the Constitution.

In response to what they believe is a fundamentally unfair and unequal society, progressives seek to build their political base by working to convince minorities and others on the middle-to-low end of the economic scale that they are victims. As victims, progressives will say, they must rely on government to be their benefactor for them to prosper and succeed. Effectively, progressives rely on what Michael Gerson once described as the "soft bigotry of low expectations"[32] to build their political base. Progressives reject the idea that all able-bodied individuals control their own destiny in American society because the "system" is racist, sexist, homophobic, and/or misogynistic. They promote the absolutist point of view that life is unfair and that only with the help of government will victims ever achieve personal and economic success.

It is important to note that many traditional liberals would disagree with this progressive point of view. For example, at a 1977 press conference, President Jimmy Carter defended the Supreme Court's ruling that the federal government did not need to fund abortions for poor women. A reporter asked Mr. Carter how fair he believed it was that women who could afford to get an abortion can go ahead and have one, yet a poor woman might be precluded from having the procedure. Mr. Carter responded:

> There are many things in life that are not fair, that wealthy people can afford and poor people can't. But I don't believe that the Federal Government should take action to try to make these opportunities exactly equal, particularly when there is a moral factor involved. [33]

—President Jimmy Carter

Mr. Carter was echoing the classical liberal point of view that recognizes the limitations of equality and fairness, particularly in a society that values Judeo-Christian morality. However, we can differentiate this point of view from the radical victimization promoted by the progressive Left. In their effort to fundamentally transform America, progressives not only seek to change policy but also to change American culture. Former Senator Patrick Moynihan, the respected liberal statesman, once commented on the influence of culture and its powerful effect on our nation.

> The central conservative truth is that it is culture, not politics
> that determines the success of a society. The central liberal truth
> is that politics can change a culture and save it from itself.[34]

—Senator Daniel Patrick Moynihan

Progressives do not just want political power, but they seek to fundamentally transform American culture into one that convinces the poor, minorities and even middle-class individuals that they are victims of an unfair world. Therefore, as progressives see it, government must expand not just to achieve equal opportunity, but also equal economic and social outcomes, even if this means adopting a double standard in how we treat people.

Many progressives defend a double standard as essential to overcoming what they perceive as the victimization suffered by the poor and minorities. For example, on July 2, 2013, the late progressive commentator Alan Colmes engaged Bill O'Reilly in a debate on *The O'Reilly Factor* program about black actor Jamie Foxx. The subject of the debate was a T-shirt that Mr. Foxx had worn to an awards event showing support for Trayvon Martin, a black teenager who was killed in February 2012 by neighborhood watchman George Zimmerman. O'Reilly asked Colmes whether it was appropriate for Foxx to wear such a shirt on national television and would it also be appropriate for a white person to wear a T-shirt supporting George Zimmerman. Without hesitation, Colmes defended the idea of a double standard.

> It probably would not have been acceptable . . . and it probably
> is a double-standard. And there's a double-standard I think
> because of disparity in this country between the perception
> that there is a white power structure. Blacks are the minority.

18

And I do believe we view things a little differently based on who really runs things in the United States . . . [minorities are] still being persecuted . . . there's still a problem in America . . . it's not just historical[35]

—Alan Colmes, Progressive Commentator

Mr. Colmes comments speak volumes for the Progressive movement and their effort to perpetuate victimization. By his logic, minorities are persecuted, and this is the primary factor that enables social and economic inequality between whites and minorities, and particularly for blacks. Colmes said nothing about how culture can play a role in the advancement of an ethnic community. This includes the cultural emphasis that a specific ethnic community or demographic group might place on making a lifetime commitment to education, a prerequisite in today's world to achieve economic advancement. Colmes also completely ignored the single most important social variable that determines whether people will live in poverty: having a child out of wedlock. He also did not consider that one in thirteen adults in America have an alcohol problem[36] and 9.3 percent of American's use illicit drugs,[37] conditions that disrupt the ability of many of our citizens to move up the economic ladder. Progressives do not weigh these factors heavily because, fundamentally, government cannot solve any of these problems. Instead, progressives rely on emotional arguments that would allow a so-called victim to shift the blame for their plight to a white majority, the wealthy "1 percent," the police, or some other group that they can target politically. In doing so, progressives open the door to their next strategy for fundamentally transforming America: redistributing wealth.

PROGRESSIVE STRATEGY NO. 2: REDISTRIBUTING WEALTH

During the term of the Obama and Trump presidencies, Americans have engaged in a great debate about the politics of rich and poor, and who is to blame for the economic challenges our nation is facing. Progressives actively entered this debate by advancing class warfare and working to convince their political base that wealthy Americans are exploiting the middle class and the poor. They argue that it is only fair that the wealthy pay more of their "fair share" of the overall tax burden because "they can afford it." This argument is an easy sell to some, even though the top 10 percent of earners in the United States today already pay more than 70 percent of all income taxes, that up from 49 percent in 1980.[38] But when the message concerning fair share comes from someone like Barack Obama, it is an argument that can have a strong influence on those not well grounded in civics and economics.

President Obama reignited the class warfare debate in December 2011 after delivering what has come to be called by some his "Fair-Shot" speech in Osawatomie, Kansas. During his speech, Mr. Obama expressed concern about income inequality, everyone doing their fair share, and everyone playing by the same rules. All of this, he said, was to focus attention on achieving a greater level of economic fairness for the middle class. There is no debate on these generic points. But then Mr. Obama proceeded to take on free market entrepreneurism by mocking America's "rugged individualism" and chiding those with a "healthy skepticism of too much government." Such comments reflect the core beliefs of Mr. Obama and most progressives that the collective interest is superior to that of the individual, and that government has a moral imperative to redistribute wealth from the rich to the middle class and poor.

Wealth redistribution is an economic strategy adopted by many western European and South American socialist countries, many of which are democracies. These countries redistribute limited public resources on generous social welfare spending, all paid for by applying punitive tax rates to an ever-shrinking base of productive taxpayers. Such policies result in a distorted set of economic incentives that encourage people to hide their income from taxation, whether legally or illegally. These policies also can lead to the kind of failed economies we have seen during the past decade in Greece, Venezuela, and Spain. Under worst case scenarios, such countries end up with unsustainable levels of public debt, chronic double-digit unemployment, and civil disorder.

Why would political leaders in these regimes adopt such harmful economic policies? One reason is that progressives, like many who do not have a competent understanding of economics, believe that there exists a fixed stock of wealth. As such, they believe that if an industrious worker or entrepreneur is making lots of money and moving up the economic ladder, then that worker or entrepreneur must be taking that wealth away from someone else who does not have enough. This type of thinking reflects economic ignorance. However, such thinking can be a convincing argument for someone who does not understand how wealth is created and shared in a free market. In fact, entrepreneurs leverage the power of free markets to create new wealth while, at the same time, sharing as much as 99 percent of this wealth with investors, the newly employed, contractors, vendors, and yes, even the tax collector.[39]

President Obama deserves to be commended for speaking out on the importance of creating opportunity for the middle class and the poor, thereby showing that his heart is in the right place. However, Mr. Obama's economic policies reflected an extraordinary lack of understanding of how the private economy works and how good middle-class jobs are created. As a progressive, Obama believes that government must control enough private resources to enable redistribution to people he believes are economic victims. The progressive Left has supported similar wealth redistribution policies since the days of FDR, without considering the unintended consequences to business formation and job creation.

Instead of demonizing the wealthy, progressives would do better to learn the lessons that FDR was forced to learn during the period leading up to World War II. FDR had to choose between waging a "class war" as he did during most of the 1930s and a "military war" against fascism. He could not do both. For FDR, this was a Hobson's choice, and he decided to partner with industry instead of waging war on them to industrialize the great

American war machine. Following World War II, free-market industrialization finally led us out of the Great Depression because incessant New Deal government interventionism had died along with FDR.

History is not clear as to whether FDR clung to the economic myth that there is a fixed stock of wealth. What we do know is that his New Deal was a response to what he saw as wealthy men acting with selfishness and greed.[40] Ironically, however, it was John Maynard Keynes, the father of Keynesian economics, that once tried to educate FDR on this point by reminding him "it is a mistake to think that . . . [businessmen] are more immoral than politicians."[41]

PROGRESSIVE STRATEGY NO. 3: WEAKENING CONSTITUTIONALISM

The Constitution was drafted to constrain the powers of the federal government and delineate the individual rights of Americans that government was instituted to protect. These constraints are inherent in the Founders' design of republican government and have been reinforced by a judicial tradition of interpreting the text of the Constitution based on its "original" intent. Given this "originalist" point of view, what are progressives to do when they cannot win public support for their own ideas and the Constitution constrains their political agenda? They employ a third strategy for fundamentally transforming America—that being to weaken the standards by which we interpret the Constitution. They do this by advocating for a "living Constitution." The Constitution is said to be "living" when judges replace the Framers' original interpretive intent of its text with arbitrary interpretation. When this happens, these unelected judges are not acting as interpreters of the law but instead like de facto legislators[42] or, as some would say, kings who have no check against their power.

Progressives are very open about their intention to evolve constitutional interpretation. In fact, many openly state their belief that the Constitution is imperfect and outdated, thereby requiring reinterpretation in a modern context to make it relevant to current circumstances. Their primary argument for loose interpretation (or "loose construction") is to suggest that the Constitution has limited relevance because the Founders could not have foreseen or appreciated the needs and struggles of our nation and its citizens in the modern world. Therefore, progressives seek to expand interpretations of the Constitution's text to accommodate their need for a larger and more intrusive federal government.

The idea that our Constitution is imperfect and will need to change and evolve over time is not new. In fact, this was something that the Framers of the Constitution had foreseen and planned for. As part of Article V, the Framers provided two methods by which amendments to the Constitution could be proposed. The first method permits Congress to propose amendments to the Constitution by a two-thirds majority vote in both houses. The other method permits two-thirds of state legislatures to authorize a "Convention of the States," a process that bypasses Congress and permits convention attendees representing state legislatures to propose constitutional amendments. Of course, any proposed amendment must also be ratified by three-fourths of the state legislatures before it becomes part of the Constitution. This process is far too burdensome for progressives as they know it will take too long—and may even be impossible—to mold public opinion to their liking. Therefore, they prefer the more expedient method of undermining the Constitution through activist judicial appointments and with executive orders.

Progressive attempts to undermine the Constitution date back to the early part of the twentieth century. President Woodrow Wilson, considered a leading progressive of his day, was an early proponent of an alternative vision for how the Constitution should be interpreted based on the opinion of a transient majority.

> It is therefore particularly true of constitutional government that its atmosphere is opinion. . . . The underlying understandings of a constitutional system are modified from age to age by changes of life and circumstance and corresponding alterations of opinion. It does not remain fixed in any unchanging form

but grows with the growth and is altered with the change of the nation's needs and purposes.[43]

—President Woodrow Wilson, 1908

What President Wilson was saying is that constitutional interpretation should always accommodate the opinions of the current political majority. In Wilson's view, that meant if a majority deem some policy or restriction of fundamental rights to be important for the public good, that majority has the power to implement that policy or restriction. President Wilson's progressivism was described in more expansive terms in his 1887 essay entitled "Socialism and Democracy."

> In fundamental theory socialism and democracy are almost if not quite one and the same. They both rest at bottom upon the absolute right of the community to determine its own destiny and that of its members. Men as communities are supreme over men as individuals. Limits of wisdom and convenience to the public control there may be: limits of principle there are, upon strict analysis, none.[44]
>
> —Woodrow Wilson, 1887

Wilson mistakenly believed that America was a democracy where majorities rule at whim and where fundamental rights can be waived by "men as communities" if they decide change is necessary. Nothing could be farther away from the vision of our Founding Fathers or what is permitted under the Constitution. The Founders insisted that their design for government would be a republic, or representative government, where those elected to represent citizens would respect the fundamental rights of minorities. These fundamental rights granted to us by God (or our Creator) cannot be undermined or taken away by secular law or majority rule. Therefore, the Constitution represents a bulwark for the protection of our fundamental rights against those in power who would seek to arbitrarily redefine or deny them. The Founders insisted on this so that no one subject to the Constitution could claim to have absolute authority, such as King George III sought over the American colonies.

Today, America has no shortage of prominent progressive activists who proclaim and defend the concept of a living Constitution. Among these are such notables as former Vice President Al Gore who advocated for liberal appointments to the Supreme Court during his 2000 campaign for the Presidency.

> I would look for justices of the Supreme Court who understand that our Constitution is a living and breathing document, that it was intended by our Founders to be interpreted in the light of the constantly evolving experience of the American people.[45]
>
> —Al Gore, 2000 Presidential Candidate

President Obama weighed in on his respect for fundamental rights as enshrined in the Constitution in his autobiography, *The Audacity of Hope*. However, comments from his early political career are even more telling about his orientation toward loose interpretation of the Constitution rather than original intent.

> The Supreme Court never ventured into the issues of redistribution of wealth and sort of more basic issues of political and economic justice in this society. And to that extent, as radical as I think people tried to characterize the Warren Court, it wasn't that radical. It didn't break free from the essential constraints that were placed by the founding fathers in the Constitution, as least as it's been interpreted, and [sic] Warren Court interpreted in the same way that, generally, the Constitution is a charter of negative liberties, says what the states can't do to you, says what the federal government can't do to you, but it doesn't say what the federal government or the state government must do on your behalf."[46]
>
> —State Senator Barack Obama, 2001

Mr. Obama's view of "negative liberties" when interpreting the Constitution is selective in nature, suggesting that if the text does not mention a certain topic, such as a right to health care, then this authorizes the federal government to be activist in the delivery of health care, and so on. But this view does not reflect a federal government whose powers are restricted to those enumerated in the Constitution, something the Founders were insistent upon. This type of thinking opens the door for progressives to dictate new fundamental rights, such as when the Supreme Court imposed a fundamental right to gay marriage upon the entire nation in *Obergefell v. Hodges.*[47]

Further, progressives often propose generous interpretations of the "General Welfare" clause, found in both the Preamble and Article I, Section 8 of the Constitution, to justify almost unlimited social service spending on their special interests. In fact, as we will see in later chapters, progressives would even seek to elevate spending on services such as health care to the status of a fundamental right. James Madison, thought of by historians as the father of the Constitution, understood the clause differently. He believed the term "general welfare" to have almost no meaning and was only applicable to spending on matters such as defense that were explicitly referenced in the remainder of section 8.[48] Madison believed that to interpret this clause otherwise would lead to Congress having unlimited power,[49] a concern that most of the Founders shared.

Today, progressives are hard at work trying to bypass both the Constitution and existing law when it suits their political objectives. As a leader of the Progressive movement, President Obama was on the forefront of undermining both in ways that violated his oath to uphold the Constitution. Here are just a few examples:

- Mr. Obama attempted to make recess appointments to the National Labor Relations Board (NLRB) using a process deemed unconstitutional by two federal appeals courts and the Supreme Court.[50]

- Mr. Obama overstepped his constitutional authority by taking executive action to implement portions of the

Development, Relief, and Education for Alien Minors (Dream) Act after Congress rejected it. This action ignored current law by unilaterally deferring deportation for 5 million illegal aliens, 1.7 million of which were brought to the United States as children.[51]

- Mr. Obama unilaterally postponed the implementation of the employer mandate under the Affordable Care Act ("Obamacare"), thereby ignoring his constitutional duty to faithfully execute the law as intended when passed by Congress.[52]

- Mr. Obama issued an executive order requiring faith-based employers, including the Catholic Church, to provide sterilization, contraceptives and abortifacients through their health insurance companies in violation of First Amendment religious freedom protections.[53]

- Mr. Obama directed the Department of Justice not to defend the Defense of Marriage Act that had bipartisan support in Congress, again refusing to faithfully execute the law.[54]

- Mr. Obama directed the Department of Health and Human Services to unilaterally waive work require-ments for those receiving Temporary Assistance for Needy Families (aka welfare).[55]

President Obama's arbitrary enforcement of existing law, as evidenced by his actions described above and many others, are equivalent to a line-item veto. No president has such constitutional power. Such power can only be granted to a president through a constitutional amendment. However, for progressives who see the Constitution as a frivolous annoyance, they say a living Constitution provides them with the flexibility to interpret the law in any way that suits their political ends.

Progressives want to weaken constitutionalism by blurring the lines between original intent and modern-day sentiments on the role and powers of the federal government. They do this because the Constitution, properly interpreted, will prevent them from fundamentally transforming America by redistributing wealth, creating greater dependency on government and achieving equal economic outcomes. If it is flexibility that progressives seek in constitutional interpretation, they should consider the words of the late Supreme Court Judge Antonin Scalia when he once made his case against a living Constitution.

> What are the arguments usually made in favor of the Living Constitution? As the name of it suggests, it is a very attractive philosophy, and it's hard to talk people out of it—the notion that the Constitution grows. The major argument is the Constitution is a living organism, it has to grow with the society that it governs, or it will become brittle and snap . . .

> My Constitution is a very flexible Constitution. You think the death penalty is a good idea—persuade your fellow citizens and adopt it. You think it's a bad idea—persuade them the other way and eliminate it. You want a right to abortion—create it the way most rights are created in a democratic society, persuade your fellow citizens it's a good idea and enact it. You want the opposite—persuade them the other way. That's flexibility. . . . If you don't believe in originalism, then you need some other principle of interpretation. Being a non-originalist is not enough. You see, I have my rules that confine me. I know what I'm looking for. When I find it—the original meaning of the Constitution—I am handcuffed . . . [and what] is the criterion that governs the Living Constitutional judge? What can you possibly use, besides original meaning? Think about that. Natural law? We all agree on that, don't we? The philosophy of John Rawls? That's easy. There really is nothing else. You either tell your judges, 'Look, this is a law, like all laws, give it the meaning it had when it was adopted.' Or, you tell your judges, "Govern us . . . You make these decisions for us." . . . [You] know I speak at law schools with some frequency just to make trouble—and I put this question to the faculty all the time, or incite the students to ask their Living Constitutional

professors: "Okay professor, you are not an originalist, what is your criterion?" There is none other ". . . *The worst thing about the Living Constitution is that it will destroy the Constitution.*[56]
—Justice Antonin Scalia, March 14, 2005

Progressives would prefer to sidestep the Constitution and be governed by unelected judges, but only by judges that share their progressive philosophy. This is precisely why judicial appointments are so politicized today, particularly those for the Supreme Court, as we saw during the Senate hearings concerning confirmation of Brett Kavanaugh in September 2018. Progressives would prefer that Left-leaning judges act like unelected kings and make decisions for us. But isn't this precisely what the Founders rejected when they wrote and signed their names to the Declaration of Independence? Instead of having to do the arduous work that goes with building public support for amending the Constitution, progressives prefer to take the easy route and simply work around it.

PROGRESSIVE STRATEGY NO. 4: DILUTING RELIGIOUS LIBERTY

America has had a long tradition of respecting the fundamental right to freedom of religion and for giving it a wide berth in its application within public policy. While no right may be considered absolute, religious freedom has come as close as any right to being treated as such in American jurisprudence. Progressives are not usually among those who share this broad-based respect for religious liberty as they hold a more "secular" view regarding such freedom. This is especially true when they see religious institutions creating barriers to achieving their agenda. Even though secular progressives might gain power and control government for a brief period, that does not mean they have the legal or moral authority to legislate away fundamental religious rights.[57]

The Framers of the Constitution understood that our unique form of republican government would recognize two different classifications of rights. "Fundamental" rights, also known as "human" or "inalienable" rights, are rights that we inherit by divine endowment from God, our Creator, or nature.[58] Transient political majorities cannot legislate away these fundamental rights because they are understood to be granted by our Creator (i.e., God) and not government.[59] A second classification of rights, as distinguished from fundamental rights, are called legislated "civil rights."[60] Civil rights are created under federal and state law are considered "alienable" in that they can be legislated into existence, modified, and legislated out of existence by majority rule, providing they are authorized within the constitutional constraints of federalism. Examples of such civil rights might include the right to education, civil protection (e.g., police and fire emergency services), or qualified legal rights (e.g., marriage).[61] Civil rights might also include specific government services that are legislated to benefit a qualifying class or group (e.g., senior citizen's benefits). However, the key point to remember is that civil rights are always subordinate to fundamental rights under our system of constitutional jurisprudence. This means that government cannot enact a law that establishes a civil right that overrides or otherwise subordinates a fundamental right.

Under the Constitution, the only way one can restrict or subordinate a fundamental right is for a compelling reason. This situation usually occurs when a court case involves a legal conflict that pits two fundamental rights against each other. For example, a parent may attempt to restrict a child's access to medical care on religious grounds. The courts will typically override the parent's fundamental religious rights and balance in favor of the child's fundamental right to life should the child's condition be life-threatening, but curable. We also see this same type of conflict on the issue of abortion where a fundamental right to life comes into conflict with privacy (or liberty) rights. To resolve such conflicts, the legislative and executive branches of government can enact laws that seek to constructively balance between fundamental rights. Likewise, the courts may step in to interpret existing laws to decide how that balance should be drawn between rights. In either case, such situations require that a balance be drawn between fundamental rights as opposed to adopting an absolutist position that chooses one right over another.

Since progressives do not adhere to originalist interpretation of the Constitution, they will not always acknowledge that fundamental rights are superior in legal status to legislated "civil rights." We saw an example of this on January 20, 2012, when Health and Human Services Secretary Kathleen Sebelius announced the Obama administration's Obamacare contraception mandate. This mandate required religiously affiliated institutions offering health plans to their employees to provide no-cost coverage for all forms of FDA approved birth control, including abortifacients and sterilization.[62] Since 1970, such services have been made available under Title X at minimal cost to the poor, and exemptions have always been guaranteed under federal law to provide churches and their affiliated institutions the broadest possible religious exemption to any mandate. Under the Obama mandate, however, exemptions were restricted only to churches and religious organizations that serve their own membership and not those serving the public at large.

Ten days after the Obama administration's executive mandate on contraception, the Catholic Church issued a pastoral letter that was read in churches across the United States openly condemning the administration for its direct assault on religious liberties. Some Catholic priests even went on to describe the Obama administration as evil and demonic in their actions.[63] Many evangelical and Jewish organizations joined with the Catholic Church in openly condemning this mandate as an attack on religious liberties. One article published in the *Wall Street Journal* and authored by representatives of the Catholic, Protestant, and Jewish faiths noted that Kathleen Sebelius's concept of how to balance between religious freedom and access to preventive health care services "stands the First Amendment on its head."[64] Yet, despite repeated attempts by the Obama administration to propose "accommodations" to religious institutions, these accommodations were rejected by the religious community for their lack of credibility.

The Obama administration's contraception mandate subordinated a historically broad interpretation of fundamental religious rights to implement their desired social engineering policy by imposing a legislated civil right. When this happens, it reflects what is called "tyranny of the majority," an action that would be found unconstitutional if challenged in any court dominated by originalists. Religiously affiliated organizations did mount a legal challenge to the mandate that worked its way up to the Supreme Court. However, on May 16, 2016, the Court sent this case and its parties back to lower courts to seek a compromise. It was reported that the Court rendered this decision given what was an expected to be a 4-4 tie should the case go forward, this in the aftermath of the death of Justice Antonin Scalia.[65]

There were other attempts by the Obama administration working through the National Labor Relations Board to disqualify Catholic colleges as religious institutions to subject them to federal labor statues.[66] The administration has also suggested eliminating the deductibility of charitable donations to churches and religious institutions as part of a broader fiscal reform package.[67] These were attempts by a progressive administration to exert authority over the religious community and dilute their influence over public policy. But to what end? All such actions by the Obama administration were designed to empower the federal government as the great arbiter of rights and morality. In effect, progressives seek to secularize standards of morality by diminishing religious influence, thereby enabling their social engineering agenda. By doing so, they strengthen their ability to achieve social and economic equality and expand government dependency.

Dennis Prager, the syndicated radio talk show host, columnist, and author, has noted that progressives, being part of the radical political Left, have long held a hostile attitude toward religion: especially Judaism and Christianity.[68] Prager has suggested that leftists practice liberalism as a secular religion,[69] one they use to displace traditional Judeo-Christian theology and the notion of a judging God with moral absolutes. He also believes the progressive leftism is hostile toward religion because it represents the major obstacle to a more widespread acceptance of their political agenda, especially when leftism encourages others to covet what wealthier people have.[70]

Prager's explanation for religious hostility may be one of several motivations for the progressive American Civil Liberties Union (ACLU) to frequently file legal challenges opposing the display of the Ten Commandments in public forums. They do this despite the influence the Ten Commandments has had on the fundamental rules of civil society and on the formation of our American legal system.

By diluting religious liberty, progressives employ a strategy of encouraging their political base to see the state as providing the ultimate standard of morality, and as the basis for their economic and social salvation. In fact, some progressives might go as far as to agree with Karl Marx who once stated that "the first requisite for the happiness of the people is the abolition of religion."[71] It is important to note that progressives do not openly state their intent to diminish religion, and many will actively deny this as their objective. However, it is clear by their actions that they will embolden and strengthen their political base by encouraging acceptance of secularism and leftist definitions of morality while, at the same time, discouraging acceptance of traditional Judeo-Christian traditions.

PROGRESSIVE STRATEGY NO. 5: SUBORDINATING THE RIGHTS OF CHILDREN

Modern-day progressives have a decidedly secular view of morality that prioritizes the social and economic interests of adults over those of children. While some may see this as a bold claim, what Americans should first be concerned with is the fact that Judeo-Christian ethics teaches exactly the opposite. Dietrich Bonhoeffer, the German Lutheran theologian and dissident anti-Nazi activist, once reminded us of whose interests we should weigh more heavily when considering standards of morality in a just society.

> The ultimate test of a moral society is the kind of world that it leaves to its children.[72]
> —Dietrich Bonhoeffer

Modern-day progressives will speak to the importance of protecting children, but their legislative priorities and political advocacy speak louder than their words. For progressives, elevating the economic interests of children offers little in the way of political payback because they do not vote. For example, in matters involving federal entitlement programs including Social Security, Medicare, and now Obamacare, we see a massive shift in wealth being taxed from current and future generations, many of whom are minors or not even born yet, so that benefits can be provided to adults who can vote. Given the unfunded liabilities inherent in these programs that burden future generations who have no say in the matter, this shift in wealth can only be viewed as fiscally irresponsible and generationally immoral. The economics behind these programs will be explored in greater detail in later chapters of this book.

Progressive priorities also subordinate the rights of children where social policy is concerned. Advocacy of late-term abortion is a high priority issue for progressives, even though this procedure will terminate the lives of viable fetuses that can live outside a mother's womb. Rather than seeking to find a constructive balance between the fundamental rights of privacy and life, progressives have staked out an absolutist position supporting a woman's right to terminate a pregnancy at any point in gestation. While many social conservatives often hold the opposite absolutist position favoring the life of the unborn, an overwhelming majority of Americans oppose either absolutist position. Instead, public opinion polls show that Americans prefer a balanced position favoring limited abortion rights prior to viability.[73] Fortunately, certain jurisdictions recognize that children inherit certain rights either from birth or from conception onward. For example, there are at least twenty-nine states that recognize the rights of the unborn and permit prosecution of offenders who harm children considered "in utero."[74]

Finally, the progressive push to legitimize gay marriage has implications for our children as well. Despite the Supreme Court's decision in *Obergefell v. Hodges,* which declared a fundamental right to gay marriage,[75] the conservative ideal that all children have a fundamental right to know one mother and one father never entered the public debate on this issue. Too often, social conservatives were sidetracked in their opposition to *Obergefell* by weak arguments about religious standards that deem homosexuality immoral and gay marriage abhorrent. These distractions gave progressives the upper hand in public debate leading up to the *Obergefell* decision. If social conservatives were to refocus their arguments by advocating that every child has a fundamental right to know one mother and father, a reality reflected in natural law, they would have had much greater success in preserving traditional marriage in the courts.

In the end, the progressive Left knows where their power base is, and it is with adults and the elderly who vote, not with children or the unborn. Even when they advocate for more public spending targeting the young, such as early childhood education (e.g., Head Start), their agenda often targets another base constituency (e.g., teachers' unions) that support their cause. Therefore, conservatives need to own the obligation of advocating for the rights of children because no other political constituency will.

ARGUMENTS THAT CHALLENGE PROGRESSIVE IDEOLOGY

References to the word "liberal" are used sparingly in this book because classical liberals are not those who are seeking to undermine the Constitution and the Founder's vision of the American dream. Classical liberals believe in respect for individual fundamental rights and economic freedom, advocacy that is consistent with the Constitution. Rather, it is the progressive Left who dominate the leadership of the modern-day Democratic Party that are attempting to fundamentally transform America by undermining the Constitution in matters of public policy. It is this growing influence of progressive ideology on the Left that explains why our politics has become so bitter and divisive, an ideology that this book seeks to challenge.

In the following chapters, this book will present a series of public policy positions advocated by the progressive Left, as well as corresponding conservative counter-arguments, to explain why progressive ideology undermines our Constitution, our economic prosperity and our national unity. Central to these counter-arguments will be discussion presented in a civic and economic framework that will enable the reader to more effectively evaluate public policy in a manner consistent with the ideas and ideals of our Constitution. Therefore, Americans concerned about progressive influence on their children and the future of our nation will come to find the following chapters to be an important reference. After reading these chapters if one finds they have begun to think differently about their own views on public policy, then this book has achieved its objective and we will all be one step closer to unifying our politically polarized nation.

PART TWO

ARGUMENTS ON ECONOMIC POLICY

3

THE MORALITY OF FREE MARKETS

The rise of capitalism brought greater morality into our relationships. There is the biblical passage, "It is as difficult for a rich man to get into Heaven as for a camel to go through the eye of a needle." That biblical phrase was quite appropriate for the time because wealth was most often acquired through capturing, plundering and looting your fellow man. But, with the rise of capitalism, people like Bill Gates are rich because they have served their fellow man. Gates has made his fellow man very happy by building Microsoft computers and software. Fred Smith with Federal Express serves his fellow man, too. The morality of the free market should be stressed because it is far superior to any other method of allocating resources.

—Walter Williams, Professor of Economics,
George Mason University.[76]

I n the early 1980s, NBC's *Saturday Night Live* put on a series of sketches called "Bizzaro World" that reflected a parallel universe, one based on the Superman DC Comic publication from the 1960s. In each sketch, the inhabitants of Bizzaro World

39

would perform everything backward, essentially reversing all logic by reflecting black as white, up as down, hot as cold, and so on. In such a world, the rules describing how the economy works might be turned on their head as well. For example, in Bizzaro World we might say that the federal government can continue to borrow and spend without destructive economic consequence, that government bureaucrats know how to invest personal wealth better than individual citizens, and that unlimited public subsidy of the poor does not encourage dependency or destroy the social fabric of families.

Unfortunately, when we look closely at the social and economic solutions that progressives propose to address poverty and manage the economy, one might think they are living in Bizzaro World. At some point during the past two decades the progressive idea that the federal government can tax, spend, and regulate our way to prosperity has taken on an air of legitimacy with some in Washington. Democratic Socialist Alexandria Ocasio-Cortez offers an example of such legitimacy as she has been pointed to by fellow progressive Democrats as the future of their party. Ms. Ocasio-Cortez defeated long-time incumbent Congressman Joseph Crowley in the 2018 New York primary by promising a plethora of government programs including Medicare for all, free college tuition, free housing, and guaranteed employment. Of course, the mainstream media has given Ms. Ocasio-Cortez plenty of coverage creating the perception that her victory is a sign of things to come. However, lost in this widely reported story was the fact that her primary in New York's 14th Congressional District only saw voter turnout of 13 percent,[77] thereby suggesting her win was really an outlier.

Of course, the progressive Left advocating the idea of creating prosperity through big government is nothing new. Progressives have sought to grow government ever since FDR first proposed the New Deal. President Obama kept this idea alive with repeated proposals for economic stimulus and other government wealth transfer schemes that included Obamacare. Even President Trump has proposed a $1 trillion infrastructure stimulus to supposedly boost economic growth.[78] However, any objective review of history shows that this type of progressive economic formula under-performs the free market, even when a weak economy is left alone to mend itself and the government does nothing.[79]

The progressive idea that big government can engineer economic prosperity may be well intended, but in practice it usually creates more problems than it solves. Similarly, progressive social engineering and economic policies may create short-term benefits, but their coercive nature often create unintended consequences in the long-run. Further, progressives do not seek policies that enable individuals to live free and independent lives, but instead they seek a utopian "nanny state" that increases dependency on government. They believe such dependency will create a greater sense of community and common purpose for our society. They also believe that human nature can be cultivated to accept this common purpose, if only the public can come to see the social and economic benefits that such engineering can deliver.

But there is a moral dimension to economic policy as well. Progressives believe their economic intentions have a higher moral purpose, and that coercion is morally acceptable to achieve their vision of the common good. They will even pursue coercive policies at the expense of individual rights. But progressives hold no monopoly on morality because they also believe the ends justify their coercive means. Dinesh D'Souza, the conservative commentator, author, and documentarian, once posed a simple but enlightening anecdote that illustrates the moral dichotomy between progressive and free market economic policy.

> [I]f you and I are walking on [a river bank] and I'm hungry and you have a sandwich . . . and I say . . . I'm hungry . . . give me your sandwich. And you say . . . yes . . . here it is. I say thank you. Now that is a moral transaction. You feel good about having done something good. I feel a sense of obligation. Maybe someday if I am doing well I'll share my sandwich with somebody else.
>
> Now here's [another] situation. You and I are walking on that same river bank. I'm hungry. You have a sandwich. And

here comes [President] Obama on a horse. He gets off that horse . . . puts a gun to your head . . . .and says . . . "turn over the sandwich to Dinesh." And so . . . you do. So, he puts his gun back and he drives away. Now . . . the outcome is the same. I mean . . . I have the sandwich. But . . . the moral content of that transaction is completely different. You deserve no moral credit . . . you didn't give willingly. I don't even feel a sense of gratitude . . . I feel a sense of entitlement. I [might even] feel that you actually owe me seven sandwiches, but you only gave me one. So . . . you can see how the whole thing is confused when you bring in the element of coercion.[80]

—Dinesh D'Souza

PROGRESSIVE MORALITY BASED ON COERCION AND CRONYISM

This simple anecdote illustrates that the morality of economic policy cannot simply be measured by outcome but must also consider the means and unintended consequences. Unfortunately, progressive economic policies fail the morality test on three key fronts. The first is the coercive nature of their policies. The second is the corruption invited by cronyism that is inevitable when government extends its influence over private economic affairs. Finally, progressive economic policies simply do not work because they are based on a misguided understanding of human nature.

A notable example of how coercive economic policies lack morality is the minimum wage. Progressive Democrats during the 2016 election cycle pressed for an increase in the national minimum wage, with some calling for a wage as high as fifteen dollars per hour.[81] Senator Bernie Sanders, a long-time advocate for the fifteen dollar minimum wage, claims that all employees deserve a "living wage"[82] and that employers have a moral obligation to provide one to their workers. But such moral arguments are always one-sided because they always ignore the private property rights of employers who must determine who to hire and how to invest their own capital. In the real world, the minimum wage is a job-killer that drives many firms to reduce head count, reduce work hours, and to replace workers with automated systems that do not require compensation or benefits.[83] Employers forced to pay an artificial minimum wage may also pass on their increased labor cost in the form of higher prices, thereby resulting in decreased purchasing power for consumers, and therefore fewer customers. Progressives rarely acknowledge these unintended consequences publicly because they do not factor labor economics into their thinking. Likewise, progressives will also simply ignore free-market principles in pursuit of coerced wealth transfer to workers. In either case, it is low-skilled workers, many of whom are minorities, that are hurt the most by minimum wage laws. Employers see these workers as being the least productive and, therefore, the first to be let go. Ironically, when minimum wage laws hurt unskilled and entry-level workers, they are harming the very people progressives will claim they are trying to help most. Given all of this, progressive minimum wage policy delivers nothing akin to what one might call a higher moral outcome.

Progressives are also prone to employ cronyism[84] as a tool to benefit those individuals and organizations that support their political agenda of wealth redistribution and political patronage. Progressives believe cronyism is morally justified to equalize the economic playing field, thereby ensuring the poor and middle class receive their "fair share "of wealth. That's because progressives view the acquisition of wealth in a free market as a zero-sum game, one where a successful entrepreneur or businessperson with rising income is somehow taking this increased wealth away from someone else. This has been referred to by economists as the "fixed pie" argument,[85] one that Nobel Prize winner Milton Friedman once described as being at the root of all economic fallacies. Cronyism enables progressives to carve up this pie into what they see as a more equitable distribution, thereby increasing government dependency for their core constituencies.

But wealth is not a fixed pie. Aggregate wealth will increase, and decrease based on several factors that include, most importantly, the incentives and burdens created by government fiscal, economic, and regulatory policies. Further, when a business brings a new product or service to market, that firm is frequently creating new wealth that did not exist before. As a business continues to grow, most of the wealth it creates is shared with employees, investors, suppliers, executives, and even the government.[86] In a business environment where the economy is free of unnecessary government intervention and regulatory burden, and where the government fulfills its proper role of enabling education and training opportunities for workers, everyone benefits including the rich, the middle class, and the poor.

Many progressives also justify cronyism because they believe successful entrepreneurs and business people owe their achievements to the opportunities provided by government itself, and not to their own private sector initiatives. For example, in 2011 while serving as an advisor to the Consumer Financial Protection Bureau, Elizabeth Warren (later a U.S. senator from Massachusetts) described what she believed were the special government privileges enjoyed by the business class.

> There is nobody in this country who got rich on his own — nobody. You built a factory out there? Good for you. But I want to be clear. You moved your goods to market on the roads the rest of us paid for. You hired workers the rest of us paid to educate. You were safe in your factory because of police-forces and fire-forces that the rest of us paid for. You didn't have to worry that marauding bands would come and seize everything at your factory — and hire someone to protect against this — because of the work the rest of us did. Now look, you built a factory and it turned into something terrific, or a great idea. God bless — keep a big hunk of it. But part of the underlying social contract is, you take a hunk of that and pay forward for the next kid who comes along.[87]
>
> —Senator Elizabeth Warren

Senator Warren's point of view is typical of progressives who argue in favor of a more invasive role for the federal government in private-business affairs to expand wealth redistribution. But such arguments do not pass credible scrutiny. To suggest that government is somehow an entity that is separate and distinct from the public it serves is backward leftist thinking that ignores the most basic lessons in civics. Citizens are not beholden to government; government is beholden to "we the people" who formed our nation through adoption of the Constitution. If government has built roads and educated our kids, it is because we as citizens have authorized it. We have no special moral obligation to the government, and no social contract exists with government. Instead, we simply owe our fellow citizens the obligation to pay our taxes, to obey the law and to fulfill the responsibilities of citizenship (e.g., voting; serving jury duty).

Finally, there is the moral consideration as to whether progressive policies work as intended, or just make our economic problems worse. If progressives want to claim the moral high ground by advocating for a managed economy, their policies must be measured not solely based on intent but also on results. Given this, President Obama provided us with an excellent case study demonstrating what progressive economics has contributed to society through higher taxation, more regulation, government stimulus spending and excessive debt. As the Obama administration transitioned out of office in January 2017, it left behind a shocking record of failure. These failures included skyrocketing poverty rates affecting 22 percent of all children (up from 18 percent in 2008),[88] a 41 percent increase in Americans on food stamps,[89] and the slowest post-recession jobs recovery since WWII.[90] Mr. Obama will also go down in history as being the first American president not to see at least 3.0 percent of annualized economic growth.[91] This stunningly poor economic record reflect policies that held back the very prosperity and higher standard of living progressives claim they are seeking for both the middle class and the poor.

When questioned about President Obama's economic record, most progressives will defend the president by either blaming Bush administration policies[92] or by suggesting the federal government should have borrowed and spent more on fiscal stimulus in response to the crisis.[93] However, these arguments have lost credibility with the passage of time. A more credible argument would be that progressives do not understand human nature well enough to discern how the incentives created by their policies will influence human behavior and economic decision making. Human nature cannot be cultivated or changed as progressives would have us believe. Human nature is immutable, and people will respond consistently based on the incentives that government policies create for them. Since progressives misunderstand human nature, the social and economic policies they advocate are poorly conceived and frequently do not work as intended. This is precisely why progressive-backed Obamacare entered a "death-spiral" as President Obama left office and why his economic policies were such a failure.

At the end of the 2016 election cycle, the American people had eight years of experience with the Obama administration's progressive economic policies. Voters soundly rejected these policies based on results. This rejection occurred because people will always place their personal individual rights and interests ahead of those of the collective state. Progressives who refuse to acknowledge this important truth are not only disconnected from reality, but they also give up any rightful claim to the moral high ground for their economic policies.

POLICY ARGUMENTS CONCERNING THE MORALITY OF FREE MARKETS

Constitutional conservatives should work towards implementing economic policy that is based on results (not intent), one that enables (not penalizes) all market participants who stand to benefit including the poor, the middle class, and the wealthy "1 percent." To do otherwise would undermine constitutionally protected private property rights and economic freedom. Therefore, conservatives must encourage economic growth through sound fiscal/monetary policies and common-sense regulation to encourage entrepreneurship and new wealth creation, while at the same time limiting the role of government in private-business affairs. Finally, government's moral obligation in a free market is not to achieve economic equality for all, for such an objective is utopian and unattainable. Instead, government is morally obligated to empower individual citizens by enabling them to obtain the self-sustaining skills they need to participate in, and benefit from, the free market.

While creating prosperity and providing a "living wage" to all Americans are admirable goals, achieving these results in a free market requires that we focus public policy on economic growth and individual empowerment. Policy makers must clearly understand that it is not just government that is responsible for creating prosperity. We as individuals must also do our own fair share to create prosperity for ourselves. First, this requires that individuals act responsibly by participating in strong marital relationships and avoiding out-of-wedlock births. That is because social scientists have noted that single-parent households contribute to income inequality and represent a major determinant as to whether one lives in poverty.[94] Prosperity also requires that individual workers make a lifetime commitment to education and training to remain productive and maintain the skills they need to deliver value in the free market. It is factors like these that the individual controls, and not government, that enable workers to move up the economic ladder.

Government does have a moral obligation to encourage individual empowerment. Such empowerment often takes the form of providing loans, grants, and other support to individual workers committed to expanding their knowledge and marketable skills. Ultimately, however, government and private employers cannot force individuals to increase their employability. Individuals must take on this responsibility themselves by doing the demanding work that education and training requires. For those who may not qualify for such government support, education can also be acquired through private certification programs, and from free online coursework such as that provided by Khan Academy[95] and iTunes U.

Of course, for the non-college bound and those individuals preferring to work with their hands, there are growing job opportunities available in industries that rely on the skilled construction and manufacturing trades.[96] Therefore, government must continue to support vocational-technical trade schools and other jobs programs specifically targeting these individuals. However, as former Senator Tom Coburn pointed out in 2013, federal funding for job training is inefficiently administered because it has been split across forty-four different programs within nine different agencies.[97] If federal job training programs are to produce a moral result, and not just reflect intent, these programs will need to be consolidated in some sensible manner to ensure funds are helping workers and not paying for unnecessary government bureaucracy.

Progressives will always reject the idea of individual empowerment because they see government as the source of prosperity. They also reject free market policies because they do not encourage dependency, thereby making it more difficult for government to use coercion to achieve equal economic outcomes. They would prefer that a government bureaucrat ride in on his white horse and tell us to whom we must give our sandwich. But free people need a free market. Free markets deliver solutions to everyday problems through voluntary transactions between parties where both benefit (aka, a win-win transaction). And in situations where one party to a transaction may be incented to exploit another (as we saw with predatory lending during the financial crisis), the government clearly has a regulatory role to play. However, for a clear majority of participants, and for most transactions, free markets will always produce greater economic prosperity and a more moral outcome for society than government coercion.

4

THE ROOT CAUSE OF THE 2008 FINANCIAL CRISIS

These two entities—Fannie Mae and Freddie Mac—are not fac-ing any kind of financial crisis . . . The more people exaggerate these problems, the more pressure there is on these companies, the less we will see in terms of affordable housing.[98]

—Congressman Barney Frank (D-MA), former ranking member of the House Financial Services Committee, September 2003

The Bush administration's regulators stood by as the financial industry engaged in some of the most catastrophic and irrespon-sible practices seen in the history of financial markets.[99]

—Center for American Progress, October 2010

Since the onset of the financial crisis in September 2008, there has been ample time to reflect on what led up to the collapse of financial markets and who was responsible. The root causes of this crisis were many, and they will not be explored in detail in this book. However, an honest accounting of history will show that politicians from both major political parties share a portion of the blame for their actions, and likewise for inaction, across the more than twenty-year period leading up to the crisis. Some individuals and institutions deserve more blame than others, and Presidents Clinton, Bush, and Obama own their respective fair share of the blame by contributing to the crisis in different ways.

For example, President Bush (a Republican) should have been more prudent when directing Fannie Mae and Freddie Mac to increase the percentage of subprime mortgages acquired from originators. Mr. Bush could also have been more vocal about the systematic risks introduced by passage of the Financial Services Modernization Act of 1999 (aka, the Graham-Leach-Bliley Act [GLBA]). This Act, as signed into law by President Clinton (a Democrat), repealed key provisions of the Glass-Steagall Act of 1933 that created regulatory barriers between the insurance, commercial banking, and investment banking businesses. When the GLBA lifted these barriers, it created an open invitation for investment and commercial banks to take on more systematic risk by leveraging financial resources across their business lines.

Passage of the GLBA also had the effect of enabling aggregated financial firms to grow to a point where the Federal Reserve would consider several of them "too big to fail." This left the Federal Reserve, and eventually Congress, in a position of having to consider repeated bailouts of failing firms for the next ten years. Therefore, it is accurate to say that many prominent Democrats who supported the GLBA, including President Clinton, economist Larry Summers and then treasury secretary Robert Rubin, shared responsibility for deregulating the financial services industry and enabling too-big-to-fail.

As for President Obama, his previous experience as a community organizer allowed him hands-on experience in pressuring banks to increase their commitments to affordable housing, particularly in minority neighborhoods. Because of this experience, Mr. Obama was aware of the role that Fannie Mae (Fannie) and Freddie Mac (Freddie) played in setting underwriting standards for mortgages. He was also aware that in 1999 Andrew

Cuomo, then president Clinton's director of Housing and Urban Development, had set a 50 percent affordable housing quota on Fannie and Freddie that mandated excessive risk taking through their purchase of subprime mortgages.[100] This provided every incentive for Fannie and Freddie to continue to lower mortgage underwriting standards, actions that also encouraged banks and private mortgage companies to originate as many subprime loans as possible. Fannie and Freddie would purchase these loans and "securitize" them as mortgage backed securities (MBS). Of course, Wall Street investment banks and other institutional investors were hungry to purchase these MBS investments as they included an implicit government guaranteed return. Wall Street would either hold these investments or resell them to their own institutional customers. Everyone in this cycle of investment origination, securitization and sale made money, and in the process passed along ownership of loans whose real level of risk was never fully understood, even by many so-called investment experts.

Knowing this, Senator Obama had an opportunity to either sponsor or advocate for legislation that would strengthen the lax mortgage lending standards that contributed directly to the 2008 financial crisis. And what did Senator Obama choose to do with the opportunity to advance such legislation? He did nothing. For example, in 2005 the Senate Banking Committee took up a Republican sponsored bill called the Federal Housing Enterprise Regulatory Reform Act. This Act would have given Fannie and Freddie's regulator, the Office of Federal Housing Enterprise Oversight (OFHEO), the equivalent authority of a bank regulator. Such authority would have included the ability to set capital requirements against their mortgage portfolios and the ability to limit issuance of certain types of risky mortgage products.[101] The Banking Committee approved the bill, but it was never called forward for a Senate vote because Democratic Senator Chris Dodd, then chairman of the committee, and other Senate Democrats threatened a filibuster. Senator Obama was silent on this legislation that would have had a major impact on the operations of both Fannie and Freddie. Of course, Fannie and Freddie rewarded Mr. Obama for this silence by making him the second highest recipient of their political action committee dona-tions by the time he announced his candidacy for President.[102] Therefore, his silence should surprise no one, and neither should his support of the threatened Democratic filibuster of the bill.

When we talk about who is responsible for the 2008 financial crisis and the resulting effects that it had on our economy, no one individual, enterprise, company, regulatory, or government agency can be said to be at fault. They were all at fault. The root cause of the crisis was a systematic problem, one with inherent moral hazards that allowed participants to take their own profits while passing on risk to the next participant in the mortgage investment food-chain. If each participant in that chain was making money or otherwise benefiting in some way, no one was willing to put their hand up and stay "STOP!"

DID THE BUSH TAX CUTS LEAD TO THE FINANCIAL CRISIS OF 2008?

During the decade of the 2000s, progressive Democrats were a one-trick pony in their criticism of President Bush's economic policy, blaming modest economic performance on what they described as tax cuts for the wealthy. Therefore, it is no won-der that when the financial crisis hit in 2008 they were ready to blame Mr. Bush again. However, the progressive argument that the Bush tax cuts led to the economic crisis would be best described as a creative non-sequitur, meaning it represented a conclusion that had no logical premise. The *Washington Post's* Fact Checker agreed. On October 10, 2012, the *Washington Post* reviewed President Obama's implied claim that the Bush tax cuts led to the financial crisis in 2008. Unfortunately for the Obama campaign, the *Washington Post* gave this a rating of "Three Pin-occhios" out of four, reflecting "significant factual error and/or obvious contradictions." However, they did cite that Mr. Bush should have been more aggressive in his regulatory focus during his term in office.[103]

The *Washington Post* also noted that The Financial Crisis Inquiry Report, a product of the national investigative commission established by Congress that was endorsed by every Democratic commissioner, made no mention of the Bush tax cuts.[104] Instead, the highly partisan report cited a number of other contributory causes of the crisis that included, but was not limited to regulatory failures, failures in corporate governance in risk management, the failure of the Federal Reserve to stem the flow of toxic mortgages, excessive borrowing, insufficient capital held by financial institutions, and the collapse of mortgage lending standards.[105]

As would be expected, the commission's two dissenting reports were critical of the majority's findings. The first dissent came from Commissioners Bill Thomas (vice chairman), Douglas Holtz-Eakin, and Keith Hennessey, who accused the majority of ignoring the global nature of the crisis. These commissioners found the Inquiry Report overlooked contributory credit bubbles in the European housing and commercial real estate markets, suggesting that the crisis stemmed from a problem that was broader than just U.S. regulatory policy.[106] A second dissent came from Commissioner Peter Wallison and accused the majority of using "its extensive statutory investigative authority to seek only the facts that supported its initial assumptions."[107] Wallison instead believed that U.S. government housing policy targeting increased home ownership by lowering mortgage underwriting standards was the critical factor leading to the crisis.[108] That policy, reinforced by the 50 percent subprime mortgage quota imposed on Fannie and Freddie by the Clinton administration, and later increased to 55 percent by the Bush administration in 2007, reflected the kind of social engineering progressives are well known for.

HOUSING POLICY IN THE AFTERMATH OF THE FINANCIAL CRISIS

One would think, given all we have learned since the onset of the 2008 financial crisis, the federal government would never want to repeat the housing policy mistakes that pushed high-risk subprime mortgages out to homeowners with questionable financial qualifications. Unfortunately, after a brief respite, President Obama returned to progressive social engineering by encouraging the lowering of underwriting standards that once again offered subprime mortgage products to low income individuals.

In January 2015, the Obama administration announced that it would begin lowering standards by reducing annual Federal Housing Administration (FHA) mortgage insurance premiums by 0.5 percentage points.[109] The FHA requires such insurance on mortgages when homeowners place less than a 20 percent down payment on their property because these buyers are deemed a higher credit risk than those with higher equity. Of course, along with reduced insurance premiums comes reduced capital reserves retained by the FHA that protect taxpayers in case these homeowners default. Later that month, the administration also announced new guidance to Fannie Mae and Freddie Mac that reduced "guarantee fees" charged to homeowners on loans that each organization acquired from originators.[110] Both of these executive actions followed a decision by Fannie and Freddie in December 2014 to begin backing mortgages with as little as a 3.0 percent down payment, a standard that was suspended in the aftermath of the financial crisis.[111] Taken together, these three actions set new underwriting standards targeting first-time and low-to-moderate income homebuyers who are known to be higher credit risks.

In its annual 2015 Survey of Credit Underwriting Practices, the Office of the Comptroller of the Currency (OCC) noted the following regarding the Obama Administration's mortgage loan underwriting practices in the banking industry.

> Underwriting standards eased at a significant number of banks for the three-year period from 2013 through 2015. This trend reflects broad trends similar to those experienced from 2005 through 2007, before the most recent financial crisis, including significantly larger numbers of banks easing standards.[112]
>
> —Office of the Comptroller of the Currency

Despite the potential risks to taxpayers, President Obama continued to pressure federal government housing agencies, Fannie and Freddie to lower mortgage underwriting standards right up to his last day in office. With encouragement from the administration, Fannie announced a new subprime mortgage product in August 2015 called HomeReady™ that lowered subprime standards even further. HomeReady enabled homebuyers to count income from an unlimited number of non-borrower household members toward the debt-to-income ratio when qualifying for a mortgage.[113] Additionally, HomeReady originators were permitted to approve mortgage applicants using alternative credit profiles that do not rely on traditional FICO-based credit histories.[114] While such policies increase taxpayer risk, they were defended by the Obama administration on the basis of fairness, citing the need for market reforms that deliver broad access to affordable mortgages and rents.[115] Unfortunately, their methods of generating artificial demand for housing among high-risk homebuyers reflect some of the same housing policies that led us into the subprime mortgage meltdown in 2007 and the resulting financial crisis in 2008.

While the socially engineered housing policies that progressives seek may be well intended, history tells us that these types of policies have generated boom-to-bust cycles in housing markets at least six times between 1800 and 1929.[116] The housing policies pressed by the Clinton, Bush, and Obama administrations were no different. It is high time we all learned from history and allow free housing markets to do what they do best: meet the demand for housing unencumbered by misguided progressive social engineering.

POLICY ARGUMENTS CONCERNING THE ROOT CAUSE OF THE 2008 FINANCIAL CRISIS

The 2008 financial crisis was not an accident. Instead, it was a failure of federal housing and financial system regulatory policies created by progressive social engineers across Democratic and Republican administrations. These administrations each overstepped their constitutional authority, as did members of Congress who enabled them, by abandoning the general welfare and choosing instead to subsidize housing for those who could not afford it. Therefore, constitutional conservatives should reject future attempts to create artificial demand for housing, including that for the poor and first-time home buyers, and instead seek to reestablish a fair and free housing market for those who can afford to buy.

A key reason federal housing policy led to the 2008 financial crisis is that authorities ignored the fact that the federal government is constitutionally restricted from engaging in spending initiatives that serve special interests. Although this was a subject of debate among the nation's Founders, the text of the Constitution's "Spending Clause" restricts spending to that for the general welfare.[117] While Alexander Hamilton argued that the federal government should have broader spending authority that would include investment in infrastructure and other internal improvements, the predominant view among the Founders was that spending should be limited to defense and the needs of the general public.[118] This interpretation of Congressional spending power was generally accepted until the New Deal era when the Supreme Court, in the 1936 case *United States v. Butler*, decided that Congress had essentially full discretion to determine what taxation and spending would be considered applicable to the general welfare.[119] This decision effectively empowered Congress to tax and spend as it saw fit without constitutional restriction, even extending beyond what Hamilton had sought. Since that time, Congress has proceeded down the slippery slope of enacting a plethora of federal social welfare spending programs that tax the public to subsidize special interests in a manner that runs counter to the Founders' intentions. Housing would certainly qualify as one of these programs given the federal bureaucracy that exists to encourage private home ownership. Such guarantees enable Fannie Mae and Freddie Mac to offer mortgages at lower interest rates than other market participants because the federal government implicitly bears any risk of default.

Since 2008, policy makers on both sides of the aisle have proposed regulatory initiatives and other reforms for the mortgage industry that would seek to head off another financial crisis created by systematic moral hazards. Some of these proposals have merit. For example, privatizing Fannie Mae and Freddie Mac would leave executives in both government-sponsored enterprises accountable to a board of directors that would respond to market demands for housing rather than social engineers in Washington. Wall Street investment banks could also be required to organize as partnerships, thereby returning to the operational model they had prior to 1970 when partners were personally liable for a firm's losses generated by excessive risk taking.[120] Both proposals, along with increased capital requirements, would create a viable incentive structure that align profit-making with risk-taking within our financial system. Such incentives would likely have prevented the 2008 financial crisis from occurring. More importantly, such proposals would help prevent social engineers from disrupting housing markets by helping to realign federal housing policy with the Founders' true intent behind the Constitution's "General Welfare" clause.

Shortly after his inauguration, President Trump decided it was time to address what he believed was the overregulation that the financial services industry was subjected to following the crisis. In February 2017, Mr. Trump signed an executive order that laid the groundwork to revise major provisions of the Dodd-Frank Wall Street Reform and Consumer Protection Act. Dodd-Frank, signed into law by President Obama in July 2010, had placed restrictions on consumer access to high-risk mortgage products and other forms of credit. President Trump's executive order authorized the Treasury Department to restructure provisions of Dodd-Frank that he believed were restricting commercial lending and holding back economic growth. House Republicans followed Mr. Trump's lead in June 2017 by passing the Financial Choice Act of 2017 (the FCA), albeit on a party line vote. The FCA sought to further pair down Dodd-Frank by authorizing greater congressional oversight of the Consumer Financial Protection Bureau.[121] The FCA also would have repealed Dodd-Frank's "Volker Rule" that had prevented banks from engaging in risky trading of cash deposits for their own financial gain.[122]

As of this writing, the FCA has not been taken up by the Senate as passage would require a 60-vote majority and it lacks bi-partisan support in its current form. Therefore, it remains to be seen what influence President Trump will have on balancing financial benefits and risks in the mortgage marketplace. However, Mr. Trump was elected saying that he intends to "drain the swamp" in Washington, DC of special interests. A good place to start would be to eliminate those interests that want to protect the status quo and the inherent moral hazards within the American mortgage financing system. Otherwise, we should expect to see recent history in the housing markets repeat itself again.

5

THE VALUE OF SUPPLY-SIDE ECONOMICS

It's kind of hard to sell "trickle down" . . . so the supply-side for-mula was the only way to get a tax policy that was really "trickle down." Supply-side is "trickle-down"' theory.[123]

—David Stockman, December 1981

The kind of [tax] plan that Donald Trump has put forth would be [supply-side] trickle-down economics all over again. In fact, it would be the most extreme version, the biggest tax cuts for the top percent of the people in this country that we've ever had. I call it trumped-up trickle-down, because that's exactly what it would be. That is not how we grow the economy.[124]

—Hillary Clinton, First Presidential Debate,
September 26, 2016

P rogressives, and even some political independents, have been highly critical of what free-market advocates have called "supply-side" economics, describing it as everything from "snake oil"[125] to "political voodoo"[126] to a "crank doctrine."[127]

Such critics are heavily vested in distorting a more authentic definition of supply-side economic theory, a distortion that includes the suggestion that it solely reflects a policy of providing tax cuts for the wealthy. Critics also say that supply-side policies put capital in the hands of a few wealthy individuals where only a small portion of this wealth will eventually "trickle-down" to the middle class and the poor. But as we will see, such myopic and cynical criticism of supply-side theory is simply a cover to distract us from misguided progressive economic theories based on socialism and class warfare.

Any intellectually honest discussion about supply-side economics must start with a more authentic description of what it is, and what it is not. Supply-side economics would be more accurately described as *incentive economics*. Economic incentives are central to policies aligned with supply-side theory, as they are based on a clear understanding of how individuals respond to incentives in their behavior, economic choices, and social decision making.

Supply-side theory recognizes a connection between high marginal tax rates and its detrimental effects on economic growth. However, the theory incorporates a much broader set of economic policies that progressives choose to ignore. In *The End of Prosperity*, Arthur Laffer, Steven Moore, and Peter Tanous provide us with an inventory of supply-side polices that are also enablers of free-market capitalism. These policies include: [128]

- Free trade
- Stable prices and sound money
- Light and efficient regulation of industry
- Reform of welfare policies to encourage work
- A generous immigration policy
- Less costly and more efficient government

These policies, combined with a commitment to low marginal tax rates, are central to what supply-side advocates believe leads to broad based prosperity for the rich, middle class, and the poor. Such advocates can build a strong defense for their supply-side argument based on economic history, both when these policies were practiced and when they were not. For example, President Franklin Roosevelt's (FDR) progressive economic policy makers repeatedly ignored supply-side tenets during his attempts to stimulate the economy during the 1930s through government works projects. Consequently, the Roosevelt administration contributed directly to extending the Great Depression for several years beyond what should have been a normal recovery.[129] Yet just a decade earlier, President Calvin Coolidge demonstrated that taxes on the highest income earners could be cut from 77 percent to 25 percent and in turn produce more tax revenue.[130] This fiscal exercise of reducing federal income tax rates while increasing revenue has been repeated at least three times since the Coolidge administration with the same results.

Progressive critics of supply-side theory unfortunately hold to a backward understanding of how the economy works, and how wealth is created and shared under free-market capitalism. Economist Thomas Sowell once commented on this backward view saying that progressive "trickle-down" theory and concern over tax cuts for the wealthy demonstrate a zero-sum understanding of our economy, one that ignores wealth creation.[131] Progressives instead choose to focus on redistributing existing wealth, unlike Presidents Ronald Reagan and John F. Kennedy whose policies focused on creating new wealth through economic growth.[132]

Most progressive leftists either do not conceptually acknowledge, or in some cases do not understand, the concept of wealth creation in the formation of their economic policy. Instead, they treat wealth as if it were a fixed-pie. For example, they believe that when an entrepreneur is building a company and generating significant revenue from sales of a product or service, then they must be taking money involuntarily from someone else's pocket. This is a flawed point of view that economist and

Nobel Laureate Milton Friedman saw as being central to all failed economic policies.

> Most economic fallacies derive from the neglect of this simple insight, from the tendency to assume that there is a fixed-pie, that one party can gain only at the expense of another.[133]
>
> —Milton Friedman, Nobel Prize Winner, Economics

The misguided notion that wealth is a fixed-pie is a widely held myth among the economically illiterate. It is important to note that such individuals are often well educated and highly intelligent people, but they simply lack a competent understanding of how the economy works. Unfortunately, progressives have a long history of exploiting economic illiteracy for political gain by advocating policies that have little to do with economic growth and job creation. Instead, they encourage people to covet what the wealthy have and work to confuse them on the issue of tax fairness by suggesting that the wealthy should "pay more of their fair share." They do this solely to encourage a philosophy of victimization and to build political support for government redistribution of wealth.

In this light, progressives have long criticized the Bush tax cuts of 2001 and 2003 using a pure class-warfare argument, describing them as part of the Republican "trickle-down" economic policies extending back to President Reagan. Unfortunately, progressives have conveniently chosen not to look all the way back to the mid-1960s when President Kennedy proposed a 20 percent across-the-board tax cut on individuals and corporations. President Kennedy cited the need to reduce rates to *increase* revenues as justification of his own tax cut proposals. [134] Signed into law by President Johnson after Mr. Kennedy's death, these tax cuts not only stimulated economic growth for a decade but also returned higher tax revenues to the federal treasury that increased at over 5 percent per year.[135]

Progressives ignore the success of the Kennedy tax cuts because they represent an intellectually honest dagger in the heart of their class warfare arguments. Among those choosing to ignore this history is progressive economist Dr. Robert Reich. Dr. Reich has advocated increasing tax rates on the wealthiest individuals to 70 percent while lowering rates on the middle class. [136] Reich defends his tax proposal saying that the economy was booming in the 1950s under President Eisenhower when tax rates on the wealthy were as high as 91 percent, therefore he believes a 70 percent rate today would be economically viable. However, there are two problems with Dr. Reich's argument:

- First, Reich is comparing a period in our history more than sixty years ago when Germany and Japan, two of our major modern-day economic competitors, were devastated by war. Additionally, two other modern-day economic competitors, India and China, had yet to develop mature economies that could compete internationally at that time. During the 1950s, America was the dominant economy on the face of the earth, a situation that is very different from what we face today. Therefore, if we implemented Dr. Reich's proposed 70 percent tax rate in today's global economy, it would severely undermine American economic prosperity. Such a tax would devastate domestic capital formation for small businesses, restrict economic growth and job creation, and ultimately hurt the middle class and the poor. [137]

- Second, Dr. Reich seems to believe that the 1950s were a period of economic prosperity, but research by economist Brian Domitrovic suggests otherwise. During the period from 1944 to 1960, the domestic economy saw an average annual growth rate of only 2.3 percent, including three recessions. One can compare this to the Kennedy-Johnson era from 1960 to 1969 where the average annual growth rate was 5.9 percent, [138] and the less than 3.0 percent annual growth during the Obama presidency. Given this, it would be very difficult to argue in favor of Reich's 70 percent tax rate since it would result in weak

GDP growth that would almost certainly push the U.S. economy into recession.

IS ECONOMIC PROSPERITY DRIVEN BY CONSUMER DEMAND?

Progressives will frequently argue that because our economy is so consumer driven, it is a lack of demand that is holding back strong economic growth and the creation of high-paying middle-class jobs.[139] Most economists would agree about the importance of consumer demand in creating a strong economy, particularly as measured by "consumer confidence" metrics.[140] Although strong consumer confidence reflects the lifeblood of a healthy economy, we cannot create economic prosperity for the middle class based on consumption alone. Incentivizing capital formation and private investment, particularly in the formation of new businesses, is really the key to expanding the economy and creating new wealth that can be shared across all economic classes.

Research by the Ewing Marion Kauffman Foundation indicates that all net new wealth and all net new job creation results from the formation of new business start-ups.[141] If this is true, then anyone who truly cares about creating middle-class prosperity and elevating the poor should support economic policies that incentivize private investors freely putting their money at risk in the capital markets. Progressive policy makers emphasize the demand side of economic activity because they see wealth as a fixed resource, and their policies result in little incentive to invest to create new products, services and wealth. Instead, they focus on redistributing the existing pool of wealth, an approach that does little to broaden economic prosperity for most Americans.

As their alternative to free-market supply-side economics, progressives say they are committed to increasing tax rates on the rich while providing reduced tax rates for the middle class. They describe this as the "middle-out" economics, a strategy that in theory will put more money in the hands of the middle class who progressives believe will spend it to increase consumer demand.

—

The fundamental problem with this "middle-out" economic strategy, and why it will not grow the economy, is the incentives it creates regarding investment. As you raise tax rates on wealthy individuals who have more discretionary income than the middle class or the poor, they have the freedom to shift their income out of economically productive investments into various tax shelters (e.g., tax-free government bonds). They may also choose to place their capital overseas in other countries that can offer investors a better return on their wealth. This shifting of capital will certainly generate a reasonable return on invested wealth, but it would also have deleterious economic side effects here in the United States, particularly for the creation of high-paying middle-class jobs.

Progressives advocate economic policies that typically ignore the issue of growth. Instead, they get sidetracked in their economic thinking by a twisted view of fairness that is obsessed with taxing the rich. There was no better example of this during the decade of the 2000s than that provided by President Obama himself during his second presidential debate of the 2008 campaign. Then Senator Obama was asked a question on capital gains taxes by the debate moderator Charlie Gibson of *ABC News*.[142]

GIBSON: Senator Obama, you both have now just taken this pledge [not to raise capital gains taxes] on people under $250,000?

OBAMA: Well, it depends on how you calculate it, but it would be between $200,000 and $250,000.

GIBSON: All right. You have, however, said you would favor an increase in the capital gains tax. As a matter of fact, you said on CNBC, and I quote, "I certainly would not go above what existed under Bill Clinton," which was 28 percent. It's now 15 percent. That's almost a doubling, if you went to 28 percent.

But actually, Bill Clinton, in 1997, signed legislation that dropped the capital gains tax to 20 percent.

OBAMA: Right.

GIBSON: And George Bush has taken it down to 15 percent.

OBAMA: Right.

GIBSON: And in each instance, when the rate dropped, revenues from the tax increased; the government took in more money. And in the 1980s, when the tax was increased to 28 percent, the revenues went down. So why raise it at all, especially given the fact that 100 million people in this country own stock and would be affected?

OBAMA: Well, Charlie, what I've said is that I would look at raising the capital gains tax for purposes of fairness.

Mr. Obama's response to Charlie Gibson expresses a fundamentally misguided point of view that true economic "fairness" has more to do with the tax rate an investor pays rather than the actual tax revenue they pay. Progressives believe a wealthy investor trading in the market makes money by simply taking it away from someone else. There is no thought given for how investment generates new wealth, what beneficial products or services such investment creates, or how efficiently money is allocated within the economy. This is the classic "wealth is a fixed-pie" class warfare argument used by progressives to promote victimization and exploit the economically illiterate. This argument makes no economic sense, and it makes even less fiscal sense because higher capital gains tax rates reduce tax revenues, thereby driving up the federal budget deficit and ultimately the national debt.

To optimally help the middle class and the poor, policy makers need to encourage investment in new business start-ups. Although some of these new businesses will fail, many will remain viable and sustainable over the long-term. To do this, it is imperative that we leave as much financial resource in the private sector as possible and grow the prosperity of the middle class by expanding job opportunities. This is precisely what supply-side advocates seek to do. Supply-side economics encourages low marginal tax rates that incentivize the movement of capital into domestic investment vehicles that can create jobs more quickly like equities (stocks), venture funds, and private savings that can be lent out by banks to entrepreneurs to start a new business. However, capital will only move to productive investments if the tax and regulatory environment provides the right incentives relative to risk and reward. That starts with low marginal tax rates.

Empirical evidence shows that reducing high-marginal tax rates on wealthy individuals will generate more tax revenue, not less, if two conditions are met. First, the tax cuts must be permanent (or very long-term) and not a one-time gimmick. A broad range of economists from diverse philosophical backgrounds including Milton Friedman and Paul Krugman have noted that such one-time tax gimmicks like rebates or temporary rate reductions do not change individual investment behavior. Secondly, nominal tax rates must be higher than the optimal tax rate as indicated by the Laffer Curve reflected in Figure B below.

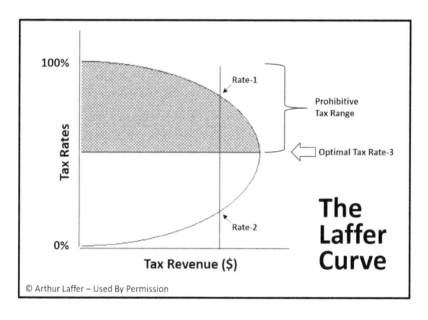

Figure B. The Laffer Curve

The Laffer Curve illustrates the real-world incentive effects of alternative tax rates on tax revenue generation. The theory suggests that at one extreme of the curve if the government sets a tax rate of zero (0) percent on income then no matter how much income an individual earns there is no tax revenue generated. Simple and logical enough. However, at the other extreme of the curve, if the government taxes a worker at 100 percent or more of the income they earn, then you eliminate all incentive for that worker to earn income. At a 100 percent tax rate, a rational individual would rather stay at home and do nothing or find a way to evade the government tax and work "under the table." In either case, the resulting tax revenue to the government would still be zero. Therefore, the Laffer Curve suggests somewhere between the tax rates of zero percent and 100 percent there is an optimal tax rate that maximizes a return of tax revenue to the government while still providing an incentive for the individual to continue to work and maximize their income.[143]

A critical point behind the supply-side argument is that if you advocate high marginal tax rates like Dr. Reich suggested (note Rate-1), you may be overlooking the fact that there is a lower tax rate (note Rate-2) at which an individual may generate and pay the same level of tax revenue. Further, there may be a third optimal tax rate (note Rate-3 above) that would return an even higher level of tax revenue if rates were set at that point. Therefore, the goal in setting marginal tax rates should be to avoid setting them above this tipping point where one would see a diminishing level of tax revenue. Supply-side economic theory is clear on these incentive effects, but the economic theories of the progressive Left do not acknowledge them.

Progressives absolutely hate to talk about the incentive principles surrounding the Laffer Curve because it distracts from their intended message about "tax fairness." However, if your objective is to have the wealthy pay more tax, then why not adopt a strategy that encourages them to generate more wealth and pay an optimal tax rate? Unfortunately, progressives instead focus on encouraging class warfare by trying to convince middle-class and poor individuals that the wealthy must pay more of their fair share. This leads back to the old "fixed-pie" argument. For someone who is economically literate enough to understand incentives and how wealth is created, this is completely illogical. But for progressives waging a class war, policy is not about logic or net tax revenue. It is about making the poor and middle class feel that they are victims and encouraging them to covet what the wealthy have. The next step is for progressives to translate feelings of victimization and envy into political support that results in more government intervention and control of the economy, thereby allowing for wealth to be redistributed.

It is important to note that some Republicans and economic conservatives have attempted to market the idea that tax cuts will always pay for themselves, implying that any tax cut is self-funding because it will always generate higher tax revenues. The reader should note that this is not, and has never been, a policy associated with supply-side economic theory. Progressives have locked on to this idea and used it to smear all advocacy of supply-side economics as being a one-dimensional "trickle-down" theory. However, The Laffer Center reminds us that tax cuts do produce other benefits such as economic growth, jobs, and higher incomes even when they do not maximize government revenues.[144]

If progressives believe they can pay for their proposed middle-class tax cuts by somehow increasing tax rates on the wealthy, they are ignoring mountains of empirical evidence that show that such policies may generate less tax revenue. Should this occur, such policies would erode the tax base, increase the federal budget deficit and, in turn, increase the national debt. Therefore, as a rule, reducing marginal tax rates on all taxpayers including the wealthy can provide a basis for optimizing tax revenues while improving economic opportunities for the middle class and the poor.

DIDN'T PRESIDENT CLINTON'S TAX INCREASES GENERATE ECONOMIC PROSPERITY?

Progressives frequently point to one historical example when the U.S. economy boomed after marginal income tax rates increased on the wealthy, one they use to justify the viability of their "middle-out" economic strategy. That example is the Clinton income tax increases of 1993 when top rates were increased from 31.0 to 39.6 percent. Progressives continue to get mileage out of this one event and sell it as a justification for every tax increase they wish to enact. Even President Obama attempted to make this argument to justify higher tax rates.

> A modest increase for wealthy individuals is not shown to have an adverse impact on job growth . . . if wealthy individuals are willing to simply go back to the rates that existed back in the 1990s . . . then we can solve this [economic] problem.[145]
>
> —President Barack Obama, July 6, 2011.

However, just as President Eisenhower's 91 percent tax rate coincided with unique fiscal and economic conditions, so did the Clinton tax increase of 1993. President Clinton was lucky enough to inherit the Internet boom during his term of office, along with a corresponding technology investment boom that most of us will only see once in our lifetime. By the mid-1990s, the Internet was being commercialized and consumers were investing heavily in all kinds of information technology and networking infrastructure. Former America Online CEO Steve Case remembers this period as one of rapid Internet expansion where consumers began purchasing personal computers and modems in large numbers, and the World Wide Web emerged to enable the public Internet to connect millions of end-users.[146] Such investment brought an incipient market to life, one that led to hundreds of technology start-ups and economic growth that by 1998 would deliver the first federal budget surplus in the United States since 1969.[147]

--

There were other factors that contributed to the boom in economic growth during the Clinton years. Republicans had finally convinced the President to support an agenda that reformed welfare and encouraged work, lowered trade tariffs, limited growth in government spending, and created a stable and strong dollar, all policies consistent with supply-side economics.[148] In the end, the momentum of the Internet boom and rabid technology investment throughout the decade of the 1990s overrode any ill-effects of the 1993 marginal tax increase on upper-income taxpayers. Of course, you will never hear this story from the Center for American Progress and other progressive organizations that choose to spin economic history. Therefore, we can look at this period concerning the Clinton tax increases as a one-off event, one that *does not* serve as an example of what we should emulate today.

POLICY ARGUMENTS CONCERNING THE VALUE OF SUPPLY-SIDE ECONOMICS

Constitutional conservatives should more accurately describe "supply-side" economics as "incentive" economics because the policies it embodies are based on free-market incentives. Supply-side policies have been put into practice successfully by both Democrat and Republican presidents, including Calvin Coolidge, John Kennedy, Ronald Reagan, and Bill Clinton. While supply-side advocates appreciate the dynamics of how lower tax rates drive economic growth, they also understand that its policies involve much more than just taxes. In short, the value of supply-side economic policy is inherently trusting in individual freedom over government control, thereby by allowing citizens to exercise their right to take risks, and to succeed or fail without undue burden or harassment from government. For when government dominates or otherwise directs the economy and prevents citizens from enjoying the fruits of their labor, our constitutional right to economic liberty is infringed.

Progressive leftists attack free markets because economic freedom does not align with their strategy of managed economies, wealth redistribution, and equal economic outcomes. They argue the idea of tax cuts that include all taxpayers allows the wealthy to gain the greatest return while offering the middle class and poor merely "trickle-down" benefits. But the concept of trickle-down has no real economic meaning. Thomas Sowell once publicly challenged anyone to name an economist, regardless of their school of thought, who had ever advocated trickle-down as an economic theory.[149] He had no takers that could offer a verifiable example. That is because the concept of "trickle-down" is not an economic theory, it is a political argument. In fact, President Obama and progressive Democrats implemented their own version of trickle-down economics to benefit their own wealthy cronies. Columnist George Will once described President Obama's version of trickle-down economics as supporting appointments to the Federal Reserve Bank who would keep interest rates near zero, thereby driving people out of bonds and into other assets, especially stocks.[150] Will noted these policies have rewarded the 10 percent of Americans who directly own 80 percent of stocks, a fact that explains why 95 percent of wealth created during the Obama presidency went to the infamous "1 percent" of Americans that progressives frequently deride.[151]

Supply-side economic policies offer the middle class and the poor greater opportunities for prosperity and advancement than any other economic policy framework because it incentivizes private investment. When private investment is focused on capitalizing new businesses, the benefits of such investment are optimized because start-up businesses must hire people immediately. We all know that while some new businesses will ultimately fail, they will eventually be replaced by others that join with successful start-ups to sustain job creation over the long-term. This type of privately funded economic growth does not burden taxpayers in the same manner as progressive "middle-out" economic policy does, thereby avoiding crony-capitalism disasters such as Solyndra (the bankrupt solar panel manufacturer), Mylan (the EpiPen pricing scandal), and Fannie Mae (the subprime mortgage crisis). By keeping government funding out of the mix of business investment, and avoiding overregulation of markets critical to our prosperity, we can achieve optimal advancement of the economic interests of all Americans and not just the top 1 percent.

One last point that cannot be ignored is that when the American economy experiences a period of strong economic growth from supply-side policies, economic inequality will not shrink but rather grow.[152] This reality does not disadvantage the poor or middle class. In fact, quite the opposite. Prosperity and economic growth will create new wealth that will eventually find its way into greater educational and training opportunities for those looking to advance economically in a growing free-market system. Progressives will ignore this fact because it does not align with their message of victimization and government dependency. However, able-bodied individuals who are concerned about their economic future will prepare themselves to participate in the free market. This includes making a lifetime commitment to education and training to acquire the skills they need to move up the economic ladder. This commitment and its cost are primarily an individual responsibility. However, government can—and should—play a role in helping to finance education and training only if there are measurable results that produce individual economic advancement.

What supply-side advocates appreciate more than anyone is that individual incentives matter and that government economic policies should reinforce personal responsibility over dependency. This includes a public-sector commitment to fund educational opportunity and to encourage individuals to develop marketable skills that will serve them in the private sector. This may be one policy area where the progressive Left and conservative Right can work together to achieve better outcomes for the middle class and the poor. After all, both should be able to agree on this: If we give someone a fish, we feed them for a day, but if we teach someone how to fish, we feed them for a lifetime. And if we can agree on this, maybe we are all supply-siders.

6

THE MYTH OF ECONOMIC STIMULUS

"There's a long history that when unemployment rises, the government steps in [with economic stimulus] to pave the way for job creation. And these policies have been effective. It's time to do so again . . ."[153]

—Heather Boushey and Michael Ettlinger, Center for American Progress, September 8, 2011

I n the aftermath of the 2008 presidential election, President-elect Obama and his progressive supporters worked tirelessly to build public support for the idea that federal spending (aka stimulus) would be critical to economic recovery from the financial crisis. For example, Vice President-elect Joe Biden made a bold claim on ABC-TV's *This Week* that expressed what would later reflect President Obama's economic policy. He said:

Every economist, as I've said, from conservative to liberal, acknowledges that direct government spending on a direct program now is the best way to infuse economic growth and create jobs.[154]

—Vice President-elect Joseph Biden, December 21, 2008

—

President-elect Obama echoed these same thoughts by trying to convince Americans that there was universal agreement among economists that a large economic stimulus was required to fix the economy and pull us out of the Great Recession.

> There is no disagreement that we need action by our government, a recovery plan that will help to jump-start the economy.[155]

—President-elect Barack Obama, January 9, 2009

Of course, this point of view harkens back to FDR's "New Deal" era that progressives look to in times of trouble to find their great economic truths. In their eyes, one of these truths is that government spending creates both jobs and prosperity. Therefore, they see stimulus as an absolute policy requirement in the event of an economic downturn. Fortunately, for the sake of intellectual honesty, POLITIFACT investigated Mr. Obama's claim of universal agreement amongst economists on stimulus, a claim they rated as "false." POLITIFACT pointed out that there were many economists that believed reductions in tax rates, smaller government, and even benign neglect were more favorable and beneficial to the economy than stimulus spending.[156]

In response to President-elect Obama's statement, The Cato Institute issued its own statement signed by more than two hundred economists, including three Nobel Laureates, criticizing President Obama's proposed stimulus package. This statement made it clear that there was not universal support for direct government spending in response to the financial crisis. The Cato statement read:

> **With all due respect Mr. President, that is not true.** There is no disagreement that we need action by our government, a recovery plan that will help to jumpstart the economy. Notwithstanding reports that all economists are now Keynesians and that we all support a big increase in the burden of government, we the undersigned do not believe that more government spending is a way to improve economic performance. More

government spending by Hoover and Roosevelt did not pull the United States economy out of the Great Depression in the 1930s. More government spending did not solve Japan's "lost decade" in the 1990s. As such, it is a triumph of hope over experience to believe that more government spending will help the U.S. today. To improve the economy, policymakers should focus on reforms that remove impediments to work, saving, investment and production. Lower tax rates and a reduction in the burden of government are the best ways of using fiscal policy to boost growth.[157]

—The Cato Institute, January 27, 2009

President Obama never acknowledged Cato's statement at the time, and he pressed forward wearing economic blinders to pass and sign his stimulus package, the American Recovery and Reinvestment Act (ARRA), on February 17, 2009. Mr. Obama defended the ARRA a week later in a speech delivered before a joint session of Congress.

As soon as I took office, I asked this Congress to send me a recovery plan by President's Day that would put people back to work and put money in their pockets. Not because I believe in bigger government—I don't. Not because I'm not mindful of the massive debt we've inherited—I am. I called for action because the failure to do so would have cost more jobs and caused more hardships. In fact, a failure to act would have worsened our long-term deficit by assuring weak economic growth for years. That's why I pushed for quick action. And tonight, I am grateful that this Congress delivered, and pleased to say that the American Recovery and Reinvestment Act is now law.[158]

—President Barack Obama, February 24, 2009

In his speech, President Obama went on to promise that the economic stimulus reflected in the ARRA would create or save 3.5 million jobs over two years, 90 percent of which he said would be in the private sector. The law called for a range of spending initiatives as varied as tuition tax credits, subsidies to state governments, so-called green energy investments, and infrastructure. One-time tax credits for individual taxpayers and a range of tax credits for business were also included as part of the package. In total, the Act authorized a total of $787 billion in stimulus spending.

Approximately one year after President Obama signed the ARRA into law, the *New York Times* reported that three independent econometric organizations, IHS Global Insight, Macroeconomic Advisors, and Moody's were claiming the stimulus had added between 1.6 and 1.8 million new jobs to the domestic economy.[159] The *Times* report also claimed that the Congressional Budget Office (CBO) had estimated that the final tally of jobs added from stimulus spending would be 2.5 million, about 1.0 million short of President Obama's stated objective. A CBO report issued at about the same time estimated that between 1.8 and 4.1 million new full-time equivalent (FTE) jobs had been created by first-quarter 2010.[160] However, the CBO offered these words of caution about its own estimates of the economic effects resulting from the ARRA:

> CBO has examined data on output and employment during the period since ARRA's enactment. However, those data are not as helpful in determining ARRA's economic effects as might be supposed, because isolating those effects would require knowing what path the economy would have taken in the absence of the law. Because that path cannot be observed, the new data add only limited information about ARRA's impact.[161]
>
> —Congressional Budget Office, May 2010

The CBO report went on to say that its own estimates of FTE job creation differ from data reported by ARRA recipients, and that such reports may be higher or lower than actual for several reasons. These reasons included counting jobs that may have been created without ARRA stimulus, incomplete reporting of jobs created by ARRA funding recipients, and the lack of measurement for tax cuts and transfer payments. Given these interpretive cautions, any reasonable person would agree that estimates concerning job creation resulting from the ARRA by the CBO and President Obama's supporters were speculative at best.

CHALLENGES TO PRESIDENT OBAMA'S STIMULUS PLAN

Economists who challenged President Obama's assertion that FDR-style government stimulus was required to jump-start the economy had concerns that were well founded. Progressive economists who defended Mr. Obama's stimulus presented an incomplete picture of the economic costs of government spending. Specifically, they failed to recognize that for every dollar the government spends there is an equal and opposite cost somewhere else in the economy. This is because government does not create wealth; it only taxes it from the private sector and then redistributes it.

Of course, progressive economists will argue against this logic by speaking to something called the "money multiplier" effect of government stimulus. Arthur Laffer, the supply-side economist and former member of President Reagan's Economic Policy Advisory Board, explains the multiplier effect in this way.

> If you give a guy $600 that he otherwise would not have had, he is going to spend more than he otherwise would have spent. And that's true; he is going to go out and buy stuff. That in turn is going to create jobs for people who are now supplying him with the goods and services that he otherwise would not have bought. Those people in turn will have higher incomes and spend more money, and there will be this cascading effect through the economy. And that will lift the economy up by the bootstraps.[162]
>
> —Arthur Laffer

However, Dr. Laffer moves on from the multiplier to explain the other half of the economic stimulus equation. That being the economic cost of taxation.

The government does not have a tooth fairy. To give command over real resources to someone based upon any characteristic other than work effort, it must take those resources from someone else. It is a zero-sum game. The government can redistribute income but cannot create it out of thin air. When resources are given to one group and taken from another, the taxpayers who lose the resources in turn will spend less. That will disemploy people who had heretofore been employed through supplying the goods and services people are no longer buying. The incomes of the newly disemployed will be down, they will in turn spend less, and there will be a cascading effect through the system on the other side that exactly offsets the multiplier effect on the stimulus recipients. For every dollar received there is a dollar lost; whenever you bail someone out of trouble, you put someone else into trouble. That's double-entry accounting.[163]

—Arthur Laffer

The progressive Left does not practice "double entry" accounting as Dr. Laffer describes it. Instead, they prefer to show only one side of their accounting ledger because it allows them to preach "free-lunch" economics to their political base. But government benefits are not free, and there is no such thing as a free lunch. That's because the government cannot spend a dollar unless it taxes it from somewhere else in the private sector. Similarly, the government has no capacity to create wealth. All it can really do is tax and redistribute existing private sector wealth.

Government can acquire private wealth in several ways. It can acquire it immediately by direct taxation imposed today, or it can borrow tax revenues by indebting someone in the future. Government may also choose to devalue the dollar through something equivalent to the Federal Reserve's recent "quantitative easing" policies, thereby creating a future tax through inflation. This has been referred to metaphorically by some economists as "printing money." Regardless of the method used to acquire private wealth, each method will eventually have an adverse effect on consumer spending, economic growth, and resulting job creation. Herein lies the zero-sum game that Dr. Laffer describes above.

Since the government cannot create wealth like the private sector can by creating new products or services, any gain from stimulus spending is offset by a reduction in wealth through taxation in some other part of the economy.

Even worse, progressive advocates of stimulus believe that their investment wisdom in acquiring and redistributing the private wealth of taxpayers is superior to that of the taxpayers whose wealth they have acquired. Therefore, they see a net benefit in taxing and spending someone else's money. One cannot say that all federal spending is wasteful because there have been many innovations that have come from government sponsored "basic" research. These include medical innovations from the National Institutes of Health, transfer of innovations created in the Defense Department that include the Internet and GPS systems, and many by-products of research at NASA. However, government's track record concerning wealth creation by investing in "applied" research and other forms of stimulus has been abysmal. Examples of such spending include giving seed money to private companies like Solyndra and A123 Systems or offering tax credits to consumers through programs like "Cash for Clunkers." These initiatives underperform private-sector investment decisions because they often become an exercise in political cronyism where resources are targeted to political supporters of those holding public office. When this occurs, any hope of investing money efficiently is lost in favor of political expediency, aggregate wealth is destroyed, and the overall benefit to the U.S. economy is often negative.

Case in point, research by Peter Schweizer of the Hoover Institution showed that approximately 80 percent of the Obama administration's stimulus funding allocated for energy loan guarantees were given to Mr. Obama's political supporters.

In the 1705 government-backed-loan program, for example, $16.4 billion of the $20.5 billion in loans granted went to companies either run by or primarily owned by Obama financial backers—individuals who were bundlers, members of Obama's National Finance Committee, or large donors to the

Democratic Party. The grant and guaranteed-loan recipients were early backers of Obama before he ran for president, people who continued to give to his campaigns and exclusively to the Democratic Party in the years leading up to 2008. Their political largesse is probably the best investment they ever made in alternative energy. It brought them returns many times over.[164]

—Peter Schweizer, *Throw Them All Out*

Given the inherent incentives for politicians to redirect government stimulus spending to their political cronies, it becomes very hard to make any reasonable case that government will be more efficient in investing private tax dollars than taxpayers themselves. For progressives, however, federal stimulus is a godsend because it is a vehicle to achieve the kind of wealth transfer they need to build their political base.

IS ECONOMIC STIMULUS MAINSTREAM ECONOMICS?

If you had a dollar for every time President Obama or his supporters proclaimed that his economic policies were mainstream, you could afford the tax increases he imposed on all of us. For those of us literate in both civics and economics, it is easy to see that Mr. Obama's policies are far left of center. This is especially true about his economic policies that have their roots in FDR's New Deal and are said by his supporters to be heavily influenced by the theories of John Maynard Keynes.

Keynes was a British economist who was a strong advocate of central government planning for the private economy. His theories on the use of fiscal and monetary policy to stabilize the normal business cycles, avoid recession, and preserve employment remain influential to this day. While Keynesian theory has always been popular with the progressive Left, economic policy as practiced by the Obama administration went far beyond anything that Keynes would have advocated. In fact, given Mr. Obama's propensity to engage in class warfare, it would be more accurate to describe them as middle-out socialist-style economics rather than Keynesian.

Middle out economics has been moved to the forefront of public debate by several liberal economists whose professional credentials are widely known and whose political point of view is unquestionably far Left. The most prominent of these economists are Paul Krugman and Robert Reich. Both men have been enormously influential among the Democratic progressive establishment. Both have long advocated the kind of higher taxes on the wealthy and spending increases by the federal government that progressives drool over. Economists including Larry Summers, Alan Blinder, Heidi Garret-Peltier, Heather Boushey, and others also defended aspects of the Obama economic agenda such as federal stimulus programs and green energy investment. But these individuals do not represent mainstream economic thought as they are pushing a fiscal policy agenda that runs counter to what Keynes advocated.

Allan Meltzer, a prominent monetary economist who served in both the Kennedy and Reagan administrations, is the author of a widely respected book on Keynesian economics called *Keynes's Monetary Theory: A Different Interpretation.* In a 2010 interview published by *CNN Money,* Meltzer has spoken publicly about how Keynes would have viewed the economic policies that were pursued by the progressive Left and President Obama during his two terms in office. Meltzer noted that Keynes was opposed to large structural deficits driven by government spending because he believed they quiesced rather than stimulated the economy.[165] Keynes, he said, viewed economic policies that stimulate *private* investment, not government spending or consumption, as the key to enduring job creation.[166] According to Meltzer, Keynes wanted deficits to be cyclical, temporary and offsetting, thereby generating sufficient tax revenues to cancel out deficits experienced during an economic downturn.[167] Clearly, these are not the economic policies we see coming from the progressive Left, or in some cases even from the conservative Right.

Meltzer's interpretation of Keynes's theories reflects that of most mainstream economists, many of whom have provided advice and critique during the writing of his interpretive book. This is important to note because Keynes is frequently, and inappropriately, cited as the justification for progressive economic policies. These policies include massive federal borrowing on top of existing structural deficits, unbridled stimulus spending and progressive tax structures that target the so-called top 1 percent. Meltzer's analysis clearly demonstrates that the economic proposals advocated by President Obama and other progressives are not aligned with the Keynes economic playbook. Rather, progressives advocate a more radical interpretation of economics that put far too much faith in the government's ability to grow the economy, create jobs, and deliver prosperity.

DID PRESIDENT OBAMA IMPLEMENT THE SAME ECONOMIC POLICIES AS FDR?

Progressives typically hold a unique perspective on the history of the 1930s when compared to traditional free-market conservatives and supply-side advocates. Progressives see FDR's New Deal, including federal spending on work projects and infrastructure, as the policy model for what government should do to boost a lackluster economy. This model includes levying higher taxes on wealthy individuals and corporations to redistribute this wealth to the middle class and the poor. While it may be said that FDR's social support offered temporary relief to those most affected by the Depression, America failed to achieve true economic recovery until well after his New Deal ended.

One example of New Deal policy failure occurred during the period from 1935 to 1938 in what would come to be known by economic historians as the "Depression within the Depression." During this period, FDR initiated aggressive intervention in the private sector using fiscal stimulus initiatives that later became known as the "Second New Deal." These initiatives included the Revenue Act of 1935 that imposed a surtax of 75 percent on incomes above $5 million.[168] This was followed by the Revenue Act of 1936 that included a new Undistributed Profits (UP) Tax that was designed to encourage corporations to distribute what FDR believed were excess profits as dividends to corporate shareholders.[169] The Second New Deal also included a range of other tax-and-spend initiatives including the Social Security Act, the Works Progress Administration (WPA), and the National Labor Relations Act. [170] It also levied punitive taxes on income, inheritances, large gifts, business profits, and property sales.[171]

FDR introduced his Second New Deal in classic class-warfare fashion in a speech on October 31, 1936, at Madison Square Garden in New York City. In this speech, FDR railed against the wealthy and the business community, pointing the finger of blame at them for the Depression.

> We had to struggle with the old enemies of peace--business and financial monopoly, speculation, reckless banking, class antagonism, sectionalism, war profiteering. They had begun to consider the Government of the United States as a mere appendage to their own affairs. We know now that Government by organized money is just as dangerous as Government by organized mob. Never before in all our history have these forces been so united against one candidate as they stand today. They are unanimous in their hate for me--and I welcome their hatred. I should like to have it said of my first Administration that in it the forces of selfishness and of lust for power met their match. I should like to have it said of my second Administration that in it these forces met their master.
> —President Franklin D. Roosevelt, October 31, 1936

In response to FDR's reinvigorated class war, private investment capital effectively went "on strike." This meant that business investors decided to wait out FDR by keeping their private capital on the sidelines instead of investing in the commercial marketplace. As a result, private domestic investment plummeted $5.1 billion in inflation-adjusted dollars (or 39 percent)[172] between 1937 to 1938, immediately pushing America back into a Depression. Progressive economist Paul Krugman has tried to point the finger of blame for extending the Depression back at FDR by saying that it was FDR's "premature attempt to balance the budget [in 1937] that helped plunge a recovering economy back into severe recession."[173] However, federal consumption/investment expenditures dropped by only $500 million in inflation-adjusted dollars (or 8.6 percent)[174] during this timeframe. By simple order of magnitude, it was the tenfold drop in private investment when compared to public spending that had the most significant economic impact during this same time-period. Therefore, it was the unintended consequences of FDR's intervention in the private sector, not a drop in public investment, that halted what had been a modest recovery, and that pushed the country back into a Depression.

The implications of FDR's policies during this period for employment were devastating. Unemployment rates skyrocketed again from 14.3 percent in 1937 to 19.0 percent in 1938, It was not until the approach of World War II when FDR faced a Hobson's choice between continuing to wage a class war on the wealthy or, alternatively, a war on fascism that he finally changed course. By the late 1930s he finally chose to partner with the wealthy business class that controlled American industry and, in the process, eliminated many of his own New Deal roadblocks to recovery.

In some respects, President Obama's progressive economic policies did reflect those of FDR in that they were both interventionist and redistributive. Both Presidents chose to wage a class war that claimed the wealthy class as the root cause of the nation's lack of economic prosperity. Both appeared to believe that wealth was a fixed-pie and that socialist redistribution and consumption would lead us out of economic crisis. Both were unsuccessful.

POLICY ARGUMENTS CONCERNING THE MYTH OF ECONOMIC STIMULUS

Among the responsibilities of the federal government outlined in the Constitution are promoting the general welfare and securing the blessings of liberty for ourselves and our posterity. Given this, the federal government does have a responsibility to enable broad based economic prosperity for the people by protecting private property rights and creating an environment within which the private economy can thrive. However, promoting the general welfare implies advancing prosperity for all citizens and not for special interest groups. Attempts at economic stimulus by progressives in both major political parties are too often corrupted by political influence and are usually counterproductive. Therefore, constitutional conservatives should limit their support for economic stimulus to those initiatives involving permanent changes in fiscal policy that encourage private-sector investment by private individuals and commercial companies.

The progressive Left will seek to justify more federal spending for several reasons, with economic stimulus being their "go-to" proposal during any economic downturn. More recently, the progressives have promoted the idea of boosting consumption spending based on "middle-out" economic theory. This theory calls for imposing higher taxes on the rich to transfer more money for consumption into the pockets of the middle class. While progressives offer many justifications for stimulus, government transfer of wealth to special interest and political cronies generally produce little economic benefit to the general welfare. Government bureaucrats, regardless of political party, simply do not have sufficient wisdom to know how to invest taxpayer wealth as wisely as the private sector. What government should do is focus on encouraging private investment as Keynes had advocated.

But stimulus can work if structured and focused properly. One important idea for how government stimulus can encourage private-sector economic growth and job creation comes from Frederick Smith, chairman and CEO of FedEx Corporation. In a Wall Street Journal opinion piece, Mr. Smith stated that *accelerated depreciation* has been rated by economists as the most effective economic stimulus tool government has employed dating back to the Eisenhower administration.[175] Smith referenced a 2001 study by the Institute for Policy Innovation (IPI) that found that every $1 in tax cuts devoted to accelerated depreciation would generate an estimated $9 of increased GDP.[176] The IPI study also noted that investment tax credits, reductions in corporate tax rates, and repeal of the Alternative Minimum Tax are all fiscal initiatives that would deliver high GDP return on investment.[177]

As an economic stimulus, accelerated depreciation does not burden taxpayers in the long-term but does drive economic growth in the short-term. One would think progressives would welcome this type of proposal because accelerated depreciation incentivizes consumption, albeit industrial consumption in the form of business investment. But alas, private industry is not a key constituency for the progressive Left, unless we are talking about industries they choose to target like green energy with one of the lowest returns on investment.[178] Instead, progressives focus their efforts on pushing middle-out economic policies that subsidize the middle class at broader taxpayer expense.

There are other rare instances when government stimulus can have positive economic returns, and specifically when spending is focused on certain types of transportation infrastructure. These returns typically arise when new infrastructure enables business and individual productivity by reducing transportation costs or, in the long-run, stimulating private investment. But while such benefits may be immediate for those gaining access to a new transportation conveyance, sustainable returns in economic growth and job creation are only achieved in the long-run. Further, one should not assume that all transportation infrastructure spending will create benefits that are sustainable. That is because the relationship between infrastructure spending and productivity is not fully understood, but rather is a topic of continued academic study.[179] Policy makers should be reminded of boondoggle infrastructure projects such as the proposed $320 million Gravina Island Bridge in Ketchikan, Alaska (aka the "Bridge-to-Nowhere"), or the $150 million John Murtha Airport in Cambria County, Pennsylvania, where the economic return on both projects was questionable. At a time when our federal government is carrying more than $20 trillion in debt, any proposed infrastructure project must be carefully targeted, and its economic benefits should be clear and readily attainable.

A wise businessperson once said that "there is always money for a sound investment; all you need to do is make a strong business case." While this is true, it is also true that those placing their own money at risk in the private marketplace are much less likely to bet on an investment that will fail. But when the economy underperforms, and progressives believe they must act, they don't call for economic stimulus and start spending their own money. Instead, they call on taxpayers to pay the bill. Given that almost 80 percent of the members of Congress lack any formal education in business or economics,[180] it is reasonable for all of us to question both their intentions and their competency when advocating such policy. After all, would you let someone without such an education invest your personal wealth?

7

THE POLITICS OF INEQUALITY

This growing inequality is morally wrong, it's bad economics . . .
When wealth concentrates at the very top, it can inflate unstable
bubbles that threaten the economy. When the rungs on the ladder
of opportunity grow farther and farther apart, it undermines the
very essence of this country.[181]

—President Barack Obama, July 24, 2013

Progressives have made an issue of how income inequality has grown in America over the past thirty years. They have been particularly vocal about the disparity they have observed growing between the middle class and the very wealthy during President Bush's term in office. President Obama himself recognized this issue in the introduction of his first budget proposal:

For the better part of three decades, a disproportionate share of the Nation's wealth has been accumulated by the very wealthy. Technological advances and growing global competition, while transforming whole industries—and birthing new ones—has accentuated the trend toward rising inequality. Yet, instead of using the tax code to lessen these increasing wage disparities, changes in the tax code over the past eight years exacerbated them.[182]

—President Obama's Budget Proposal, February 26, 2009

Mr. Obama was the preeminent cheerleader for highlighting the problem of income inequality during his two terms in office. He and other progressives claimed that inequality is reflected in a shrinking middle class and a reduction in consumer demand, factors they see as the root cause of America's sluggish economy during his presidency.

No one denies the importance of a vibrant and thriving American middle class or that there is growing income inequality between the wealthy, the middle class and the poor. And to their credit, progressives have been willing to acknowledge that the causes of inequality include the disruptive effects of economic globalization and business investment in technology. These factors have hit the traditional middle-class job market hard as automation replaces many middle-management functions, and as cheap labor has motivated manufacturers to outsource operations overseas. However, there remains much disagreement between progressives and free-market conservatives as to how inequality should be addressed.

It is important to acknowledge that growing income inequality is not a problem that is unique to the United States, but rather a global phenomenon. Research by the Organization for Economic Cooperation and Development (OECD) has shown that most of its thirty-four-member countries have seen growing income inequality over the past twenty years.

Over the two decades prior to the onset of the global economic crisis, real disposable household incomes increased by an average 1.7% a year in OECD countries. In a large majority of them, however, the household incomes of the richest 10% grew faster than those of the poorest 10%, so widening income inequality. Differences in the pace of income growth across household groups were particularly pronounced in some of the English-speaking countries, some Nordic countries, and Israel.[183]

—OECD, Divided We Stand: Why Inequality Keeps Rising

Given this global observation, to conclude that income inequality is a phenomenon that is unique to America or that it is a problem created by the Bush administration's economic policies would be a mistake. In fact, it is a paradox of history in that the wealth gap between economic classes typically grows wider during periods of prosperity led by strong economic growth. Therefore, progressives might do better to emphasize the importance of enabling income mobility between economic classes as one of its core political objectives.

RESEARCH ON INCOME EQUALITY

During the past decade, there have been several academic research studies that have attempted to explain the nature and root cause of income inequality. Research by Dr. Emmanuel Saez, a French economist and professor at the University of California at Berkeley, has probably been the most publicized on this subject in mainstream media. Dr. Saez updated his research findings pertaining to income inequality in the aftermath of the 2008 financial crisis by noting the following:

> Top 1% incomes grew by 31.4% while bottom 99% incomes grew only by 0.4% from 2009 to 2012. Hence, the top 1% captured 95% of the income gains in the first three years of the [recent] recovery . . . Note also that part of the surge of top 1% incomes in 2012 could be due to income retiming to take advantage of the lower top [income and capital gains] tax rates in 2012 relative to 2013 and after . . . A number of factors may help explain this increase in inequality, not only underlying technological changes but also the retreat of institutions developed during the New Deal and World War II— such as progressive tax policies, powerful unions, corporate provision of health and retirement benefits, and changing social norms regarding pay inequality.[184]
>
> —Dr. Emmanuel Saez, UC Berkeley

Dr. Saez's research, along with that conducted with Professor Thomas Piketty of the Paris School of Economics, has frequently been referenced by progressives as the basis of their claim that income inequality is a growing problem. For example, President Obama's 2009 budget proposal referenced Piketty/Saez's 2003 research to claim that the top 1 percent of earners have been increasing their share of wealth.[185] But caution should reign whenever such studies are reported in the mainstream media, if for no other reason than journalists often share the same level of economic illiteracy as the general public. Further, there are inherent challenges in focusing solely on income statistics without considering a more important measure of the quality of a person's life: that measure being one's "standard of living."

Current research on the topic of income inequality will typically reference at least one of four distinct types of raw income statistics.[186] These include: (1) Internal Revenue Service (IRS) data; (2) U.S. Census Bureau data; (3) the Congressional Budget Office (CBO); and (4) custom research data such as that developed by Dr. Richard Burkhauser, an economist from Cornell University. These four income statistics, summarized in Table 7.1, are differentiated by what raw data they measure and how income is aggregated (or excluded) to affect living standards.

Table 7.1 – Sources of Raw Individual Income Data

Source	Measurement Targets	Income Metric	Identified Exclusions
US Internal Revenue Service (IRS)**	Pre-tax, pre-transfer cash income (e.g., wages, salary, reported tips, interest income)	Tax Unit[187]	Excludes cash impact net of taxes and credits; Excludes capital gains; Ignores value of employer provided health care and other in-kind benefits; Excludes government cash and non-cash transfer payments. Ignores household demographic changes.

US Census Bureau	Pre-tax, post-transfer cash income (e.g., includes social security)	Household Income[188]	Excludes cash impact net of taxes and credits; Excludes capital gains; Excludes value of employer provided health care and other in-kind benefits. Excludes certain government non-cash transfer payments (e.g., food stamps, Medicare, Medicaid).
US Congres-sional Budget Office (CBO)	Post-tax, post-transfer cash income, business income, value of employer provided health insurance, capital gains, other capital income (e.g., interest and rental income).[189]	Size Adjusted Household Income[190]	Ex-ante value of health insurance and other in-kind benefits.
Burkhauser (1979–2007)	Post-tax, post-transfer cash income including in-kind employer pro-vided health-care benefits.[191]	Size Adjusted Household Income	None identified given that the broadest definition of income has been con-sidered.
NOTES:	** IRS data is the most frequently cited by progressives, includ-ing Piketty and Saez (2003), and reflects the least representa-tive data available upon which to draw conclusions on income disparity.		

Research from Dr. Burkhauser and the CBO suggests that income inequality is not accurately measured based on what one earns as pre-tax income alone without certain adjustments. These adjustments include net post-tax retained earnings, capital gains income, government transfers or subsidies, the value of employer-provided health insurance, and other support. Such adjustments clearly have a direct effect on an individual's standard of living, yet they have largely been ignored by both Piketty and Saez.

While any economic study of income inequality since the 2008 financial crisis may offer unique insights about the short-term, the more important policy lessons must come from longer-term analysis. Economists study long-term policy implications to avoid distortions created by cyclical trends in markets, and to focus on intergenerational trends in living standards. For example, the period between 1980 and 2008, when America generally prospered between economic downturns, has been researched extensively by economists with an interest in income inequality. The progressive Left would argue that policy makers should have imposed "middle-out" tax increases on the rich that subsidize the middle class during this period to address increased inequality between these two groups. Dr. Brian Domitrovic, an economic historian and Assistant Professor at Sam Houston State University, has argued against such subsidies by suggesting the middle class did better during this period than progressives might suggest. Dr. Domitrovic has noted that from 1980 to 2012, living standards and income measured in real terms rose for almost everyone. [192] He also has noted that when tax increases are imposed on the wealthy, the overall economy may respond in a manner that reduces inequality but that also creates a decline in living standards for those in lower income brackets. [193] Therefore, one might view reducing inequality as a pyrrhic victory that is not in the interest of any income group. This is but one of many of the unintended consequences typical of middle-out economic theory.

Progressives focus their political debate on income inequality because they mistakenly believe that when the rich are increasing their wealth they are doing so at the expense of the middle class and the poor. This is the classic "fixed-pie" or "zero-sum" argument that ignores the wealth-creating benefits of entrepreneurs taking risks, starting new businesses, and creating new products and services in a free market. In fact, recent studies confirm that the wealthiest Americans earn most of their income through a combination of business and investment (aka, entrepreneurship), not employer compensation. [194] Therefore, the rich generally add to America's total pool of wealth by creating new wealth that did not previously exist while, at the same time, contributing to economic growth by sharing that new wealth with all economic classes.

While progressives emphasize raising taxes on the rich, legislating mandatory employer benefits, and raising the minimum wage to reduce inequality,[195] they simultaneously ignore the disincentives that these policies create pertaining to risk taking and entrepreneurship. While the need for some type of taxation is inevitable, it is imperative that tax policy be efficient so that it does not penalize the wealth creation effects of new business start-ups. The Ewing Marion Kauffman Foundation has noted that it is entrepreneurs and innovators in our society that are responsible for generating all net new wealth in a free market. Kauffman also notes that despite what some may perceive, entrepreneurs typically only keep a small fraction of the wealth they create relative to that which is eventually shared with investors, stockholders, vendors, employees, customers, and the government.[196] Therefore, when progressives advocate high taxes on the wealthy, they ignore empirical evidence showing how such policies suppress the capital investment required to grow our economy and create new jobs that economically elevate both the middle class and the poor.[197]

Ultimately, it is the middle class and poor that suffer disproportionally from the "tax-the-rich" policies advocated by progressives. The best evidence of this is the fact that taxation was a major contributing factor for why the U.S. median household income dropped during the Obama presidency from $55,627 in 2007 to $51,017 in 2012.[198] This was a reduction of over $4,600. On top of this, in 2014 the IRS forced the middle class and poor to either pay for Obamacare health insurance policies or pay their so-called Shared Responsibility tax, thereby further reducing the standard of living for these groups.

HOW IS THE MIDDLE CLASS REALLY DOING?

Dr. Burkhauser has drawn from his own research on income inequality to show that the middle class is doing much better than most progressives would suggest, primarily because he looks past the limited window of "earned income." Burkhauser's research focuses on the period from 1979 to 2007 and includes a broad set of income measures that directly contribute to living standards, as noted below:

> Hence, these more inclusive measures of access to economic resources suggest that income inequality increased in the United States not because the rich got richer, the poor got poorer and the middle-class stagnated, but because the rich got richer at a faster rate than the middle and poorer quintiles, primarily during the 1980s. Growth was substantial in all quintiles [between 1979 and 2007] once the influence of government tax and transfer policy as well as the shift in compensation from wages to health insurance provided by employers and the shift to increased in-kind health insurance by government is recognized.[199]

—Burkhauser, Larrimore, and Simon, 2012

Table 7.2 summarizes Burkhauser's findings as published by the *National Tax Journal* in March 2012.

Table 7.2 – Burkhauser 1979–2007 Mean Income Growth (Percent)—By Income Quintile[200]

	Tax Unit Pre-Tax & Pre-Transfer	Household Pre-Tax & Post-Transfer	Household Size-Adjusted Pre-Tax & Post-Transfer	House-hold Size-Adjusted Post-Tax & Post-Transfer	Household Size-Adjusted Post-Tax & Post-Transfer + Health Insurance
Top 5%	37.9	38.0	48.7	63.0	65.4
Top 10%	36.7	37.3	46.1	56.0	58.8
Top Quintile	32.7	34.6	42.0	49.4	*52.6*
4th Quintile	12.3	23.0	29.2	34.6	*40.4*
Middle Quintile	2.2	15.3	22.8	29.5	*36.9*
2nd Quintile	0.7	11.1	15.6	22.4	31.3
Bottom Quintile	-33.0	9.5	9.9	15.0	26.4

As highlighted, based on the most inclusive definition of income, the middle quintile (or middle class) saw income growth of 36.9 percent over the period from 1979 to 2007. We can contrast this finding with the fourth-quintile and top-quintile at 40.4 percent and 52.6 percent growth respectively. Obviously, these findings paint a very different picture of how well the middle class has fared during this period than was suggested by either the Obama administration or progressive economists.

Given the narrow focus of the progressive Left on Piketty/Saez measures of income, there is one obvious question that should come to mind. That question is "can progressives paint an accurate picture of how the middle class is doing relative to other economic classes when they limit their analysis to the narrowest definition of income measures?" The answer is they cannot. Progressives use the Piketty/Saez research because its narrow scope of data and analysis bolsters their class-warfare arguments that paint the American middle class as being victims of the rich.

For example, one weakness of the Saez research is its focus on income inequality with the top 1 percent of earners. By contrast, other researchers at Pew, the OECD, and other institutions will typically focus on measuring income quintiles, or even deciles, that reflect broader trends in income distribution. By focusing solely on the top 1 percent, one can easily exaggerate the implications of the short-term marginal change in income of the super-rich relative to that earned by America's poor and middle class, particularly since the 2008 financial crisis. This is also true for 2012 when many wealthy individuals incurred capital gains by selling stock and other assets to avoid increased tax rates. These one-time events distort more credible conclusions that might be drawn about income distribution when viewed across longer business cycles.

HOW TO HELP THE AMERICAN MIDDLE CLASS

Is it true that the number of middle-class Americans is shrinking? It seems we always hear this as a by-product of progressive class-warfare arguments. And it would seem intuitive that as we experience greater global economic competition and reductions in middle-management jobs based on technology displacement that middle-class job security and wages would be under threat. Not according to Dr. Mark Perry, professor of economics at the University of Michigan. Writing in his blog for the American Enterprise Institute, Dr. Perry noted the following:

> America's middle-class did start largely disappearing in the 1970s, but it was because they were moving up to a higher-income category, not down into a lower-income category. And that movement was so significant that between 1967 and 2009, the share of American families earning incomes above $75,000 more than doubled, from 16.3% to 39.1%. [One of my readers] commented that although "many prominent people like Paul Krugman claim that the middle-class has been in decline since the 1970s, that assertion is incredibly and verifiably wrong" . . . I think [my reader] is exactly right.[201]
>
> —Mark Perry, University of Michigan

America needs a thriving and prosperous middle class for many reasons. One of the most important reasons is that it signifies we are achieving social and economic justice in America. When the middle class thrives, it drives our economy forward and creates opportunity for all economic classes. Therefore, it becomes critical that as a nation we adopt public policies that encourage economic growth, job creation, and ultimately prosperity for the middle class along with advancement opportunities for America's poor.

The progressive Left would like to tell us that the answer to social and economic justice is more government involvement in our lives. They believe that it is government that should direct our national economy and allocate resources to ensure that everyone receives their "fair-share" of wealth and prosperity. But this belief reflects a deep and fundamental misunderstanding of human nature, particularly in how incentives affect human behavior and individual decision making. Progressives often fail to "look past stage one" as Thomas Sowell is famous for saying, thereby creating through their activism a host of unintended consequences when their policies are enacted. Obamacare's ever-increasing health insurance premiums are a perfect example of this, particularly when President Obama promised Americans a $2,500 reduction per family.

To truly help the middle class and the poor, what is really needed is more economic freedom and less governmental interventionism. Many progressives deny this reality, even though there is ample research available that shows less government intervention in economic affairs means greater prosperity. For example, both the Heritage Foundation and The Fraser Institute publish an annual index of economic freedom, indices that provide prosperity metrics for more than 140 countries around the globe. The research performed annually by these organizations demonstrates invariably the inverse relationship between the level of government intervention in economic affairs (including taxation, corruption, and regulation) and a country's economic prosperity. Therefore, the next time a progressive asks you what you think government should do to end poverty and advance the middle class, an appropriate response might be to tell them to get government out of the way.

Policy Arguments Concerning the Politics of Inequality

While the Constitution guarantees equality for certain rights, constitutional conservatives know that equal economic outcomes is not one of them. In a free society with free markets, economic inequality is inevitable. This will never change, nor should it. Instead, society should invest in each individual citizen by encouraging them to develop the skills and capabilities with which God has uniquely endowed them and that make them valuable and employable in a free market. Such investment may not guarantee prosperity for every individual. However, history has shown the best way to enable economic prosperity for the overwhelming majority of Americans is to ignore the debate over income inequality and to encourage both individuals and commercial enterprises to invest in themselves, and the free market.

In certain respects, the debate over economic inequality is a canard. Progressive leftists raise this issue as a means of encouraging victimization, which is typical of their political playbook. However, as Burkhauser and Domitrovic have shown, the middle class is not being victimized economically but instead is doing well. However, enabling the upward migration of those on the lower end of income ladder has become more challenging given trends toward globalization and technology displacement. While we should expect these trends to continue well into the Trump administration and beyond, it does raise the question of how we can enable those in poverty to migrate upward and fill the ranks of the middle class.

We know that personal responsibility and commitment to marriage are the key foundations for individual economic advancement and remaining out of poverty. Multiple studies of U.S. Census Bureau data have reported that incidents of poverty are highly correlated with women having children out-of-wedlock.[202] Additionally, drug and alcohol addiction are inextricably linked to poverty.[203] These types of personal concerns cannot be solved by progressive policies that simply redistribute wealth. While counseling and treatment programs offer some promise, ultimately individuals must take responsibility to put their own lives in order if they are to take full advantage of the opportunities the free market offers them.

We also know that having the right kind of education and marketable skills is a poverty killer. Those looking for a brighter economic future may wish to listen to billionaire investor Mark Cuban, who was recently quoted saying that "creative" and "critical thinking" skills will come to the forefront of those which employers are looking to hire. Cuban believes in ten years employers will need people with liberal arts degrees more than they will need computer science or engineering credentials.[204] The skills acquired in liberal arts degrees cannot be automated, and once they are acquired they can give an individual a competitive advantage over another potential hire. The importance of a liberal arts background was also something that Steve Jobs advocated based on his own life experience. While neither Cuban or Jobs would have discounted the importance of technical or engineering training, it is the ability to combine these skills with creativity fostered in a liberal arts education that make some individuals extraordinarily valuable as employees.

Thomas Friedman, Pulitzer Prize-winning columnist for the *New York Times*, has made arguments similar to that of Cuban and Jobs for years, but with a slightly different twist. Friedman speaks to the importance of thinking entrepreneurially because the nature of employment is evolving so quickly.[205] Friedman has noted that employers are increasingly less concerned about whether an employee acquires their skills from self-study, online or formal university training, but instead are concerned about how an individual can add value to their organization.[206] Innovation and creativity are central to entrepreneurial thinking, and these skills are not an inherited trait but can be developed through the right kind of education and mentorship.

To escape poverty in an automated world where cheap labor is readily available overseas, one must also make a lifetime commitment to education and training. But the skills acquired as part of this commitment must be focused on closing the gaps between what employers want and the value that an individual employee can deliver. This commitment is even more important for those who are not college bound, as the limited skills gained in many entry level positions may not provide the foundation upon which an individual can advance in their working careers. That means unskilled workers may need to look beyond their current employer for opportunities to acquire job training and the essential skills that will allow them to advance economically.

Finally, there is one important trend that is having a direct and negative impact on the ability of the poor to advance into middle-class America, a trend that has not been widely reported in the mainstream media or fully understood by politicians in Washington. That trend is the decline in new business start-ups dating back to the 1980s.[207] This decline has directly hurt the creation of middle-class jobs because research shows that all net new wealth and job creation comes from start-up companies.[208] Without an improved climate for entrepreneurship and new business formation in America, we as a nation will not be able to create enough good paying jobs upon which we grow the middle class. In fact, the greatest predictor of economic growth in a society is the number of new companies that are created by that society each year.[209] Therefore, reversing the thirty-year long-term decline in new business start-ups[210] is critical to protecting middle-class prosperity here in America and elsewhere.

Unfortunately, there are many on the progressive Left who give lip service to the idea of supporting entrepreneurship because they regard successful entrepreneurs as part of the "1 percent" who take more than their fair-share of wealth. The best evidence of this is President Obama's famous comment during the 2012 campaign telling small-business owners "you didn't build that,"[211] implying that government was responsible for successful small-business enterprises. Other progressives downplay the importance of innovators and entrepreneurs as job creators, claiming that it is only middle-class consumers that create jobs when they act upon their needs.[212] This is classic left-wing progressive gibberish that works against middle-class prosperity every day in America.

Sensible Americans should be concerned about enabling the prosperity of all economic classes, not just the middle class or the poor. Prosperity is best enabled by doing everything we can in the public and private sector to encourage entrepreneurs to take risks, innovate, and invest, thereby driving economic growth. There is good news here for the jobless. Unlike large firms that work to reduce head count where they can, new businesses must hire immediately, or they cannot begin operations. Therefore, when domestic unemployment is high, or when middle-class jobs become scarce, encouraging entrepreneurship becomes a means by which we can create jobs today and not wait for the next business cycle.

The American Dream has always been about providing equal rights and equal opportunity for all Americans so that individuals can pursue their personal and professional ambitions. This dream was never about guaranteeing individual success, but rather about empowering Americans to be self-sufficient. The progressive Left has been working diligently to fundamentally transform this vision of the American Dream by encouraging an attitude of victim-ization and encouraging universal commitment to government dependency. Eight years of an Obama presidency gave us great insight into what this progressive vision looks like. It leads to sluggish economic growth, higher taxes on all Americans, massive wealth-transfer from programs like Obamacare, and overbearing regulatory burdens that discourage entrepreneurial activity.

The progressive Left would do better to heed the words of former President Calvin Coolidge if they truly want to address the problem of economic inequality. Coolidge once reminded us: "The wise and correct course to follow in taxation is not to destroy those who have already secured success but to create conditions under which everyone will have a better chance to be successful."[213] In this one sentence, "Silent Cal" says it all.

PART THREE

ARGUMENTS ON HEALTH-CARE POLICY

8
THE PROGRESSIVE VIEW OF MORALITY AND HEALTH CARE

[Obamacare] is a government takeover of our health-care system. It is the government basically running the entire health-care system, turning large insurers into de facto public utilities, depriving people of choice, depriving people of options, raising people's prices, raising taxes when we need new jobs. And they're taking all this money out of Medicare and they're not using it to make Medicare more solvent, they're treating Medicare like a piggy-bank to fund this other entitlement.[214]

—Congressman Paul Ryan, March 23, 2010

Since their movement began in the late nineteenth century, progressives have postulated the moral superiority of the rights of the state over those of the individual, often seeing the state as the vehicle for socializing what they interpret as Judeo-Christian values. Early progressives believed that a just society had a moral imperative for activist and interventionist government, an ideological view that progressives maintain to this day. Their view is that government activism must elevate and evolve the morality and actions of the average citizen by coercing them

109

into becoming enablers and providers of social welfare. As they see it, to do otherwise would simply be to endorse the mercenary pursuits of what they call "hyper-individualism,"[215] a philosophy they see as exploitive of humanity and natural resources, and as fostering economic inequality.

One of the best expressions of the progressive point of view on morality and the role of government comes from the Center for American Progress (CAP). Founded in 2003 by John Podesta, President Bill Clinton's former White House Chief of Staff, CAP has become the leading think tank for progressive policy advocacy in America. CAP describes the philosophy behind the progressive agenda in economic terms, suggesting that consideration of the common interest of Americans elevates the values we embody in public policy to a higher moral purpose.

> Progressive economics is primarily concerned with striking a proper balance between private and public action to ensure greater stability and equitable growth in the economy and better achieve national goals... In terms of values, progressive economics often stresses the importance of social cohesion and cooperation over pure self-interest as the basis for a more stable and just economic order. [For example,] Modern progressive economics, building on environmentalism, also promotes sustainability as a core value underlying our society. Since the 1970s, progressives have warned about the practical and moral costs of the misuse of natural resources, rising pollution, global warming and other environmental disasters, and violations of human rights in pursuit of corporate profits. These alternative economic values have been incorporated into the emerging progressive focus on national indicators that go beyond mea-surements of aggregate national output.[216]
>
> —Center for American Progress

As an advocate of modern-day progressive morality, CAP's view of a "more stable and just economic order" was on full display during the public debate over Obamacare. In fact, CAP was one of the primary authors of Obamacare legislation, and its progressive values were reflected throughout the final work product. In its final form, Obamacare reflected one of the largest wealth transfer initiatives in American history, a transfer from the young and healthy middle class and upper middle class to the uninsured. This is totally consistent with the redistribution strategy that progressives have long advocated.

PROGRESSIVES AND THE NOBLE LIE

One would think progressives operating on a higher moral plane would not need to resort to intellectual dishonesty to achieve their political ends. Unfortunately, the history of the Progressive movement, and recent history of the passage of Obamacare legislation suggests otherwise. That is because progressives have long used health care as their primary political wedge to divide the nation between rich and poor, even if they need to lie to achieve their ends.

For example, during his attempts to rally the country around the Obamacare, President Obama repeated several promises to the American people about how the new law would affect their lives. Mr. Obama's most well-known promise to the American people was that "if you like your [health insurance] plan you can keep your plan . . . period."[217] President Obama repeated this promise over and over without equivocation. He did so even though he and his administration knew as early as June 2010 that Obamacare legislation was designed specifically to push people out of their existing employer-based and individual health insurance plans. According to the Federal Register, the Obama administration estimated that by 2013 between 39 and 69 percent of all employer-based health insurance plans would be cancelled because of Obamacare's passage, thereby forcing people to purchase different insurance.[218] The administration also acknowledge the existence of multiple studies showing between 40 and 67 percent people who carried individual health insurance would also lose their coverage.[219] The late columnist Charles Krauthammer once pointed out that President Obama's claim that he was unaware that Obamacare would force cancelations of

111

private health insurance policies lacked credibility. Krauthammer, along with many Congressional Republicans, pointed out that pushing people out of their private insurance and forcing them to pay for unnecessary benefits was a fundamental principal of how Obamacare was supposed to work.[220]

Unfortunately, progressives throughout their history have resorted to intellectual dishonesty as a political tactic, or what some have termed the *noble lie*.[221] Most reasonable people today would consider the term *noble lie* an oxymoron. However, in the mind of a progressive elitist who feels unconstrained by the Constitution, and who believes the state must elevate society's ethical values through public policy, the noble lie is often justified to achieve what they see as being in the public's best interest. This is precisely why President Obama lied at least seven times to the American people about key aspects of Obamacare. After telling Americans they could keep their health plans, his six additional lies included:

- "No matter how we reform health care, we will keep this promise to the American people: If you like your doctor, you will be able to keep your doctor, period."[222] We now know that Obamacare approved insurance policies have completely revised physician networks, and many people have been forced to find new physicians to provide care.

- "In an Obama administration, we'll lower premiums by up to $2,500 for a typical family per year."[223] According to a 2013 Manhattan Institute study of forty-nine states, Obamacare premiums were expected to increase by an average of 41 percent.[224] In October 2016, the New York Times reported that such premium price increases would continue into 2017, with the average increase being another 22 percent.[225]

- "I can make a firm pledge. Under my plan, no family making less than $250,000 a year will see any form of tax increase. Not your income tax, not your payroll tax, not your capital-gains taxes, not any of your taxes."[226] We now know that Obamacare included eighteen different revenue increases including an "individual mandate" that the Supreme Court called a tax.[227]

- "I will not sign a plan that adds one dime to our deficits—either now or in the future."[228] According to a U.S. Government Accountability Office Report release in January 2011, an alternative cost projection showed that Obamacare would increase the primary deficit by 0.7 percent of GDP over a seventy-five-year period.[229]

- "So, this law means more choice, more competition, lower costs for millions of Americans."[230] According to the Heritage Foundation, we now know that in most states the number of exchange carriers is less than the number of market carriers that previously sold policies. For example, in 2013, 35 percent of U.S. counties had only two health insurance carriers to compete in an exchange, and in 17 percent had only one.[231] In May 2016, the *Washington Free Beacon* reported that insurer participation in the Obamacare exchanges was down by 27 percent, a trend that would continue into 2017.[232]

- "I will protect Medicare."[233] Unfortunately for President Obama, Medicare's chief actuary, Richard Foster, saw the implications of Obamacare differently. According to Mr. Foster, "providers for whom Medicare constitutes a substantive portion of their business could find it difficult to remain profitable and, absent legislative intervention, might end their participation in the program . . . roughly 15 percent of Part A [hospital insurance] providers would become unprofitable within a 10-year projection period."[234]

Each of President Obama's promises was made to persuade a skeptical public to support the passage of Obamacare legislation. Yet, at the time it was signed into law on March 23, 2010, not a single opinion poll showed a majority of Americans

—

supporting the legislation. President Obama and his fellow progressive Democrats pushed this legislation because they believe government should be empowered to achieve the greater good for society. They were not concerned about public opinion or how Obamacare might affect the rights of individual citizens. For example, as of November 2013, it did not matter to President Obama that for every person choosing to sign up for Obamacare, fifty other Americans with active health insurance would have their policies canceled.[235] What was important to progressives was that Obamacare expanded government control over a larger share of private sector health-care resources. They wanted such control to enable wealth transfer to one of their core political constituencies: the uninsured.

Progressives did not invent the noble lie or other intellectually dishonest tactics during the political battle over Obamacare. We can point to many historical examples of how the Progressive movement saw fit to use such tactics to achieve their political ends. This applies equally to progressives whether they be Democrat, Republican, or those from an independent party, because progressives come in all political stripes. However, by order of magnitude, it is the progressive ambitions of the Far Left that have posed the greatest threat to our constitutional republic, and therefore deserve special attention in this text.

THE EARLY PROGRESSIVE MOVEMENT AND THE FOUNDATIONS OF HEALTH CARE REFORM

The progressive Left, and their philosophy of "progressivism," is an existential threat to the ideas and ideals given to us by the Founders as described in our Constitution and Declaration of Independence. It is important that we explore progressive philosophy because the ideology is radically different from what we know as America's first principles, and its adoption would lead our nation to establish a very different version of the American Dream. Such exploration can be seen in how progressives employ the noble lie to manipulate public opinion, tactics that most of us would consider objectionable and unethical.

Ethics and morality are important themes we continually hear in the early writings of progressives. For example, CAP has written about the origins of the Progressive movement by positioning its founders as having commonality with Christian social values and ethics. While on the surface this may seem a reasonable comparison, it is interesting to see CAP's positioning of Dr. Richard Ely (1854–1943), an academic economist and one of the movement's founders. CAP describes Ely as "evolutionary" in his thinking, but the term "revolutionary" may be more appropriate.

> Beginning in the late 19th century, progressive economics developed as a non-socialist alternative to the limitations and failures of the classical tradition. Prior to the dominance of Keynesian thought in the late 1930s, progressive economics centered on the historical model of Richard Ely and the institutional school associated with John R. Commons, Thorstein Veblen, and Wesley Mitchell. These early progressive economists shared several beliefs about the interaction of society, politics, and the economy. Many spent time studying at German universities focusing their scholarship on the evolutionary development of economics within particular political and cultural environments. Some were influenced deeply by Christian ethics and social gospel reform efforts (see "The Role of Faith in the Progressive Movement") that challenged the exploitation of people and communities for profit.[236]
>
> —Center for American Progress

CAP's identification of Richard Ely as a founding economic progressive is most interesting, and at the same time quite troubling. Ely's academic career led him to become a major influence on progressive thinking in university circles as it pertained to morality, social reform, and the integration of both with economic policy. After studying at Dartmouth and Columbia College where he received a BA in philosophy, Ely moved on to Germany for his graduate studies. It was in Germany that his focus turned to the study of economics at the Universities of Halle and Heidelberg. After receiving his PhD, he returned to the United States in

1880 and eventually accepted a position as instructor in political economy at Johns Hopkins University in Baltimore. During his tenure, Ely earned a national reputation as a reformer, becoming a proponent of several social welfare causes that included child and adult labor laws, industrial safety regulation, and the rights of labor unions. By 1885 he would go on to establish the American Economic Association (AEA) and eventually serve as its president. For all of this, and for his research focus in political economic theory, he eventually became known as the "Dean of American Economists" and later the founding proponent of progressive economics.[237]

From the mid-1880s through the early part of the twentieth century, Richard Ely enjoyed a considerable influence on public policy and on the direction of the Progressive movement. One notable example of such influence was one his students, a radical progressive by the name of Woodrow Wilson, who would go on to be elected president of the United States in 1912. Ely was also a prolific author with more than twenty books on topics as varied as basic economics, political economy, socialism, the labor movement, taxation, and matters of church and state.

However, given Ely's belief that public policy should reconcile economic theory with his moral philosophy, there are legitimate reasons to be concerned about his influence. Ely was heavily schooled in the academic tenets of German historicism that held there are no universal "laws of economics" around which policy might be formed. Instead, Ely put forth that all economic facts are relative and evolutionary,[238] suggesting policy can only be crafted based on current social and economic conditions at a given place and time. Ely also believed that to achieve social and economic advancement, a society should appoint a group of intellectual elites who would be responsible for implementing what he called "coercive philanthropy."[239] In such a world, government central planners would define social priorities and programs, they would tax an unlimited amount of private wealth to support these programs, and they would allocate resources in a manner to coercively develop human potential.

—

Although Richard Ely considered himself a devout Presbyterian Christian, it is hard to reconcile some of Ely's writings on public policy with any reasonable interpretation of mainstream Christian theology. His coercive philanthropy might best be described as Christian socialism because it gave little consideration to the rights of the individual who he believed needed to be elevated from poverty, or to the citizen whose taxes paid for such elevation.[240] Ely, along with Margaret Sanger the founder of Planned Parenthood, was also an advocate of eugenics, a science whose goal was to encourage controlled breeding, particularly among the poor, to achieve hereditary improvement of the human race. [241]

> As a part of the preparation of our human material we shall give increasing attention to eugenics. We know very little about race betterment as yet, but we do know some things of significance. We do know that heredity is a force which sets limits to all our activities, and which, if entirely neglected, leads to decay and ruin in the nation. [Therefore,] we have got far enough to recognize that there are certain human beings who are absolutely unfit and who should be prevented from a continuation of their kind.[242]
> —Richard Ely, 1918

Ely's point of view was a perversion of both Christian theology and Judeo-Christian ethics, both of which elevate the worth of the individual through respect for human rights, including the right to reproduce. In Ely's mind, however, he believed the greater good of society was served by elevating the human condition from what he called "pauperism." One could also say the methods Ely advocated for implementing his social reforms reflected a radical form of religious statism.[243]

> Now, it may rationally be maintained that, if there is anything divine on earth it is the State, the product of the same God-given instincts which led to the establishment of the Church and the Family. It was once held that kings ruled by right divine, and in any widely accepted belief, though it be

afterwards discredited, there is generally found a kernel of truth. In this case it was the divine right of the State . . . The Christian ought not to view civil authority in any other light than a delegated responsibility from the Almighty. When men come to look upon their duty to the state as something as holy as their duty to the church, regarding the state as one of God's chief agencies for good, it will be easy for government to perform all its functions.[244]

—Richard Ely, 1885

Even when interpreting Ely's words in their historical context, it is hard for one to conceptually distinguish such statist commentary from similar ideas expressed today by religious political fanatics such as the Muslim Brotherhood, ISIS or the Taliban. Yet, Ely believed in the sovereignty and sanctity of the state above all else, because he believed God worked through the state to achieve a higher moral purpose. Consider the following:

It is seen in general that there is no limit to the right of the State, the sovereign power, save its ability to do good. Duty, function, is co-extensive with power. The State is a moral person.[245]

– Richard Ely, 1889

God works through the State in carrying out his purposes more universally than through any other institution . . . All great and glorious deeds of men have taken place within a State, and the highest achievements of the mind of man have been preceded or accompanied by a large and expanding national life.[246]

—Richard Ely, 1896

Although Ely denied absolute authority for the State in some of his writings, he did not sway from the possibility that the State had the right to choose socialism or that all private property was subject to State redistribution.

[T]he state, like the church, has divine rights. But these rights . . . are vested in the people . . . Their rights are derived from God through the social body . . . We may have a paternal theory of the state, and at the same time advocate very limited functions of the state; or we may advocate very extensive functions of the state, going even to the extreme of Socialism.[247]

—Richard Ely, 1898

Clearly, Ely did not grasp the concepts of limited government and tyranny of the majority, or the political and economic risks inherent in socialism. He was naïve enough to believe that a large benevolent government would always remain so, suggesting that his views were desperately out of touch with those of the American Founders, and with the limitations imposed upon the federal government by our Constitution. As columnist Jonah Goldberg put it:

Ely's determination to meld Christianity and economics while claiming that science was always on his side undermined the authority of Christianity while accelerating the growth and increasing power of the state. The "pragmatist razor" that trims away needless superstition sliced away Christianity whenever it got in the way of statist imperatives. With time, the state became the golden calf.[248]

—Jonah Goldberg, 2009

Richard Ely's influence over progressive thinkers continued to grow into the early part of the twentieth century, and the intellectual residue of this thinking permeates that of the modern-day Progressive movement. His influence spawned a new generation of progressive activists during this period who called for increased power of the state and a new form of social thinking, one that deviated dramatically from the ideas and ideals of the American Founders. Central to this thinking was the need for improved public health services for the working class.

PROGRESSIVE INFLUENCE ON NATIONAL HEALTH INSURANCE

Progressives have had a long history of advocating for socialized medicine in America. Specifically, passage of national health insurance legislation reflects the core political strategy progressives have pursued to achieve their wealth redistribution objectives. Early attempts to enact socialized medicine began with Franklin Roosevelt who pushed for several national health-care programs as part of his New Deal. These programs were eventually removed from the Social Security Act before its final passage in 1935. Roosevelt had little choice in this matter because objections from the American Medical Association and other activists led him to believe they would jeopardize the Act's passage.

However, beginning in 1939, Senator Robert Wagner of New York launched what would become the first in a series of attempts by progressives to pass federal health insurance legislation in Congress. Wagner's bill, called the "National Health Act of 1939," sought to establish a compulsory health insurance program administered through the states. This bill would later die in committee. Similarly, in 1945, progressives would see their first major push for national health insurance from a sitting President. On November 19th of that year, President Harry Truman sent a presidential message to Congress proposing a new national health-care program.

In my message to the Congress of September 6, 1945, there were enumerated in a proposed Economic Bill of Rights certain rights which ought to be assured to every American citizen. One of them was: "The right to adequate medical care and the opportunity to achieve and enjoy good health." Another was the "right to adequate protection from the economic fears of . . . sickness . . . Millions of our citizens do not now have a full measure of opportunity to achieve and enjoy good health. Millions do not now have protection or security against the economic effects of sickness. The time has arrived for action to help them attain that opportunity and that protection.[249]

—President Harry S. Truman, Message to Congress

Progressive Democrats in Congress would continue to introduce proposals for national health insurance through 1949 without legislative success, most of which called for some form of universal compulsory coverage.[250] The results of the 1950 elections saw incumbents supporting compulsory insurance soundly defeated, resulting in a net loss of Democratic seats.[251] This changed the political calculus for some progressive Democrats who saw compulsory universal insurance as unsalable, leaving them to consider alternatives that would limit proposals for health coverage that only target the elderly and the poor.[252]

By the mid-1960s, the political landscape would change once again. The 1964 presidential election saw President Lyndon Johnson's victory over Republican Senator Barry Goldwater carrying with it long coattails. The shift in Congress left Democrats with a two-thirds majority in the House (295–140) and a filibuster-proof majority in the Senate (68–32). No longer would progressives have to adopt a strategy of incrementalism in pushing for national health care, for their party now controlled the executive and legislative branches. Johnson had asked for a mandate during the 1964 campaign and he received it, thereby giving him the opportunity to lead both progressive and moderate Democrats to pass his Great Society agenda. That agenda would include passage of Medicare providing limited health insurance coverage for senior citizens and Medicaid providing limited coverage for qualifying uninsured.

POLICY ARGUMENTS CONCERNING THE PROGRESSIVE VIEW OF MORALITY AND HEALTH CARE

The constitutional limits imposed by federalism do not authorize the federal government to establish a national health-care system or health insurance program. However, precedent was set with the passage of Medicare and Medicaid in 1965, and conservatives chose not to challenge the constitutionality of these programs in the aftermath of the Butler decision. Unless the American people choose to eliminate these programs, or modify them to fit within constitutional boundaries, they will remain intact. However, both programs are examples of Richard Ely's "coercive philanthropy" that ignores constitutional limits in favor of a government run by educated elites. Constitutional conservatives should remind their fellow citizens that adherence to the Constitution requires that both Medicare and Medicaid be reformed to place them on a sound Constitutional footing, as per the General Welfare clause. At the same time, citizens should be cognizant of the ethical motivations of progressives and why their utopian vision for American society is neither practical, legal, or moral.

The passage of Medicare and Medicaid in 1965 was a watershed event for progressives, as both programs would radically alter federalism by creating greater dependency on the federal government for the average American. However, for every increase in government dependency, Americans lose freedom. That is precisely why we have a Constitution. The Constitution preserves freedom by protecting Americans from intrusive government by limiting its power, and from public officials who abuse that power. Unfortunately, progressives choose to ignore such Constitutional restrictions when they gain power, as President Obama did when he attempted to "fundamentally transform America" by increasing government dependency with Obamacare. Now in hindsight, we see that Mr. Obama's utopian vision for health-care reform was not clearly thought out, and the Trump administration and Congress have been forced to stabilize the Obamacare insurance exchanges while at the same time eliminating what many consider to be an unconstitutional individual mandate. Had President Obama backed a constitutionally consistent health-care reform proposal, one that did not require his use of the noble lie to gain its passage, it is possible that such reform would have been a boon to his legacy and not a bust.

Progressives believe their case for nationalized health care goes beyond moral debate and is also a legal obligation tied to what is called the Constitution's "General Welfare" clause. Former progressive Congressman Dennis Kucinich of Ohio has made this point very clear in a letter he wrote to his constituents.

The Preamble to the United States Constitution and Article I, Section 8 of the U.S. Constitution both describe an originating purpose of our United States: to promote the general welfare. Health care is a legitimate function of our government. Health care is a basic right in a Democratic society. It is no more a privilege based on ability to pay than is the right to vote, which was once accorded only to property owners. Health care is also a moral imperative.[253]

—Congressman Dennis Kucinich, September 9, 2009

The debate over the meaning of the phrase "general welfare" in the Constitution traces its roots back to the founding of this nation. In fact, early debates raged between James Madison and Thomas Jefferson on one side, and Alexander Hamilton on the other, over how to interpret this clause.[254] This issue was never fully resolved by the Founders, and the context for this debate remains the same today: a choice between a limited central government espoused by Madison and Jefferson, and a strong central government with wide latitude for infrastructure spending that was preferred by Hamilton.

However, our Constitution establishes limits on the authority of the federal government and its role in the lives of all Americans. Therefore, even a liberal interpretation of the General Welfare clause consistent with Hamilton's view is not a call for government offering unlimited social welfare, even when there is a need. Therefore, we must ask ourselves *how much government welfare is permissible given the constraints of our Constitution?* The late American philosopher and author Mortimer J. Adler provides some insight on the answer to this question. Adler believed that introducing the adjective "economic" into the phrase "general welfare" would clarify its legitimate purpose as one component of the common good.[255] In doing so, Adler believed that the general welfare would be served in a manner consistent with what President Lincoln once argued.

"[It is] the legitimate object of government, is to do for a community of people, whatever they need to have done, but cannot do, at all, or cannot, so well do, for themselves - in their separate, and individual capacities. In all that the people can individually do as well for themselves, government ought not to interfere."[256]

—President Abraham Lincoln, July 1, 1854

The true meaning of the General Welfare clause should be viewed as promoting the general economic welfare, not a call for massive wealth redistribution by a federal welfare state that guarantees individual success and happiness to special interests. A progressive's interpretation of this clause would have us establish a mythical utopian society where the government responds to provide benefits for every specialized personal need of the individual citizen. Progressives have encouraged incremental steps in this direction with Social Security and Medicare, both of which are compulsory programs. However, by 2018, the federal government has mismanaged these programs to the point where their unfunded liabilities now total $13.2 trillion[257] and $37.7 trillion[258] respectively. Such mismanagement indicates that both programs operate in a manner that is fiscally irresponsible and generationally immoral. Because of these liabilities, bankruptcy looms for both programs as baby boomers now retire at an ever-increasing rate. Yet progressives would have us add more generous benefits like Obamacare on top of these outstanding liabilities, a policy that continues to add to the federal debt.

All reasonable and compassionate Americans should agree that there are some individuals in our society who, due to no fault of their own, need government support. However, when we see senior citizens receiving on average of three times the Medicare benefits that anyone could reasonably justify based on the FICA taxes they paid during their working years, we should know something is not right.[259] Such a program is unsustainable, and it cries out for "means testing" that progressives refused to consider in 1965 when the program was enacted. Instead, progressives advocate for even more benefits to provide for the general welfare. Maybe a more prudent approach would be for all Americans to take a step back and look at how we are allocating limited health care and social spending resources and fix what is broken first before spending more on programs like Obamacare.

Since the early days of their movement, progressives have long eyed a government run health-care program as a primary national political objective. Medicare, Medicaid and Obamacare were only stepping stones toward this objective. Had Hillary Clinton won the 2016 presidential election, we might be hearing her tell a story about how we tried market-based health-care reforms and they did not work. Therefore, she might say, a single-payer system is the next logical step in American health-care reform. But as we will see in later chapters, much of what is wrong with America's health-care system cannot be fixed by government. That is because the root cause of most of the problems in our health-care system are related to market disruptions that were created by government. Progressives will never acknowledge this because they believe government is smarter than markets, if only they can put the right elitist bureaucrats in place to manage health-care resources. If this is true, common sense would dictate that progressives should first demonstrate their wisdom by fixing a broken single-payer system at the Veteran's Administration or finding a way to mend Medicaid so that doctors would choose to participate in the program instead of avoiding it.

In the mind of a progressive leftist, equality is more important than morality.[260] This is why many on the left will revere and defend tyrannical Marxist regimes who aspire to equal outcomes over America with its commitment to fundamental individual rights.[261] Therefore, one should expect that anytime the progressive Left achieves power in America, or elsewhere for that matter, true morality will take a back seat to their hyperbolic outcry over the need for economic equality and universal government-run health care.

9

THE MEDICARE HEALTH
INSURANCE SCAM

A major driver of the cost of health care in the United States is a compromise that was reached with the American Medical Association in the 1960s when Medicare was first established. ... [As part of this compromise] the government agreed to compensate doctors on a fee-for-service basis. Now what that means is the more services doctors provide, the more income they make. And the more complicated and expensive the services that they provide are, the more income they make. And the fee-for-service system essentially pours gasoline on the fire of health-care cost inflation ... because when we guarantee that we will reimburse them for whatever they do and whatever it costs, they're just incentivized to offer more and more and more.[262]

—Clayton Christensen, Harvard Business School

On July 30, 1965, President Lyndon Johnson signed two health-care bills into law that established what we in America know as Medicare and Medicaid. Medicare established a system of national compulsory health insurance for senior citizens that most of us are familiar with today, a system providing hospital and physician services partially funded by payroll taxes. Medicaid was a means-tested program complimentary to Medicare, but for uninsured citizens with low incomes. Both programs were a central part of Johnson's Great Society agenda, much like those that had been pushed by progressive Democrats since the days of FDR.

Not much has been written or spoken about in recent times concerning how Medicare, and its sister program Medicaid, were rushed through the legislative process in Washington and how that process deviated from the norm. However, a brief review of the legislative history of Medicare will serve as an example of how intellectually dishonest the progressive Left can be when they find themselves blessed with political power.

Charlotte Twight, professor of economics at Boise State University, has conducted extensive research on the political history of Medicare. Her research offers important insights on the arguments used by progressive lawmakers to win Medicare's passage. One of Dr. Twight's most important insights involve the gap between what the Johnson administration told the public about Medicare's catastrophic coverage, and what the text of the bill would de facto provide seniors as written.

> The gulf between what the public thought and what was actually in the [Medicare bill] was enormous. The most pressing rationale for compulsory health insurance continually put forward by government officials and echoed by the public was the specter that responsible older people could be ruined financially by catastrophic illness. Yet neither the 1963 nor the 1965 proposal provided coverage for catastrophic illness . . . Yet the very element that government officials [including President Johnson's HEW Secretary Anthony Celebrezze] continued to cite to win public support for Medicare was deliberately omitted from the administration's bills. [263]

—Charlotte Twight, PhD, Boise State University

The progressive Left has never been immune to using the noble lie to achieve what they see as their utopian society with universal health care. After all, they believe as elites they are working on behalf of people they see as "victims" who were being oppressed by the wealthy class. While such tactics were effective in building political support for Medicare's passage, they may not have been necessary. At the time Medicare was passed by Congress, public opinion polls were already showing growing support for a national health plan.[264] Despite this, the Johnson administration sought to build public support for Medicare by misrepresenting the financial demographics of seniors, thereby suggesting the program would alleviate their economic suffering. It is a widely promoted progressive myth that most senior citizens in America are poor. However, this myth is not borne out by reality. In fact, today's senior citizens have the lowest net poverty rate of any demographic group in America, not only due to their ownership of financial assets but also due to income received from Social Security.[265] As Dr. Twight notes, the fiscal condition of seniors in 1965 was not that dissimilar.

> Misrepresentation of the financial condition of the elderly helped to paint this portrait, as government officials advocating Medicare repeatedly cited statistics showing lower incomes received by the elderly in comparison with other age groups. Yet the income statistics by themselves were misleading because they did not include asset ownership, and the elderly as a group had more substantial assets than other segments of the populace . . . The pro-Medicare pitch was that this presumptively deserving, and financially precarious group should receive medical benefits without regard to need in order to protect elderly persons from the indignity of a means test. However . . . a 1960 University of Michigan study showed that "87 percent of all spending units headed by persons aged 65 or older" had assets whose median value matched asset ownership of people aged 45–64 and exceed the asset ownership of people under age 45.[266]

> —Charlotte Twight, PhD, Boise State University

The real political motives of the progressive Left and their push to pass Medicare had little to do with their concerns over financial security for the elderly. Instead, progressives understood in 1965, as they do today, that senior citizens will vote while young people are generally less engaged in the political process. Therefore, as conceived of by its authors, Medicare would be passed as a program that takes payroll taxes from young working people to curry favor with seniors who would receive health-care benefits. The fact that America's working poor would wind up subsidizing wealthy Medicare recipients did not matter. Instead, for progressives, President Johnson's Great Society was the more important goal because it increased government dependency and control over not only more health-care resources but also more votes. The politics of victimization, as played out in the perceived plight of seniors, gave progressive Democrats more control over a sizable and committed voting block that they would continue to count on in future elections.

WHERE IS THE MEDICARE TRUST FUND?

Possibly the most unethical misrepresentation that the progressive Left used to build political support for Medicare involved what the public was told about how their Medicare payroll taxes would be used.

> The payroll taxes were to be put into a "trust fund" that was 'separate' from the OASDI Social Security trust fund. People were told during their working years they would be paying for "insurance" to defray the costs of illnesses in their old age . . . In their view, the taxes were not even taxes: according to government officials, they represented an "opportunity" to make "contributions" . . . many voters did not understand that, far from putting funds into a paid-up insurance policy, they would be taxed today to pay for other people's benefits today, with no guarantee that the program would pay comparable benefits to them when they reached age 65.[267]
>
> —Charlotte Twight, Ph.D., Boise State University

Despite claims by the Johnson administration, a segregated operational trust fund was never established as part of Medicare. Instead, Medicare operates with two budget accounting entries that are often, but erroneously, described as "trust funds." One accounting entry is for "hospital" insurance (HI) and a second entry is for "supplemental medical" insurance (SMI). While Medicare payroll taxes have historically been used for their stated purpose of paying for HI and SMI benefits, there is no legal guarantee or obligation that these funds will continue to be used for this purpose in the future. We saw an example of how these funds could be misappropriated with the passage of Obamacare legislation that appropriated more than $700 billion in Medicare funding to subsidize its own medical benefits.[268]

Republicans, who generally opposed Medicare's passage in 1965, may have challenged the program more successfully had the House Ways and Means Committee opened congressional hearings on program amendments to the public. However, Democratic Congressman Wilbur Mills, chairman of the committee, insisted that all hearings on Medicare (and Medicaid) amendments be closed.[269] Despite strong objections calling for open public hearings, Republicans could not force the issue because Democrats outnumbered them on the Ways and Means Committee by more than two to one. Medicare was eventually passed out of committee on a party line vote of 17–8, reflecting Republican dissatisfaction with the methods by which this bill was managed and brought to the House floor.[270]

Progressive Democrats made other misrepresentations about Medicare in 1965 that were not unlike those we heard during the more recent debate about the passage of Obamacare. For example, we know that Medicare's proponents ignored credible actuarial warnings about how the Johnson administration had underestimated the long-term cost of the program. Among those citing actuarial warnings was Dr. Barkev Sanders, a respected government statistician who held several key research positions during more than thirty-five years in government service, including that of chief of the Division of Health and Disability Studies in the Office of Commissioner of Social Security. Dr. Sanders publicly challenged official Medicare cost projections coming from Johnson's Department of Health, Education and Welfare (HEW), citing multiple reasons why "their calculations are low to a remarkable degree."[271] What Dr. Sanders understood from his analysis of HEW's assumptions, and from separate observations he made of Canada's nationalized health-care system at the time, was that patient utilization of benefits would skyrocket under Medicare and lead to inflationary effects on health-care costs .[272] In fact, Dr. Sander went on to accuse the government officials of deliberate deception in calculating their cost projections.

> [T]he Social Security Administration has been concealing the truth by means of its actuarial estimates . . . If a sound realistic health program cannot be accepted by the public on its merits it should not be imposed upon them by the government.[273]

—Dr. Barkev Sanders

The Johnson administration and progressive members of Congress refused to heed the fiscal warnings of Dr. Sanders and others. Ultimately, Sanders's worst fears were realized as health-care inflation was ignited following the introduction of Medicare and Medicaid services in 1967. Prior to that time, over 75 percent of America's health-care expenditures were funded by the private sector,[274] and individuals paid nearly 50 percent of these as out-of-pocket costs.[275] Since the commencement of Medicare and Medicaid programs, and the subsequent enactment of HMO Act of 1973, only about 50 percent of health-care expenditures are funded by the private sector[276] while third-party payment for these expenditures has expanded to the point where out-of-pocket costs in 2015 dropped to about 10.5 percent.[277] Therefore, based on government action starting in 1967, there has been a fundamental change in the economic efficiency of how health-care markets price medical products and provider services. This change was created by the third-party payment system that desensitized consumers to the cost-benefit decisions normally made in an efficient and properly functioning health-care marketplace.

—

There is ample empirical evidence that demonstrates consumers will want to utilize more health care when they bear less
of the cost, thereby driving up demand for care and health-care
inflation as well.[278] The inverse is also true, that as consumers
bear more of the cost of health care they will consume less of
it, and health-care inflation recedes. Therefore, by empowering
third-party insurance providers in 1967 instead of individual
consumers, the federal government disrupted normal patterns
of consumer health-care demand and set the stage for increasing
health-care costs.

According to the Bureau of Labor Statistics, between 1945
and 1965, health-care inflation averaged about 4.0 percent per
year.[279] From 1966 through 2008, health-care inflation increased
on an average annual basis of 6.6 percent, about a 65 percent
increase in the aftermath of Medicare and Medicaid's passage.[280]
When benchmarking health-care inflation between 1945 and
1965 against the broader Consumer Price Index (CPI), health-care
inflation ran approximately 1.0 percent higher than the CPI.[281]
Similar benchmarking between 1966 and 2008 saw health-care
inflation running close to 2.0 percent above the CPI, an increase
of about 100 percent.[282] This increase in health-care inflation has
been compounding annually from 1966 onward. This is one key
reason why in 2015 the OECD observed that the United States
spent more than twice as much per capita ($8,713) on health
care when compared to the average OECD country ($3,453).[283]

State governments have also played a significant role in driving
up health-care inflation given that they regulate the business of
insurance subject to federal law under the McCarran–Ferguson
Act. Progressive-leaning state legislatures have enacted regulations requiring insurance carriers to cover a plethora of services
of questionable medical value that drive up health-care utilization
and cost. Such services include massage therapy, hair prosthesis,
acupuncture, contraceptives and other complementary and alternative medical procedures that have nothing to do with treating
a disabling condition.[284]

Despite assurances given by members of the Johnson administration, actuarial projections pertaining to the long-term cost

of Medicare have been shown to be totally unrealistic. According to a 1965 report published by Robert J. Myers, chief actuary for the Social Security Administration from 1947 to 1970, the projected cost of the Hospital Insurance portion of Medicare in 1990 would be $9,061 million.[285] We now know the actual cost of Medicare HI in 1990 was $66,997 million,[286] a whopping 739 percent margin of error. In an article Myers authored in 1994, he suggested that a more valid comparison would be to compare Medicare costs as a percentage of taxable payroll, similar to the way a corporation measures industry comparable costs based on operating ratios. Such a comparison would need to account for certain program adjustments between 1965 and 1990 including costs of extending new disability and renal disease benefits, and adjustments to maximum taxable earnings base. Accounting for these adjustments, Myers noted the following:

> The appropriately modified cost rates for 1990 were thus 2.94% of taxable payroll for the actual experience and 1.11% of taxable payroll for the estimate made in 1965, a ratio of 2.65 to 1. So, the actual experience was 165% higher than the estimate, after all necessary adjustments to achieve consistency were made. A deviation such as this is nothing to be proud of; it is however, much better than that based on the dollar values alone. Nonetheless, the only thing for me to do now is to commit hari-kari![287]
>
> —Robert J. Myers

Because Medicare has never been placed on a sound financial footing since its inception, the system has accrued unfunded liabilities that as of 2018 total at least $37.7 trillion.[288] These liabilities represent the cost of promises made to current and future senior citizens that exceed any reasonable projection of Medicare payroll tax revenues that would be used to pay for benefits. To ensure Medicare survives over the long-term, Congress will need to take some form of action to either fully fund these promises through future tax increases on our children and grandchildren, or we can expect to see benefit reductions of some sort when a future political consensus is reached.

What has led America to this point are progressive politicians, primarily on the political Left, who gave no thought to fiscal responsibility or actuarial accuracy when promising government largess. Their only consideration was promoting the politics of victimization and government dependency, wealth redistribution and enabling economic equality through government coercion and control.

Policy Arguments Concerning the Medicare Health Insurance Scam

Government is not the solution to creating a better American health-care system, it is the source of most of its problems. This is a bit ironic, given that the Constitution does not authorize the federal government to establish a national health insurance program. Therefore, constitutional conservatives should oppose further expansion of both Medicare and Medicaid entitlements until these programs can be reformed to place them on a sound constitutional and financial footing. Further, a quality American health-care system requires the reintroduction of credible market reforms that address the entire system and not just insurance. Only a free and efficient health-care marketplace will lead to a system that simultaneously improves quality, expands access, and reduces cost.

True reform for Medicare also requires that we fulfill the promises of its original proponents by requiring Medicare payroll taxes to be placed into a real trust fund. However, the trust fund should be designated for the individual taxpayer alone for that person's future medical needs, with any remaining funds being passed on to the individual's estate upon death. This is the only way to stop politicians from promising health-care benefits the nation cannot afford.

For progressives, Medicare was only the first stepping stone toward their end-game for health-care reform. Even Obamacare was just another interim step toward their ultimate goal of implementing a universal single-payer health-care system.[289] Single-payer is a government-financed monopoly on health-care delivery where citizen participation is compulsory, not optional. Under single-payer, the government controls the allocation of health-care resources and services while individuals are given either a limited choice, or no choice, in selecting or scheduling services and providers. As a monopoly, single-payer often makes the availability of private sector competition in health care illegal because progressives believe such competition fosters inequality. They believe this even when health-care services are purchased with private funds or paid for through private third-party insurance.

Further, progressives advocate for a single-payer system on the assumption that the government can administer and distribute health-care resources more cost-effectively and efficiently to ensure broader coverage for citizens of a particular jurisdiction. Progressive economists such as Paul Krugman have pointed to Medicare as an efficient single-payer model that should be expanded to serve all Americans.[290] These progressives advocate for expanding Medicare even though the system has already promised tens of trillions of dollars in benefits to current and future seniors that have no projected basis in funding. It is interesting to note how many progressives advocate for expanding Medicare without even addressing the financing issues pertaining to these unfunded liabilities. That's because their financing plan typically calls for a combination of higher taxes and service rationing, much like we see in Canada and the United Kingdom. But this approach does little to improve quality of care, and higher taxes will inevitably reduce an individual health-care consumer's standard of living. For the individual, their taxes go up and then they must wait weeks or months for rationed services or seek other providers outside their local jurisdiction. In short, a true single-payer system treats health-care delivery as a zero-sum game because private markets are not allowed to expand the pool of medical resources available to serve patients.

Single-payer also breeds a multitude of other problems that affect quality and availability of care, and not just here in America. For example, the Canadian government operates a single-payer system that provides public financing for hospital and physician services, but each province decides whether dental services, pharmaceuticals, and other supplemental benefits will be offered.[291] Canada also rations care, resulting in wait times for services that are reported to be the worst among OECD countries.[292] According to the Fraser Institute, average wait times across all ten Canadian provinces for patients seeking a referral from a general practitioner to a medical specialist increased from 9.4 weeks to 10.2 weeks between 2016 and 2017.[293] Likewise, wait times between seeing a specialist and receiving actual treatment rose from 10.6 weeks to 10.9 weeks between 2016 and 2017. In combination, wait times of 21.2 weeks are the longest the Fraser Institute has reported since they began surveying health-care practitioners in 1993. Canadians can also experience lengthy wait times for diagnostic tests. For example, Canadian wait times to receive an MRI scan averaged 10.8 weeks in 2017.

Despite the progressive push in America for socialized medicine under the single-payer model, Canada has been slowly moving in the opposite direction. The tide began to turn in 2005 with the Canadian Supreme Court decision in *Chaoulli v. Quebec*. This decision struck down a Quebec law that prohibited its citizens from paying privately for health-care services or from purchasing private health insurance.[294] Dr. Jacques Chaoulli, a physician himself, brought his case to the Canadian court system because Quebec law had prohibited him from paying privately for a hip replacement. Chief Justice of Canada Beverly McLachlin and puisne justice John Major who wrote the decision were very clear in their criticism of the Canadian health-care system:

> The evidence in this case shows that delays in the public health care system are widespread, and that, in some serious cases, *patients die as a result of waiting lists for public health care.* The evidence also demonstrates that the prohibition against private health insurance and its consequence of denying people vital health care result in physical and psychological suffering that meets a threshold test of seriousness . . . In sum, the prohibition on obtaining private health insurance, while it might

be constitutional in circumstances where health care services are reasonable as to both quality and timeliness, is not constitutional where the public system fails to deliver reasonable services.[295]

—Supreme Court of Canada, *Chaoulli vs. Quebec*, 2005

Although the *Chaoulli v. Quebec* decision only applied to Quebec Province, the decision set the stage for future court challenges throughout Canada to other provincial health-care laws. Dr. Chaoulli would later comment he believed the decision implied the unconstitutionality of similar prohibitions in other provinces because they violate a Canadian's rights to life, security, and liberty as reflected in both the Quebec Charter and Canadian Charter.[296]

The Chaoulli decision forever declared the Canadian single-payer health-care system as flawed and, in certain cases, dangerous enough to lead to the loss of life. The decision also encouraged health-care providers to speak out about the need for reform. For example, in 2009, Dr. Anne Doig, a former president of the Canadian Medical Association described the Canadian health-care system as *"imploding."*[297]

We all agree that things are more precarious than perhaps Canadians realize . . . [Canadians] have to understand that the system that we have right now—if it keeps on going without change—is not sustainable. [298]

—Dr. Anne Doig, Former President, Canadian Medical Association

After *Chaoulli vs. Quebec*, Canada legislated changes to its health-care system that have introduced a limited set of market reforms in all ten provinces. For example, while the purchase of private health insurance for general physician services and other forms of mixed medical practice remains prohibited by law, Canadians can now purchase private supplementary health insurance that compliments Canadian Medicare.[299] Although supplemental insurance does provide for a limited number of surgical treatments including cataract removal, knee replacement and hip replacement, the market for such insurance has been slow to evolve due to the high cost of coverage. Additionally, Canada continues to have long wait times for these services even when individual consumers carry private insurance.

Canada will face some tough choices about their next phase of health-care reforms should the trends toward longer wait times and operational inefficiencies continue. However, they will not be alone. While Canadian health care is unique in some aspects of its administration and financing, it shares common problems with many other nations that have instituted single-payer systems. Michael Tanner, director of Health and Welfare Studies at the CATO Institute, has said that almost all universal health-care systems worldwide have problems like the United States, including increasing costs and a lack of access to care. Inclusive of Canada, Tanner has noted the following drawbacks of universal health-care systems from around the globe: [300]

- Health-care costs are rising for all nations, not just the United States, resulting in tax increases, benefit cuts, and increasing budget deficits;

- Having health insurance and universal health care coverage are not the same thing. Nations offering universal coverage often have lengthy lead times to receive treatment because they ration care;

- Nations that emphasize government-controlled health care create obstacles to quality treatment including restriction on physician choice and long waiting lists for treatment; and

- Nations achieve greater success with national health-care systems when they integrate market reforms such as competition, consumer choice and market pricing.

Progressive critics of the U.S. health-care system will tell you that we also ration care here in America: not in terms of health-care service, but instead based on who can afford to purchase health insurance. While there may be some truth in this, we have already explored in this text why the high cost of U.S. health care is making insurance less affordable to those who need it. The primary reason for higher costs is excessive government intrusion into the private health-care markets, starting with the introduction of Medicare and Medicaid in 1965. Obamacare has only exacerbated the problems involving quality of care and increasing cost of health insurance.

While the U.S. health-care delivery system has its challenges, replacing it with a government monopoly called single-payer would introduce a whole new set of problems. Dr. Michael Porter, professor at Harvard Business School and Dr. Elizabeth Olmsted Teisberg, professor of Community and Family Medicine at Geisel School of Medicine at Dartmouth College, identify some of the problems single-payer would introduce:

> A single-payer system would create serious, and in our view, fatal, problems for health care value. It would eliminate independent health plans, and thereby eliminate competition among health plans to add value by serving subscribers in their quest for excellent care… competing health plans can play crucial roles in value-based competition that are inconceivable from a monolithic government entity. A single-payer system would create a government monopoly with absolute bargaining power relative to other participants. With the inevitable and irresistible pressures to control its budget, the single-payer would undoubtedly engage in major cost shifting to providers, suppliers, and patients. In time, rationing of services and deterrents to the adoption of innovative new approaches to care would seem inevitable, as we have seen in other countries.[301]

—Michael Porter and Elizabeth Olmsted Teisberg

Former Democratic Senator Daniel Patrick Moynihan once reminded us that "the single most exciting thing you encounter in government is competence, because it's so rare."[302] Competence, or more appropriately the lack thereof, should be the primary reason why the federal government should adopt a minimalist perspective on regulating health-care delivery in America. One could argue that the progressive Left would agree with this lack of competence, and that is why they chose to deceive the American people when pressing for passage of Medicare and Obamacare, this instead of selling each program on its merits. Given that health-care delivery is almost 18 percent of our national economy, [303] it would seem more reasonable that we could agree on one tool that we know from history can help fix our broken health-care system: that of reintroducing free market competition.

10

THE CASE FOR REAL HEALTH CARE REFORM

[Health care] is the cause of my life. It is a key reason that I defied my illness last summer to speak at the Democratic convention in Denver . . . to make sure, as I said, that we will break the old gridlock and guarantee that every American . . . will have decent, quality health care as a fundamental right and not just a privilege . . . [I]t goes to the heart of my belief in a just society.[304]

—Senator Edward (Ted) Kennedy, July 2009

For a new right to be considered fundamental under our Constitution, three-fourths of the state legislatures in the United States must pass a constitutional amendment. Therefore, for someone to declare that something like health care is a fundamental right is essentially meaningless because it does not carry the weight of law. You may have an opinion that health care or health insurance is a fundamental right, but nothing constitutionally obligates the United States to provide such to all citizens.

The late Senator Ted Kennedy believed that health care was a right that all Americans owed to each other, one important enough to be elevated to a fundamental right. Most on the progressive Left believe this as well, and it is this belief that led President Obama to push for passage of the Affordable Care Act. However, caution must reign any time politicians advocate for fundamental rights that cost money, and for good reason. Any constitutional entitlement requiring unbridled federal spending could bankrupt the country. This is particularly true for health care where the propensity to consume services is almost unlimited. The implications for medical professionals would also be significant as they become subject to federal obligations to deliver services, effectively ending private medical practice. All of this would eventually force the implementation of a single-payer health-care system with all the associated drawbacks that would come with it.

America has an alternative to treating health care as a fundamental right, particularly for the poor; that alternative is to make health care a social service priority. Medicaid was conceived of as one compassionate alternative to providing health care to the poor and uninsured. The progressive Left,[305] and even some moderate Republicans,[306] have been almost religious in their commitment to government sponsorship of Medicaid, particularly as part of Obamacare's expansion of the program. But spending money on health care to make Americans feel better about themselves is not the same thing as providing quality care for those in need. Government health-care programs must improve health if they are to be considered viable and worthy of public investment.

While Medicaid may have been an honorable attempt to serve the poor, there have been several controlled studies that show the program does not improve health outcomes. For example, a 2013 study published in the *New England Journal of Medicine* carried out by researchers in Oregon measured no significant improvement in health conditions of participants during the first two years the study was conducted.[307] Although the Oregon study noted that Medicaid patients enjoy an increased use of preventative services and increased rates of diagnosing diabetes, Medicaid had no significant effect on diagnosing other conditions including high cholesterol and hypertension—or in the use of medications to treat these conditions.[308] Likewise, a 2010 study by the University of Virginia (UVA) reviewed mortality outcome data for patients undergoing eight types of surgical procedures from 2003 to 2007. Adjusting for patient specific risks, the UVA study found that uninsured patients had a 74 percent higher post-operative mortality rate when compared to those with private insurance, an outcome that one might expect. However, those insured by Medicaid had a 97 percent higher mortality rate than those with private insurance.[309] In effect, *Medicaid patients had higher mortality rates than the uninsured.* Other studies investigating other aspects of health-care delivery for Medicaid patients have drawn similar conclusions, suggesting either equivalent or worse outcomes for Medicaid recipients.

For most of us, the idea that the uninsured would see better medical outcomes than those on Medicaid seems counterintuitive. However, when we look a bit deeper at the underlying incentives created by Medicaid, the story becomes clearer. Prior to becoming a chief architect of Obamacare, MIT economist Jonathan Gruber coauthored a 2007 study that analyzed compensation data from four thousand physicians to understand how much uncompensated care they were providing. Gruber's analysis revealed that most physicians received higher compensation from uninsured patients who pay directly than they receive from patients on Medicaid.[310] Medicaid fee-for-service rates for physicians are notoriously low, even lower than that for Medicare. Add to this the lengthy delays physicians experience in receiving Medicaid payments from the government, it is no wonder so many physicians are unwilling to accept new Medicaid patients.[311] These incentives create inherent barriers for Medicaid patients to access treatment. As a result, many on Medicaid end up being treated later in the care cycle when health outcomes are sub-optimal.

For these reasons, it is right that we should question whether Medicaid is helping or hurting America's poor. It is especially important to ask this question because Medicaid expansion was a central feature of Obamacare that progressives continue to defend. Much of Obamacare's new Medicaid enrollment came at the expense of employers pushing their employees off private insurance coverage, thereby placing these new enrollees at risk of substandard health outcomes. Heritage Foundation analysis revealed that for the first six months of 2014, 71 percent (or about 6.1 million) of those enrolled in Obamacare gained coverage through Medicaid as opposed to private health insurance.[312] During this same period, the number of insured receiving coverage through employer group plans saw a net decrease of 3.8 million, or about 61 percent of all new Medicaid enrollments.[313] Recognizing this shift from private insurance to Medicaid, a reasonable person might be concerned about this trend leading to diminishing quality of health outcomes in America. This concern was given credence in 2016 when the CDC's National Center for Health Statistics reported that U.S. life expectancy declined for the first time since 1993, with age-adjusted mortality rate increases in eight of the top ten leading causes of death.[314]

Despite all of this, progressives continue to push for broader federal coverage of the uninsured through Medicaid. Both Hillary Clinton[315] and President Obama[316] expressed their desire to expand Medicaid funding during the 2016 presidential campaign. In fact, President Obama has often spoken about the need for government to provide health care for those without, even suggesting it is a moral obligation.

> I consider [health care] to be a core ethical and moral obligation, and that is that we look out for one another, that I am my brother's keeper, I am my sister's keeper. And in the wealthiest nation on earth right now, we are neglecting to live up to that call.[317]
> —President Barack Obama, August 19, 2009

What is missing from President Obama's glowing lecture on morality here appears to be his understanding of the law. Federal law already requires emergency services to be rendered to individuals at hospitals regardless of a patient's ability to pay.[318] This demonstrates why any time you hear a politician speak about morality, regardless of their political stripe, one should scrutinize their words carefully. In a pluralistic society, there can be different definitions of morality, even for those who subscribe to Judeo-Christian ethics. For example, Catholic and Protestant Christians know there is a difference in theological opinion concerning the morality of using birth control. However, when we hear a progressive like President Obama speak about health care and he tells us that we have an *"ethical and moral obligation"* to provide it, we should be cautious. As a progressive, he believes this moral obligation requires government to provide equal access to health-care resources and that government should control and allocate these resources under some form of universal health-care system.

If you believe that the federal government has a moral obligation to guarantee universal health care for everyone in America, be careful what you wish for. Judeo-Christian ethics teaches us that we are all God's children, or in other words, we are all neighbors. Neighbors are not just the people living down the street, but they are also those people living in your town, your state, your nation, and even those living around the globe. If one were truly making a moral argument for universal government health care, recognizing that America is one of the wealthiest nations on earth, the scope of that commitment must include everyone including the poor from around the world. After all, God's morality does not recognize provincial borders. Under true universal health care, the United States and other wealthy industrialized nations would have a moral obligation to pay for global universal health care to be delivered to all the world's poor. And of course, if you are a progressive you would insist that everyone's quality of care be equal.

There are several problems inherent in attempting to make this type of moral argument in favor of government health care, particularly on a global scale. First, the United States and other wealthy nations collectively do not have enough wealth to export and deliver equal and comprehensive health-care services for all the world's poor. These nations would also have to institute massive tax increases to raise enough capital for global health-care delivery. They would also have to manage the problem of variances in the quality of care that you find between countries, particularly for the variance in skill sets for physicians and other skilled providers.

This would require establishing and funding a global health-care quality administration to ensure equity. Global universal health care would also require America to make available our own medical practitioners to deliver treatment around the world. And while U.S. doctors are serving patients world-wide, they would not be available to serve patients here at home. For all these reasons and many others, making a moral argument to obligate us to establish Global universal health care is impractical, both politically or economically.

Although some radical progressives (e.g., businessman George Soros) support the idea of an "open borders" society with global access to health care as a public good,[319] most progressives in America are a bit more pragmatic. The progressive Left has opted to focus on addressing domestic health-care needs only. They had hoped that Obamacare would be a transitional reform that would eventually collapse the broader American health-care system, thereby creating a need to move our nation to a single-payer model.[320] Unfortunately, by limiting their focus to the domestic United States, progressives create a moral quandary for them-selves by abandoning the needs of poorer nations. Not to worry however. For these leftists, political pragmatism ranks as a higher priority than any commitment to morality.

Free-market conservatives would likely agree with President Obama on one key point. That point is that as a society founded on Judeo-Christian ethics, we have an obligation to do what we can to provide basic health care to every citizen that is in need. The question is not on the "what," but "how." Conservatives do not see health care as a fundamental right or as a primary obligation of the federal government. Instead, conservatives see health care as a primary responsibility of the individual, with government focusing on assisting those individuals truly needing a social safety net.

Fortunately, we do have options for reforming our American health-care system to address the needs of the poor and uninsured. Effective reform requires that we discard progressive notions of economic equality and social justice that lead to the wrong incentives in health-care delivery. It also requires that we look past the myopic notion that health-care reform is just about insurance reform. Insurance myopia was a fundamental mistake that progressives made as part of their 1965 push for Medicare and Medicaid, and in 2009 for Obamacare. Real reforms must leverage the power of free markets that time and again have shown that they lead to improved product and service quality, reduced cost and expanded access for consumers. Free markets can achieve these three goals simultaneously in the health-care marketplace as well, but only if this market is unburdened from the distorted incentives created by intrusive government regulation.

POLICY ARGUMENTS CONCERNING REAL HEALTH CARE REFORM

Constitutional conservatives, as well as all Americans, should understand that while government may have a compelling interest in promoting quality health care for its citizens, our health care system is far too complex to be managed efficiently and effectively by any centralized government agency. Further, despite precedent that has been set with Medicare and Medicaid, the federal government is not Constitutionally authorized to administer such programs. Individual states, based on the constraints of their respective state constitutions, may have more legal flexibility in establishing public health-care programs. Therefore, the states should be taking the lead in the administration and delivery of publicly funded health care programs.

Constitutional conservatives should also oppose further expansion of the existing Medicaid system because it has not produced better health outcomes for the poor. Instead, conservatives should support a federal role in ensuring that a free market exists for health-care delivery, one that encourages competition, enables innovation in treatment methods, expands access and reduces cost. The federal government should also block grant existing Medicaid funding to the states while, at the same time, giving them broad latitude to experiment with innovative approaches in health-care delivery. All of this must be established within a constitutional framework that does not expand the welfare state but instead creates incentives for individuals to eventually take responsibility for their own health-care needs. Finally, the federal government should encourage, but not mandate, a standard way of measuring, monitoring and reporting on health-care outcomes across all fifty states. This will empower both health-care consumers and insurers to identify the best providers, an operational prerequisite to any viable and efficient health-care marketplace.

Free markets can be a powerful force in health care because they will enable the creation and delivery of new products and services that improve our quality of life and health at continually lower cost, all while encouraging availability to the broadest base of consumers possible. Michael Porter of the Harvard Business School and Elizabeth Olmsted Teisberg of Dartmouth College describe how free markets can work in health care to benefit all participants.

> In a normal market, competition drives relentless improvements in quality and cost. Rapid innovation leads to rapid diffusion of new technologies and better ways of doing things. Excellent competitors prosper and grow, while weaker rivals are restructured or go out of business. Quality adjusted prices fall, value improves, and the market expands to meet the needs of more consumers. This is the trajectory of all well-functioning industries—computers, mobile communications, consumer banking, and many others.[321]
>
> —Michael E. Porter and Elizabeth Olmsted Teisberg

We see the power of free markets on full display in the delivery of Lasix surgery and plastic surgery, both of which are health-care related services but are not covered by third-party insurance. In both markets, competition and continued innovation have led to improved quality of care along with reduced delivery cost and expanded access for consumers. This virtuous cycle, as described by Porter and Teisberg above, is a simplified description of how a free market would also create value for patients as health-care consumers.

Despite this, the progressive Left continues to oppose the idea of free-market health care. For example, progressive economist Paul Krugman has noted two aspects of free markets that he believes make a consumer driven health-care market nonsensical. The first is that consumers cannot predict when they will need care, and when you do need care it will be too expensive to purchase out of pocket.[322] Secondly, Krugman says that health care is too complex to rely on consumers to shop for the best providers,[323] something that is essential for any market to function efficiently.

Krugman appears to confuse how insurance manages the risk of catastrophic health events versus predictable health expenses that we all routinely incur. Those schooled in risk management will tell you that insurance is a tool that is used to transfer the financial risk associated with unpredictable events. For example, any homeowner knows that there are ongoing expenses to maintain and upgrade one's home. These expenses might include an occasional paint job, replacing one's windows, upgrading a kitchen or bathroom, or caring for your front lawn. None of us would expect insurance to pay for such maintenance to our home. We pay them because they are predictable expenses we all incur as homeowners. Yet, a wise homeowner will buy insurance that protects them financially against events one cannot predict: events like a fire, basement flooding, a tree falling on one's roof, or a break-in and theft. These events are random in their occurrence and cannot be predicted in advance, but still represent credible threats to one's home whose financial implications can be managed using insurance.

Krugman believes that free markets do not work in health care because of unpredictability. However, many common health-care expenses are predictable, although they may be different for each of us in any given year. For example, we all visit our doctor's office, take medicine, get blood work, and maybe request an annual physical. Many of us plan to have children, schedule preventative services, or may suffer minor injuries that need medical treatment. These predictable expenses are consumptive, not catastrophic, and we don't need traditional insurance to pay for them. Instead, we can use Health Savings Accounts (HSA). HSA's are high-deductible health plans that are funded with dollars normally paid out as premiums for traditional health insurance. Once an HSA has been funded, it empowers its owner to make cost-benefit decisions when purchasing consumptive health-care services, while at the same time providing a back-stop in the form of coordinated catastrophic health insurance coverage. Therefore, the HSA owner is incentivized to avoid unnecessary health-care expenses and preserve as many HSA dollars as possible for their future needs. In turn, we all would benefit from broad-based adoption of HSAs because they eliminate the incentives and administrative overhead created by traditional "third-party-payment"[324] insurance that historically have contributed to health-care inflation.[325]

Krugman also speaks to the complexity of our health-care system, suggesting that it is too complicated for the average person to compare the quality of service offered by competing providers. While we all know that the health-care delivery system is complex, we also know that other complex markets (e.g., computers, automobiles, financial services) operate efficiently as free markets with consumers relying on third-party analysis (e.g., Consumer Reports) to help make product choices. Krugman is right about complexity, but the free market has been responding to this concern without government intrusion by migrating towards a Value-Based Health-Care delivery that will be discussed later in this chapter.

HEALTH SAVINGS ACCOUNTS: A KEY ENABLER OF HEALTH-CARE REFORM

Fortunately, most economists are much wiser than Paul Krugman because they understand how the right kind of consumer incentives can bring down the cost of both health care and insurance by containing excessive consumption. Among the reasons these incentives are important is that despite America's higher per capita health-care spending relative to other industrialized nations, we are not healthier because of it.[326] Therefore, it is important that health-care consumption focus on those treatments that measurably improve health. That is exactly how Health Savings Accounts (HSA) add value because they create the proper incentives for account owners to consider cost-benefit when consuming health-care products and services.

HSAs must be part of any realistic health-care reform proposal for the rich, middle-class, and the poor because they create the right incentives for individuals to consume health-care resources judiciously. These incentives directly address the problems created in 1965 with the passage of Medicare and Medicaid, and later the HMO Act, that have brought us unbridled health-care consumption. Without such incentives, health-care inflation will continue to be a problem that will haunt us in America for the foreseeable future.

When both Republicans and Democrats finally face up to the failed economics of Medicare, Medicaid, and Obamacare, there will be a need for Washington to move in a different direction for health-care reform. Free markets and vehicles such as HSAs can do much to bring down health-care costs, and to realign U.S. per capita spending on health care with other industrialized nations. However, federal and state funding for health-care services will require a new financing and benefit delivery approach, including that for Medicare and Medicaid. Further, we should not assume these reforms need to be reinvented. We know that approaches to public subsidy to assist the poor to purchase private insurance are working well in other nations and jurisdictions. We should consider what is working elsewhere, such as in Switzerland and Singapore,[327] and adapt these solutions to a broader reform program here in the United States.

MEDICARE AND ITS EFFECT ON THE POOR

Reform of the Medicare system should address more than just its inherent incentives that encourage enrollees to consume health-care services. It must also rectify a moral quandary that was built into the system from its inception. That quandary is the fact that the working poor in America are subsidizing very wealthy Medicare recipients. What? How can this be? There are multiple sources of analysis showing the average Medicare recipient receives benefits that far exceed the Medicare taxes they paid during their working years. In 2012, former Senator Tom Coburn was interviewed about his own analysis that showed the average American senior couple received over $330,000 in Medicare benefits, but only contributed on average about $110,000 in Medicare taxes during their working careers.[328] There may be some seniors who still cling to Lyndon Johnson's sales pitch that they are only receiving back what they paid into the Medicare "Trust Fund," but they are denying reality. The fact is that wealthy Medicare recipients are being heavily subsidized by taxpayers, many of whom are the working poor, under the current pay-as-you-go system.

Then there is the problem of Medicare's solvency. The 2018 report of the Trustees of the Medicare system highlighted the fact that the Medicare Trust Fund is scheduled to become insolvent by 2027, three years earlier than the Trustees reported in 2015.[329] This leads to the obvious question, what needs to be done to set the Medicare program on a sound financial footing? Medicare payroll tax increases have been tried in the past, most recently with Obamacare's 0.9 percent surtax on high-income earners. However, such tax increases have never balanced the system's financials. A more effective answer to stabilize Medicare's financing is to adopt former Governor Mitt Romney's proposal for means-testing benefits. Means testing would simultaneously resolve Medicare's fiscal problems, as well the moral quandary of the working poor subsidizing the wealthy seniors.

However, there is one problem that means-testing Medicare will not solve; that problem is the propensity of our elected officials to promise more health-care benefits than the Medicare system can afford to pay. This problem will never go away under Medicare's pay-as-you-go financing mechanism because that system reinforces the kind of government dependency that the progressive Left covets so dearly. There is only one strategy to break this dependency cycle and place Medicare on a sound financial footing and keep it there. That strategy involves transitioning the Medicare system to a forced savings program for the benefit of an individual participant's future health-care needs.

Given the current state of the systems financing, Medicare's transition to a forced savings program cannot happen overnight. Instead, this transition would require a multigenerational commitment on the part of the American people, and Congress, to slowly migrate off the current pay-as-you-go model. Medicare's transition over a 40-year migration period would be a reasonable time frame that avoids significant disruption to the system. However, current retirees and those within ten years of retirement would be exempted from this transition and would remain on traditional Medicare. HSAs would also become an important feature of this program that enable the transition of Medicare to a forced savings plan. During this transition period, a growing but pro-rated percentage of Medicare taxes would be deposited into HSAs owned by individual participants, with residual taxes being retained to fund traditional Medicare. At the end of the 40-year transition, 100 percent of each worker's Medicare taxes would be deposited into the HSA account they own for their use at retirement age. These funds could then be annuitized upon retirement to provide a steady stream of tax-free income that would cover a worker's cost of private health insurance. In short, Medicare's transition to a forced savings plan would not only protect the system from political manipulation, it would also reinforce the principle of self-reliance in that individuals would take personal responsibility for their own health-care needs.

Finally, there is one last, but very important reason for transitioning from the current pay-as-you-go system to one that redirects Medicare taxes to individual HSA accounts: The Constitution, and the constraints it imposes via the General Welfare clause. One can easily make the case that both Medicare and Medicaid are systems that tax one group of people to fund other special interests. Originalist interpretation of the General Welfare clause would imply that the federal government can only fund concerns that apply to the "general" economic interest; In other words, all citizens share in the benefits. However, by mandatorily redirecting one's own Medicare taxes into an HSA owned by the individual, we can overcome this constitutional hurdle. Some on the progressive Left may draw parallels between forced savings accounts and the individual mandate under Obamacare. However, forced savings should have far more appeal to the average American than the Obamacare mandate because individuals would directly benefit from the Medicare taxes deposited into their own HSA accounts.

REFORMING HEALTH CARE AT THE STATE LEVEL

State participation in the Medicaid program carries with it regulatory obligations that many governors and health experts complain have hamstringed innovations in cost-effective service delivery. In 2016, a spokesperson for then-Wisconsin Governor Scott Walker once noted that "[the Governor] believes block-granting Medicaid will help end the one-size-fits-all Washington mandates that do not work for Wisconsin and result in worse outcomes and higher costs to taxpayers."[330] By block granting Medicaid funds to individual states, each state can experiment with their unique ideas for financing health care or health insurance, and for enabling access to providers. For example, some states might choose to offer tax credits to qualifying individuals or provide direct subsidy payments that go directly into an individual's HSA, thereby enabling them to purchase health insurance or health-care services on the open market. Other states might choose to invest in public health clinics as a vehicle to deliver basic health-care services to the uninsured.

Other state-level proposals for health-care reform have come directly from the medical community itself. In the State of New Jersey, Senate bill 239 (NJ S239) was introduced as the "Volunteer Medical Professional Health Care Act." NJ S239 was the brainchild of Dr. Alieta Eck, a physician in private practice in Piscataway, New Jersey. In addition to her private practice, Dr. Eck is also the founder of the Zarephath Health Center, a free health clinic for the poor and uninsured in Somerset, New Jersey. Dr. Eck is very familiar with the need to expand health-care services for the poor, particularly for those who rely on Medicaid and cannot find a participating doctor. The challenge, however, is in meeting the growing need to provide uninsured patients with access to high-quality care while New Jersey's Medicaid budgets, along with that other states, are failing to meet demand. That is where NJ S239 comes in.

NJ S239 would put in place a state administered program to replace traditional Medicaid that changes how New Jersey delivers charity care to the poor and uninsured. This legislation would offer physicians (including dentists) in New Jersey a win-win arrangement by providing them with limited civil immunity for tort claims in exchange for an ongoing commitment to volunteer in free clinics. Physicians certified by the state to participate would agree to commit no less than forty-eight hours of volunteer service per calendar quarter. In return for this commitment, the State of New Jersey would indemnify these physicians from most malpractice claims. Should a participating physician become subject to a claim of malpractice (i.e., absent an act of omission, gross negligence or misconduct), the State of New Jersey would be responsible to defend the physician in court. The benefit to physicians in this arrangement is a significant reduction in their malpractice insurance costs.

In 2011, then-Governor Chris Christie of New Jersey described the need for more community health centers as "extraordinary,"[331] citing the growing population of Medicaid patients. NJ S239 would not only expand health-care service for the uninsured in New Jersey, but also save billions of dollars by replacing Medicaid with charity care. Dr. Eck explains:

> At our clinic, here at Zarephath, we have no problem in getting volunteer nurses or administrators to support our operations. We receive generous donations of pharmaceuticals and medical supplies from drug and health care manufacturers. What we really need to scale our operations is physician participation as volunteers. I believe that NJ S239 gives them the right incentive to participate in charity care as it will compensate them with reduced costs for professional liability coverage.

That is a win-win in my book and will allow New Jersey to offer an example to the rest of the nation on how realistic and cost-effective charity care can be.

—Dr. Alieta Eck, Zarephath Health Center, Somerset, New Jersey

While NJ S239 has enjoyed bipartisan support in the New Jersey Senate, it continues to come up against progressive special interests as it works its way through the legislative process. However, this legislation represents a real-world example of how states and private individuals can challenge entrenched support for a failing Medicaid system. It also demonstrates how a bit of creativity can deliver cost-effective health-care reform for the poor from outside of Washington.

WHAT DOES CREDIBLE MEDICAID REFORM LOOK LIKE?

Optimal reform of the Medicaid system would not be unlike reform of the broader health-care system. It must include a method of subsidizing the poor and working poor to provide a level of basic health care along with some level of catastrophic insurance coverage. Beyond this requirement, Medicaid should be reformed by combining it with Medicare into a single program the individual manages through their HSA. Both Medicaid and Medicare were established as separate government programs so progressive Democrats could appeal politically to two very different and highly coveted constituencies. However, real reform of both Medicaid and Medicare should lead the nation to consider merging these two programs into one under a common financing mechanism; that mechanism would be to require every American to have an HSA. For purposes of this narrative, we will call it the "USA-HSA."

The USA-HSA would be held as a private asset of every individual citizen, with funding contributed to each account coming from various sources. One source would be an individual worker's own Medicare taxes that would be retained for use upon retirement, subject to the forty-year transition plan previously described. Employers would also fund an employee's USA-HSA just as they previously paid for an employee's group health insurance, thereby permitting an employee to pay for catastrophic health insurance and other medical expenses. Employers who today cannot afford comprehensive insurance coverage for their employees might be able to provide a limited USA-HSA contribution to help pay for basic health-care expenses. Likewise, churches, charitable organizations, and even individuals themselves could make contributions to an individual's USA-HSA, with limited tax deductibility applying to the contributor. One could even use a "GoFundMe" page to request contributions.

From the perspective of the individual recipient, the USA-HSA would be a portable account that would follow the individual from employer to employer, so that any funds contributed to an account would move with the employee on a permanent basis. The USA-HSA would also have an annual limit of tax-free contributions that one could accept from all sources. For illustration purposes, assume this limit is $10,000. Individual USA-HSA owners would incur a tax penalty for contributions received that exceed this limit. Individuals would also be required to use HSA funds to first purchase a catastrophic health insurance policy before any other direct health-care expenses. Let's say this cost for catastrophic coverage is $2,500 per year. The remaining $7,500 would be available to the individual to pay for authorized health-care expenses incurred by themselves and their families. The individual would retain any funds not spent each year for future health-care expenses. Should a USA-HSA owner die, any remaining HSA funds would be passed on to one's spouse or designated heirs as part of their estate. Therefore, the individual is incentivized during their lifetime to spend USA-HSA funds judiciously on consumptive health care, while at the same time retaining as much funding as possible for future use.

As for the poor and uninsured (including former Medicaid participants), they would receive a subsidy from their participating state governments (possibly from Medicaid block grants), deposited into their USA-HSA accounts based on a means-tested formula. Formulas for graduated subsidy would need to be structured so as not to discourage economic advancement of the poor as they transition into the middle class.[332] These subsidies would come in the form of a tax credit or direct grant, with funds being deposited directly into the individual's USA-HSA. If the individual finds that their USA-HSA funds designated for primary health-care services runs out in a specific year, but their medical condition does not qualify for catastrophic coverage, the individual would rely on residual funds in their USA-HSA, state-funded charity care or other state-run health-care programs. States that establish a program such as the Volunteer Medical Professional Health Care Act (NJ S239) would be able to provide charity care by reallocating potentially billions of dollars in Medicaid funding for this purpose.

MOVING TOWARD A VALUE-BASED HEALTH CARE MODEL

The USA-HSA introduces the right incentives to ensure individuals will consider cost-benefit when consuming health-care services. However, if health-care markets are to function efficiently, there is a need to improve the way in which we measure patient outcomes so that consumers can identify the best and most cost-effective providers to treat their medical conditions. That is where a reform model called Value-Based Health Care (VBHC) comes in.

VBHC is a method of organizing, delivering, measuring and reporting on health-care service delivery that recognizes the economic principle that better health is less expensive in the long-run.[333] VBHC also recognizes that like any efficient marketplace, the consumers need a basis for determining which providers are producing the most cost-effective products and services. Therefore, measuring and reporting on provider health outcomes is an inherent part of making health-care markets more efficient. Using such information, consumers can identify which providers are producing the best medical outcomes for the dollars they spend (i.e., the best value).

America's current health-care delivery system based on fee-for-service is subject to dysfunctional zero-sum competition based on misaligned economic incentives. These misalignments inhibit market efficiency and drive up health-care costs, thereby offering consumers sub-optimal value. To turn this system around, VBHC does not focus on a single dimension of the health-care system, such as President Obama and progressive Democrats tried to do by overregulating insurance. Instead, VBHC addresses reform requirements holistically for all market participants including providers, consumers, insurance companies, government, and other stakeholders. VBHC offers a vision for how health-care reform can achieve "positive-sum" competition where all participants benefit from any transaction involving patient care.[334]

But how do we operationalize VBHC delivery? Michael Porter of the Harvard Business School has identified a strategic agenda focused on both government and private-sector participants that will encourage adoption and implementation of VBHC. These six agenda items include:[335]

1. **Organize Care into Integrated Practice Units (IPUs) Around Patient Medical Conditions:** IPUs incorporate a multidisciplinary team of doctors, technicians, and other providers that deliver health-care services across an entire lifecycle-of-care for a given medical condition. These lifecycle elements include initial diagnosis, inpatient and rehabilitative care, patient education, and outpatient services.

2. **Measure Outcomes and Cost for Every Patient:** VBHC measures health-care processes, costs and outcomes across the lifecycle-of-care for a given medical condition. Highly efficient markets are created when consumers are empowered with information on both quality and cost. Fixing broken health-care markets requires that similar information on patient outcomes be collected and reported so that consumers can make informed choices about which providers are offering the best quality of care. Quality is

further enabled as providers will seek to emulate those of their peers who are obtaining the best outcomes.

3. **Reimburse through Bundled Pricing for Care Cycles:** VBHC replaces the administrative overhead of "fee-for-service" billing with a one-time fee charged by the IPU to patients (or their insurance company) to cover all services delivered across the entire lifecycle-of-care. Under this payment arrangement, the IPC becomes accountable for both outcomes and managing the cost of service delivery.

4. **Integrate Care Delivery Across Separate Facilities:** VBHC rationalizes health-care delivery differently than one finds at community hospitals that are prone to offer one-stop shopping. IPU service rationalizes delivery of care across facilities to optimize utilization of medical equipment and other resources, thereby increasing the volume of specialized services treating specific conditions. Value is improved as medical teams gain greater experience by seeing more cases of the same medical condition and as innovations for treatment are discovered more quickly.

5. **Expand Areas of Excellence Across Geography:** As outcomes improve and IPU teams become more experienced, providers integrate affiliates across geography to expand knowledge sharing and offer greater access to high-value care.

6. **Build an Enabling Information Technology Platform:** Information pertaining to patient diagnosis, treatment, and outpatient care must be recorded along with the costs of delivery to enable accurate measurement of health-care outcomes and value. Therefore, computer systems become a critical enabler to both IPU operations and patients seeking information about which providers can deliver the highest quality service.

Elements of the VBHC framework described above have slowly been adopted over the past fifteen years by health-care providers and leading hospital networks that believe it holds the promise of better-quality care for patients. Private industry was well on its way to implementing the VBHC model without the intervention imposed by the federal government via Obamacare. Therefore, it is the private sector, and not government, that continues to lead the way in developing standards by which the quality of health-care delivery can be measured and improved.

WHAT ABOUT PRE-EXISTING CONDITIONS?

What may be the most challenging problem in reforming the American health-care system is how to address the care requirements of those with pre-existing medical conditions. There were several strategic proposals presented during the 2016 Presidential campaign debate to address this issue. These proposals countered the approach taken by Obamacare, which simply guaranteed everyone the right to purchase health insurance at will. While extending coverage in this manner may have had a noble intent, Obamacare was fundamentally flawed in terms of the economic incentives it created. For example, the law's pricing strategy charged both the healthy and the sick the same premiums,[336] thereby creating every incentive for healthy consumers to avoid obtaining insurance until they suffer a serious illness or injury. After a consumer becomes seriously ill, obtains coverage, and is treated, this consumer could then turn around and cancel their insurance and pay the annual Obamacare penalties that are typically less expensive than policy premiums, if not avoiding the penalties altogether. These incentives undermined the financial viability of Obamacare's state health insurance exchanges, resulting in an ever-increasing number of insurance companies withdrawing from these marketplaces. Companies that remained in the exchanges have been forced to continually increase their premiums and deductibles, thereby making Obamacare insurance less and less affordable. This is what led to Obamacare's so-called death

—

spiral, in which an increasing number of people are being forced onto Medicaid or to go without insurance coverage altogether.

A viable solution to address pre-existing conditions will require a restructuring of how health insurance premiums are priced, and how public subsidies are allocated. There has been growing acceptance among many conservatives about the need for some form of federal and/or state subsidized premium support. Even the much-maligned House Freedom Caucus has seen many of its conservative members come to accept the need for such subsidies.[337] The question is what form subsidies should take.

Both Obamacare, and Republican health-care proposals put forward in 2017, called for means-tested premium subsidies paid to insurance companies to make coverage more affordable. Similarly, "age band ratings[338] have been in use for many years, ranging from the Obamacare's 3:1 to the more historically common 5:1 ratio which would help adjust premiums downward for young and healthy. Such adjustments create incentives for consumers to enter the health insurance markets earlier in life when they consume less care. However, there is another dimension of subsidies to be considered based on health status that would encourage the participation of private insurers in state-run high-risk insurance exchanges. This practice known as "risk adjustment," which has been used successfully under the Medicare Advantage program,[339] would pay federal subsidies to insurance companies participating in state-run high-risk pools. These subsidies would be based on capped federal appropriations to avoid creating a new federal entitlement program. But how large should these federal appropriations be to ensure subsidies are sufficient to cover those in need?

In 2010 and prior to the passage of Obamacare, health-care economists James Capretta and Thomas Miller presented an analysis of the cost to fully fund high-risk pools for individuals under the age of 65 who do not qualify for Medicare. Their analysis used credible estimates of between two and four million people with pre-existing conditions.[340] The Capretta-Miller estimate of up to four million can be contrasted with the Obama administration's exaggerated claim that almost 50 percent of

Americans (more than 150 million) could be uninsurable due to pre-existing conditions.[341] Others such as the Kaiser Family Foundation have estimated as many as 52 million Americans may have some condition making them uninsurable, but the vast majority of these are already covered by employer insurance or are enrolled in Medicaid.[342] Therefore, their coverage would remain intact under existing federal and state law. Based on the four million assumption, Capretta-Miller used the 2008 average state high-risk pool subsidy of $4,341 and other variables to estimate that it could cost between $15 and $20 billion to fully fund high-risk pools.[343]

In 2010, the House Committee on Energy and Commerce also provided a pre-Obamacare estimate on the cost of care for pre-existing conditions. The Committee determined that, on average, about 200,000 applicants each year were turned down for health coverage between 2007 and 2009 due to pre-existing conditions.[344] Additionally, about 135,000 were enrolled under Obamacare's transitional Pre-Existing Condition Insurance Plan (PCIP) during the 2010 to 2014 time frame.[345] Assuming some overlap between these estimates, and the fact that some who applied for individual coverage may have been turned down more than once, the Committee assumed that between 500,000 to 600,000 individuals might need to participate in state-run high-risk pools due to pre-existing conditions. Based on Center for Medicare and Medicaid Services average annual cost estimates of approximately $32,000 to fully fund the medical needs of one PCIP enrollee,[346] the Committee's estimated cost ranged between $16.0 billion and $19.2 billion per year to cover pre-existing conditions. Although these Committee estimates are viewed from a distinct perspective, they are extremely close to Capretta-Miller's estimates of subsidies required to fully fund pre-Obamacare state high-risk pools.

Assuming a high-end estimate of $20 billion annually to fully fund high-risk coverage for pre-existing conditions is correct, three things are worthy of note. First, Obamacare legislation as passed by the House only appropriated $13.8 billion annually ($130 billion plus an additional $8 billion over ten years) to fund high-risk pools.[347] Therefore, the states and individual enrollees would need to make up the difference. Second, this $20 billion figure can be contrasted against 2016 federal budget of $588 billion for Medicare and $368 billion for Medicaid (or $956 billion total) for health-care spending.[348] To fully fund a federal commitment to cover pre-existing conditions would require a 2.1 percent increase in such spending. Finally, most Americans with pre-existing conditions already have health insurance through their employers or through government. This coverage cannot be canceled, even if these individuals transition between employers.[349] Therefore, the problem of providing affordable health coverage for those with pre-existing conditions is a manageable one assuming both the federal and state governments participate in funding the solution.

GETTING IT RIGHT—OR WRONG

On March 6, 2017, Congressional Republicans, under the leadership of Speaker Paul Ryan, presented their long-awaited health-care reform alternative to the American people: the American Health Care Act of 2017 (AHCA). The AHCA was presented by Speaker Ryan as the first of a three-step reform process designed to repeal and replace the Affordable Care Act (aka "Obamacare"). True to their word, AHCA as proposed complied with Republican promises to eliminate the individual mandate to purchase insurance, the employer mandate, and many of Obamacare's new taxes.[350]

Almost immediately upon its presentation, the AHCA came under heavy criticism from both congressional Democrats and the conservative Republican House Freedom Caucus. Among the criticisms levied by the Caucus was that the proposed legislation would leave intact most of Obamacare's regulatory obstacles that drove up the cost of basic health insurance. These regulations obligated insurers to provide coverage for services many consumers did not need and want, in effect nullifying the cost-benefit incentives of HSAs that the AHCA also included. Given that only 17 percent of Americans supported Speaker Ryan's AHCA

—

proposal,[351] the Freedom Caucus also knew that the initial draft of the AHCA represented a political nonstarter.

The Freedom Caucus and most conservatives should agree on one point; that health-care reform must not be allowed to create a new middle-class entitlement. America has already promised tens of trillions of dollars more in benefits under Medicare and Social Security than the country can afford to pay based on current unfunded liabilities. Given that our nation also now carries more than $20 trillion in debt, or more than $60,000 per American,[352] adding to this debt burden by creating a new entitlement would be fiscally irresponsible and generationally immoral. Credible health-care reform must deliver change that is grounded in sound fiscal discipline.

On April 26, 2017, House Speaker Ryan announced that a compromise has been reached between moderate Republicans and the House Freedom Caucus over details of the AHCA. The full House passed the bill in a party-line vote of 217–213 on May 4, 2017. This compromise offered greater latitude to the states in applying for exemptions from essential health benefits, managing pre-existing conditions using high-risk pools, and in setting policy pricing by using a combination of both age and community rating.[353] As such, the House version of the AHCA moved us closer to the conservative view of federalism by empowering the states with greater latitude to address the health-care needs of their citizens.

On June 22, 2017, Majority Leader Mitch McConnell followed the House lead by presenting the Senate Republican's version of health-care reform legislation called the Better Care Reconciliation Act (BCRA). Like the AHCA, the BCRA called for eliminating the individual mandate, employer mandates, and Obamacare taxes.[354] Several attempts to amend the BCRA were required to gain the support of moderate Republicans opposed to Medicaid cuts, including the final "Skinny-Repeal" version (renamed the Health Care Freedom Act). Ultimately, Republican Senators Murkowsky (R-AK), Collins (R-ME), and McCain (R-AZ) joined forty-eight Democrats to reject this final attempt to repeal Obamacare.[355] Therefore, as of this writing,

GOP health-care reform in both the House and Senate has been deferred in favor other legislative priorities.

Regardless of what direction America's final health-care legislation takes, any new reform that is passed and signed into law by President Trump must seek to undo the economic damage that Obamacare has done to our health insurance markets. Reform should also seek to better align the federal government's role in health care with the constraints imposed on it by our Constitution. We also need to take special care to ensure that reforms to Medicare and Medicaid will be undertaken carefully and compassionately, given the dependencies that have been created for many Americans by precedent. Building public support for such reform will not be easy. However, by grounding more Americans in the basics of civics and economics, we stand the best chance of achieving constructive reforms we know free markets can deliver to what has been historically the greatest health-care delivery system in the world.

PART FOUR

ARGUMENTS ON SOCIAL POLICY

11

THE TREATMENT OF YOUNG BLACK MEN BY POLICE

How do black people protect themselves not against simply the bullets of a police officer, but the metaphors, the stereotypes, the tropes that operate in that police officer['s] imagination that are equally lethal because they lead to trigger-happy cops or at least . . . hair trigger decisions where cops [end] up believing that they must use lethal force to contain a threat that is not even real, or if there is a real threat, resort to the most lethal form of resolution of the conflict as opposed to trying other things like driving away, like using mace, like tasing, like calling for help and the like. So, when we think about all of this, this is the dehumanization of African-American people. This is the failure to recognize our fundamental rights to exist in the state. This is using state authority to legally execute black people on the streets of America.[356]

—Professor Michael Eric Dyson, PhD,
Georgetown University

P rogressive activists on the left are always calling for an "honest conversation about race" as if to suggest that Americans are unwilling or incapable of such dialog. U.S. Attorney

171

General Eric Holder offered an example of this when, shortly after taking office in 2009, he spoke to Justice Department employees in honor of Black History Month by saying:

> Though this nation has proudly thought of itself as an ethnic melting pot, in things racial we have always been and continue to be, in too many ways, essentially a nation of cowards . . . And yet, if we are to make progress in this area we must feel comfortable enough with one another, and tolerant enough of each other, to have frank conversations about the racial matters that continue to divide us. [357]

—Eric Holder, Former U.S. Attorney General

Conversations about race are important, but they are only valuable and worthy if they are intellectually honest. An honest person should expect that these conversations include fact-based criticism of police engagement with the black community to ensure that legitimate public concerns about racism are explored in their entirety. One such concern is the very prominent accusation by many black progressives that police have abused their authority when engaging with the black community, and specifically when using violence against young black men. Given America's racial history, it is wise not to jump to conclusions in defense of how police across the country treat black Americans. However, defending such an accusation requires facts and credible analysis, not the appeal to victimization we hear far too often from the progressive Left.

In October 2014 the investigative journalism organization ProPublica published an analysis of Federal Bureau of Investigation (FBI) data on police shootings that found black men between the ages of fifteen and nineteen are at twenty-one times greater risk of being shot dead by police than whites. Coming in the immediate aftermath of the Michael Brown shooting by a white police officer in Ferguson, Missouri, ProPublica's findings generated much consternation and debate in the mainstream media. For example, Chuck Todd of NBC's *Meet the Press* highlighted ProPublica's analysis to suggest that blacks were at higher risk of being shot.[358]

Another journalist, former Fox News host Bill O'Reilly, challenged ProPublica's findings saying that available data suggested the opposite. O'Reilly pointed to 2012 data from the Centers for Disease Control showing only 123 African-Americans versus 326 whites were shot dead by police.[359] However, he also noted that 2013 Federal Bureau of Investigation data showed that blacks committed murder at a significantly higher rate per capita (1.0 per 8,037 persons) than whites (1.0 per 56,466 persons).[360] Given that blacks are engaged in a higher rate of violent behavior including murder, O'Reilly suggested that blacks would experience more frequent contact with police, thereby resulting in a higher proportion of fatal police shootings than whites.[361]

Several fact-checking organizations, prominent experts, and journalists were quick to challenge both Mr. O'Reilly's analysis and that of ProPublica. In general, these challenges suggested that source data on police shootings published by the CDC and FBI was unreliable because both organizations were heavily dependent upon self-reporting of such incidents. For example, John Lott, an economist and frequent author on the topic of crime, criticized ProPublica's conclusions by describing them as exaggerations that poisoned relations between police and the black community.[362] Mr. Lott argued that ProPublica's claims were based on data that is worse than unreliable given that about 17,000 police departments don't file reports on fatal police shootings.[363] Without reliable data on police shootings, most intellectually honest persons would say one cannot draw firm conclusions about the treatment of blacks by police. We are left only with anecdotal evidence and opinion, much of which is colored by the racial attitudes of pundits and journalists.

A leading pundit among black progressives is Dr. Michael Eric Dyson, Professor of Sociology at Georgetown University. Dr. Dyson is well known for his criticism of police and has been quoted saying they have been given state authority to execute black men in the street. But Dr. Dyson is not alone. Dr. Marc Lamont Hill, a political contributor for CNN, once claimed that in America a police officer shoots some unarmed black person every 28 hours.[364] Likewise, noted commentator Tavis Smiley has been highly critical of both the tactics being used by police officers against black citizens, as well as the grand jury system he believes weighs in favor of the police in cases where a black person has been killed.

Mr. Smiley has been particularly vocal about the case involving Eric Garner, a low-level street offender that died in police custody on July 17, 2014 after being arrested on Staten Island by the New York Police Department (NYPD). One officer who participated in the Garner arrest used a choke hold to subdue him, a police tactic that has been prohibited by the NYPD since 1993. Prosecutors later convened a grand jury to investigate the circumstances of Garner's death. Even though a New York City coroner ruled Garner's death a homicide, the grand jury chose not to indict any of the police officers involved.[365] Smiley, while being interviewed on Fox News about Garner's death, commented that the case shows that for police it's open hunting season on black men.[366] Such points of view are common among black progressives who take every opportunity to make their case that the actions and attitudes of white police officers is a primary driver behind violence in the black community.

Not all black progressives point to police as a primary cause of violence experienced by young black men, at least not directly. Some see the cause of such violence as historically based, having its roots in the violence experienced by blacks under slavery and Jim Crow. President Obama made this same argument when speaking to the White House press corps about the acquittal of George Zimmerman in the shooting death of Trayvon Martin.

> Now, this isn't to say that the African American community is naïve about the fact that African American young men are disproportionately involved in the criminal justice system; that they're disproportionately both victims and perpetrators of violence. It's not to make excuses for that fact—although black folks do interpret the reasons for that in a historical context. They understand that some of the violence that takes place in poor black neighborhoods around the country is born out of a very violent past in this country, and that the poverty and

dysfunction that we see in those communities can be traced to a very difficult history.[367]

—President Barack Obama, July 19, 2013

Jason Riley, senior fellow at the Manhattan Institute and member of the *Wall Street Journal* editorial board, specifically challenged President Obama's comments about the Zimmerman verdict by decrying them as an impediment to black advancement:

Obama was doing exactly what the Left has been conditioning blacks to do since the 1960s, which is to blame black pathology on the legacy of slavery and Jim Crow. This is a dodge. That legacy is not holding down blacks half as much as the legacy of efforts to help. Underprivileged blacks have become playthings for intellectuals and politicians who care more about reveling in their good intentions or winning votes than advocating behaviors and attitudes that have allowed other groups to get ahead. Meanwhile, the civil rights movement has become an industry that does little more than monetize white guilt.

Martin Luther King and his contemporaries demanded black self-improvement despite the abundant and overt racism of their day. King's self-styled successors, living in an era when public policy bends over backwards to accommodate blacks, insist that blacks cannot be held responsible for their plight so long as someone, somewhere in white America, is still prejudiced. The more fundamental problem with these well-meaning liberal efforts is that they have succeeded, tragically, in convincing blacks to see themselves first and foremost as victims. [368]

—Jason Riley, Senior Fellow, Manhattan Institute

Mr. Riley has frequently pointed to the fact that the leading cause of death among young black men is homicide,[369] not police officers, the effects of racism, or poverty. Further, Riley points out that if racism was the root-cause of black violence, why were black crime rates lower in the 1940s and 1950s when racial discrimination was rampant and legal, and black poverty was higher.[370] Riley's point is that higher rates of direct encounters between police and young black males are the effect of violent crime being committed by young black men, not racism.[371] As a result, young blacks are exposed more frequently to circumstances where engagement with the police may lead to a shooting.

Media commentator Larry Elder has also spoken publicly about what he sees as the false claims of black activists who say there is an epidemic of white cops shooting unarmed black men, particularly when the number of blacks killed by police are down significantly in America over the past 30 years.[372] Mr. Elder believes such claims advance the agenda of Democrats who assert that blacks remain the victims of racial injustice, while other black activists like the Rev. Al Sharpton simply use these claims to seek continued relevance.[373]

One thing becomes very clear when exploring the opinions of both progressive and conservative black leaders, and the black community at large. That is black Americans are not monolithic in their attitudes toward police, or in what they see as the root-cause of violence among young blacks.

POLICY ARGUMENTS CONCERNING THE TREATMENT OF YOUNG BLACK MEN BY POLICE

Police officers, like all American citizens, are entitled to a presumption of innocence until proven guilty in matters of criminal justice. Constitutional conservatives should defend this principle in the court of public opinion as well and be prepared to criticize false notions of bias in how police officers conduct themselves on the job in the absence of credible proof. This means being willing to challenge progressive activists in the grievance industry when they offer anecdotal evidence as opposed to facts to defend their point of view.

What is clear from available data is that no one can make an objective case that says white cops in America are intentionally targeting young black men for execution. Research data from the FBI, the CDC, and other sources are sufficiently incomplete or inadequate to enable anyone to draw such conclusions. In fact, if we rely on relevant academic studies to shed light on police shootings, the conclusions one draws support the counterargument suggesting that white police are not predisposed to shoot black men. For example, a 2016 Washington State University research study called The Reverse Racism Effect concluded that officers were slower to shoot armed black suspects than white suspects.[374] Likewise, a July 2016 study from Harvard University concluded that even though blacks and Hispanics were more than 50 percent more likely to experience some form of nonlethal force when interacting with police, researchers found no racial differences regarding when police officers used lethal force.[375]

Progressive critics claimed small sample sizes that were used in the Washington State and Harvard studies prevented the authors from reaching valid conclusions. Nevertheless, the results of both studies contradicted the expectations of many who assumed blacks are being targeted by police. If fact, the author of the Harvard study, Dr. Roland G. Fryer Jr., who is black and holds the title of Henry Lee Professor of Economics at Harvard, said that he considered his findings to be the most surprising result of his career.[376] Dr. Fryer's research concluded that no racial bias was present in the more than one thousand shootings across the ten major police departments studied.

Instead of arguing with progressives about white police officers targeting blacks, conservatives can make a stronger counterargument by refocusing public debate on the critical risk-issue at hand: violent crimes committed by blacks against blacks. Looking at the matter solely from the perspective of personal risk to a young black man in an urban environment, black-on-black homicide is the real threat. This claim is not without academic support. For example, Dr. Andrew Papachristos, Professor of Sociology at Yale University, has spent the past 12 years studying data from the City of Chicago to develop predictive models of social networks that explain who can be expected to perpetrate or experience that city's gun violence. His research analyzed Chicago arrest records from 2006 to 2014 for 138,163 individuals (about 30 percent of total arrests), arrests that included 11,123 gunshot incidents

177

and 9,773 individuals who were victims of gunshots. The average age of these victims was 27 years, while 82.0 percent were male, and 75.6 percent were black.[377] Papachristos concluded that 63.1 percent of the gunshot incidents he analyzed were accounted for by the social interaction between networks of people who knew each other or otherwise had some form of contact.[378] These findings would suggest that for certain social networks in Chicago, particularly those in the black community, blacks are at higher risk of gun violence from other blacks.

Progressives and racial hucksters will dismiss this issue of black on black crime, and instead claim that the actions of police officers are a higher priority for concern because they have been granted special powers by the state. They also say that police have special obligations of restraint when engaging with violent criminals, even if such engagement puts their own lives at risk. While the tactics used by police when engaging with a potentially violent criminal is a legitimate topic for debate, injecting race as a factor becomes a red herring as it distracts from a more credible discussion about black-on-black violence. Jason Riley put an exclamation point on this by saying the media constantly reports that blacks don't trust police, this even though blacks will call the police more frequently than other racial groups.[379] Therefore, when they respond to such calls, police are not demonstrating that they are targeting blacks but rather that they are concerned about the safety and security of the black community.

For those whose priority concern is how police treat young black men, it would seem reasonable they could agree with conservatives on one thing. That would be the need to educate young people of all colors on how to safely engage with, and take instruction from, the police. Legislators in North Carolina, Illinois, New Jersey and other states have already sponsored legislation requiring driver's education curricula in public schools to instruct students on how to safely engage with police during traffic stops. To further mitigate risk of a violent conflict, public school curricula should be expanded to educate students on how to handle engagement with police during traffic stops and when called to their homes. Such education would seem to be a logical fit as part of local community policing initiatives where lesson plans could be developed for minimal cost.

In short, until there is clear and objective evidence of a wide-scale problem with racial bias that is driving white police officers to target young black men with violence, our police officers deserve the benefit of the doubt. Anything else is simply good old-fashioned racial politics.

12

THE TREATMENT OF BLACKS BY THE JUSTICE SYSTEM

We know that in our criminal justice system, African-Americans and whites, for the same crime … are arrested at very different rates, are convicted at very different rates, [and] receive very different sentences.

—Barack Obama, Democratic President Debate, January 21, 2008.[380]

There is an urgent need to address the astronomical growth in the prison population, with its huge costs in dollars and lost human potential… The criminal justice system is broken, and conservatives must lead the way in fixing it.[381]

—Newt Gingrich, Former U.S. House Speaker

Michelle Alexander's book, *The New Jim Crow: Mass Incarceration in the Age of Colorblindness*, has received due attention since its publication in 2010. In the preface, Ms. Alexander explains that she wrote *The New Jim Crow* for people sharing her deep concern that today's mass incarceration

181

looks and feels a lot like an era America supposedly left behind.[382] In comparing the American criminal justice system's effects to that of the Jim Crow era in the old South, she makes a case for criminal justice reform that is both compelling and provocative. However, activists on both the progressive Left and conservative Right have been critical of Ms. Alexander's work by suggesting that her arguments are incomplete, albeit for different reasons.

Among her progressive counterparts, writer and social justice advocate Joseph Osel criticized *The New Jim Crow* as having presented an analytical framework that omits critical aspects of black history. For example, Osel has pointed to the exploitation of blacks under capitalism, economic imperialism, and colonialism that he believes affect incarceration rates.[383] Similarly, Greg Thomas, associate professor of Global Black Studies at Syracuse University, criticized *The New Jim Crow* for having left out important historical anchors that he believes explain the treatment of blacks in the criminal justice system. Thomas questions whether Alexander's comprehension of mass incarceration effectively describes the entire condition of black oppression under what he believes is the current era of white racist rule.[384]

Osel and Thomas apparently believe Alexander weakened her case for reform by focusing solely on the effects of the government's "War on Drugs" that began under President Nixon, bypassing discussion of the historical basis for racism they believe has been institutionalized within the criminal justice system. Most progressives, whether they be black or white, would agree with this broader assessment as leftists are often quick to blame society at large for social ills while ignoring personal responsibility for one's own behavior. These criticisms aside, Alexander is sharp and direct when attacking the motives of politicians and law enforcement behind the War on Drugs. She cites her belief that the War's escalation against crack cocaine during the 1980s under President Reagan was a key factor leading to current black incarceration rates.[385] Alexander believes the Reagan administration launched this War to capitalize politically on white racial resentment against blacks, something she believes would not have taken place if most crack users and dealers were white.[386]

Alexander and other progressives argue that blacks have been specifically targeted as part of the War on Drugs because of what appears to be a disparity between those who use drugs and those who are arrested for drug crimes. According to a 2013 U.S. Department of Health and Human Services study, blacks were found to have essentially the same rates of illicit drug use as whites and other ethnic groups.[387] Given this, studies since 1990 have also shown that blacks are arrested for drug use in greater numbers than whites by an average ratio as large as 4.5 to 1.0.[388] This higher arrest ratio and resulting higher incarceration rate establishes a pattern of felony convictions that Alexander believes has created a permanent under-class keeping many young blacks out of mainstream society.

Criminologists who have studied the growth in violent crime and drug activity from the late 1960s onward have concluded that it is growth in violent crime, not drug offenses, that drove up incarceration rates since the mid-1970s.[389] For example, Heather Mac Donald, a Fellow at the Manhattan Institute who writes extensively on crime and criminal justice reform, furthers this conservative argument. Ms. Mac Donald makes the case that the War on Drugs had nothing to do with racism or police targeting nonviolent drug users within the black community. Instead, Mac Donald has criticized Alexander's book, *The New Jim Crow*, as having pushed several ideological myths that include the notion that blacks are being targeted by federal drug prosecutions in disproportionate numbers.[390] To defend her point, she has noted that in 2013 Hispanics made up 48 percent of drug offenders sentenced in federal court, while blacks comprised 27 percent and whites 22 percent.[391] She goes on to say that reducing prison populations would require reducing sentences for violent offenders, not casual drug users.[392]

Independent data on both federal and state incarceration rates confirm Ms. Mac Donald's findings, but this does not satisfy the progressive Left. Alexander states that the "vast majority of those arrested for drug crimes are not charged with serious offenses, and most of the people in state prison on drug charges have no history of violence or significant selling activity."[393] Yet,

183

Bureau of Justice Statistics (BJS) tell us a different story. In 2012, the BJS reported that of the 16.6 percent of prisoners in state institutions who were incarcerated for drug violations, only 4.1 percent were sentenced for drug possession, many of whom had successfully plea bargained down from drug trafficking.[394] The remaining 12.5 percent were sentenced for drug trafficking and other drug related offenses.[395] At the federal level, less than one percent of prisoners who were incarcerated for drug violations were sentenced for possession, with the other 99 percent being held for drug trafficking.[396]

Many progressives will also argue that drug trafficking is a nonviolent crime, suggesting somehow that punishment via incarceration does not fit the crime. Instead, they believe those engaged in the sale of drugs should be considered for restorative justice[397] during sentencing to reduce incarceration rates. However, the U.S. Department of Justice has noted that drug trafficking in many ways contributes to violent crime. This includes scenarios where drug dealers compete for local territories and markets and often resolve disputes with weapons and other violent means.[398]

Despite Alexander's thesis that the War on Drugs was an intentional strategy to incarcerate black men, the black community is hardly monolithic on this issue. Black support for the War on Drugs can be traced back at least to March 1971 when Congressman Charles Rangel led the Congressional Black Caucus (CBC) to lobby President Nixon for executive action on restricting the flow of narcotics into the inner cities.[399] With CBC backing, this lobbying effort led Nixon to publicly declare his own War on Drugs just three months later and to create the Drug Enforcement Agency two years after that. In 1986, the Reagan administration launched their own War on Drugs with the passage of the Anti-Drug Abuse Act (ADAA) of 1986. This legislation enacted what are now controversial minimum sentencing provisions for drug possession, provisions that progressives believe account for growing black incarceration rates. At the time of the ADAA's passage, it won the support of the CBC with sixteen of nineteen members cosponsoring the bill.[400] Even today, many in the black community continue to support tough anti-crime, anti-drug measures, yet this support does not receive the same level of attention from the mainstream media that so-called black leaders in the Progressive movement do.

POLICY ARGUMENTS CONCERNING THE TREATMENT OF BLACKS BY THE JUSTICE SYSTEM

Constitutional conservatives should distinguish between enforcement, prosecution, and sentencing when considering changes to criminal justice policy. Law enforcement efforts should be focused on mitigating violence where it exists, along with enforcing broader public policy goals on controlling drug use, without regard to its impact on, or engagement with, any particular ethnic group. Likewise, prosecutors should enforce the law aggressively given that the U.S. Department of Justice has acknowledged a strong relationship between drug trafficking and violent crime. However, conservatives should consider support of alternative sentencing programs for other nonviolent drug offenders that emphasize not just punishment, but also restitution to crime victims, drug treatment, personal responsibility, rehabilitation, and reintegration into society. Conservative policy groups such as Right on Crime are currently advocating such policies.[401]

Progressive activists will continue to push their narrative that the root cause of high black incarceration rates is racism, whether it is reflected in the War on Drugs or other historical and social factors. While some progressives may be sincere in this belief, there will be others with a vested interest in ignoring credible alternative explanations. Chief among these alternatives is a social pathology that has its roots in President Lyndon Johnson's Great Society. The Great Society's social programs famously expanded the welfare-state that began during the Kennedy administration and, in the process, set off a great debate as to whether they helped or hurt minorities and the poor.

In a commencement speech at the University of Michigan on May 22, 1964, President Johnson launched his Great Society by calling on Americans to join his "battle to give every citizen an escape from the crushing weight of poverty.[402] This call led to the passage of the Economic Opportunity Act of 1964 and a plethora of other wealth transfer programs that were couched in the progressive values of economic equality. Albeit with the best of intentions, Johnson's Great Society would turn out to be a social bust, and the first signals that things were going awry came from his own administration.

Former Democratic Senator Patrick Moynihan of New York, then an assistant secretary in Johnson's Labor Department, published a report in March 1965 entitled "The Negro Family: The Case for National Action." The so-called *"Moynihan Report"* warned that the structure of the black family in urban America was "crumbling," keeping a large number of unskilled and poorly educated blacks within a "cycle of poverty and disadvantage."[403] The report noted that rates of nonwhite families where husbands were not present had increased between 1950 and 1960, and that rates of illegitimacy for blacks skyrocketed between 1940 and 1963 from 16.8 percent to 23.6 percent. Similar findings were reported for divorce rates as well. As these levels of family disorganization increased, the report noted, breakdown in the black family structure led to a "startling increase in welfare dependency."[404]

But Johnson administration officials ignored Moynihan's warnings. Instead, they continued to roll out their Great Society initiatives unabated, exacerbating the trends that Moynihan identified within black families that penalized marriage and encouraged single-parenthood.[405] The Great Society eliminated the need for fathers to anchor the economic success of families, giving mothers every incentive to replace them with a government paycheck. Effectively, the progressive Left used the Great Society to replace Jim Crow with a new form of "plantation politics" that expanded welfare dependency by ignoring the effect of incentives created by government transfer payments. This was particularly evident for black families, and the results have been devastating. In 1965, 24 percent of black children and 3.1 percent of white children were born to unwed mothers.[406] Today, more than 70 percent of black children are born to unwed mothers compared to 29 percent of white children.[407]

While one might be able to identify many causal factors that contribute to higher black incarceration rates, research suggests that the single most likely factor contributing to juvenile delinquency is the single-parent family where a father is absent.[408] For black families, this is a more plausible explanation than racism as to why young black men are being incarcerated at rates higher than whites. Recent data from the Department of Justice shows that while blacks make up just 13 percent of the population, they were responsible for 52.5 percent of murders between 1999 and 2008, and 65.6 percent of drug-related murders during this same time frame.[409] Blacks continue to underperform whites in math and reading skills, an academic achievement gap that has changed little since the 1960s.[410] Blacks also consistently lag behind whites in high school graduation rates.[411] These are cultural indicators that do not translate well into personal and economic success.

Finally, progressives will remind us that "broken windows" policing initiatives and "stop-and-frisk" policies used in urban communities ultimately create a higher level of engagement between the black community and police. As a result, blacks are subject to higher arrest rates for drug possession and trafficking compared to suburban whites, even though studies indicate that drug usage and trafficking rates are approximately the same. This makes logical sense and may help to explain why blacks are seeing higher rates of incarceration. However, one must also recognize that police focus greater attention on urban black neighborhoods because of high crime rates, and they are encouraged to be there because of the higher number of calls they receive from black residents seeking police help. Therefore, a more likely explanation is that higher engagement by police in black neighborhoods is a symptom of a much deeper cultural problem.

Ms. Alexander's book serves a constructive purpose in that it has helped to foster a national dialog on race and equality within the criminal justice system, something that all sides of the political spectrum should consider a positive outcome from her work. However, to suggest that historical racism or the War on Drugs are the primary reasons for mass incarceration of blacks while ignoring the implications of black culture and the chaotic domestic environment created by welfare dependency is shortsighted. Progressives will often default to cries of racism when they run out of other explanations for outcomes that don't align with their political agenda, including that of explaining black incarceration rates. In this case, we have other explanations that are more credible. Only when we incorporate factors that include culture and the incentives created by the modern-day welfare state into our conversation about race will we begin to have honest discussion about how to improve the lives of young black men in America.

13

THE CREDIBILITY OF WHITE PRIVILEGE

To pay attention to the American political process, and what the candidates for this nation's highest office have to say and not say about the issues that are of importance . . . you would get the impression that the issue of race, that the issue of racism, that the issue of discrimination, and certainly that the issue of white racial privilege were non-existent issues; that they were of really no importance. . . Yes, they talk about poverty and occasionally they talk about schooling and education. They talk about health care. They talk about all of those things, but not once have any of those candidates tried to directly connect the role that racism, the role that racial discrimination, the role that institutional racial oppression and white privilege play in regard to health care, in regard to housing, in regard to schooling. It is as if those issues exist in a vacuum and have no relationship to color, have no relationship to race, have no relationship to a history of racial subordination.[412]

—Tim Wise, Author, *White Like Me*

White privilege has become a growing rhetorical theme being pushed by the progressive Left during the past decade, one that seemed to have hit its stride during the Obama presidency. Like most manifest accusations of racism, progressives claim that white privilege reflects a set of immunities and benefits that white people receive in American society that are not otherwise enjoyed by nonwhites. As such, privilege is often viewed by progressives as the flip side of overt discrimination. Whether consciously recognized or not, progressives claim that privilege allows whites to enjoy a higher social status and fewer societal burdens. Such claims align directly with the progressive strategy for promoting victimization because they see white privilege as inherited from birth and not something that is earned. Therefore, they believe, it unfairly inhibits the social and economic advancement of nonwhites.

To help us gain a better understanding of white privilege, progressives will frequently point to an academic article by Dr. Peggy McIntosh, associate director at the Wellesley Centers for Women, entitled *White Privilege: Unpacking the Invisible Knapsack.*[413] Published in 1988, Dr. McIntosh's article lists twenty-six examples of privilege she says whites enjoy, but that her black coworkers do not. These examples are too numerous to list here in their entirety. However, the impact of these examples of privilege on inhibiting black advancement, either socially or economically, ranges from negligible to nonexistent. Among the more ridiculous examples Dr. McIntosh cites is that whites can purchase a bandage from a retail pharmacy that matches their skin tone, but blacks cannot. Blacks may encounter this so-called problem based on the marketing strategy of their local pharmacy, but this is hardly an impediment to their advancement. Dr. McIntosh also cites an example of privilege that may offer whites a negligible advantage, such as the higher likelihood of blacks being stopped by a police officer. This privilege might be seen disadvantaging blacks in some urban communities where stop-and-frisk police tactics are still used and possibly with traffic stops in other geographies. However, this higher likelihood is more often a result of the high crime rates one would find in predominantly black urban neighborhoods.

Dr. McIntosh believes unearned privileges become interlocking oppressions (i.e., additive in nature) that confer dominance of whites over blacks and other minorities. In her perfect world, we would redesign social systems to acknowledge privilege and then somehow promote equality. Dr. McIntosh is less specific about solutions to the problem, but she does suggest the strategy of using one's unearned advantages to weaken privilege.

In more recent years, one of the leading exponents of white privilege is Tim Wise (who is white), a career political activist and author of *White Like Me*. In his book, Mr. Wise advocates for recognizing white privilege as a serious form of discrimination, suggesting that "those who reap the benefits of past actions—and the privileges that have come from whiteness are certainly among those—have an obligation to take responsibility for our use of those benefits."[414] No reasonable person could— or should— argue against the biblical concept that "to whom much is given, from him much will be required."[415] Arguing against this concept would be unreasonable in a compassionate and just society that seeks equal opportunity. However, Mr. Wise takes his argument a step further by stating the following:

> To be an American and to be white is to be told in a million different ways that the world is your oyster; it is to believe, because so many outward signs suggest it, that you can do anything and be anything your heart desires. Although people of color and folks in other countries have rarely had the luxury of believing that mythology, white Americans have.[416]
>
> —Tim Wise

Mr. Wise echoes the belief of most progressives that America is not a meritocracy and that adoption of "rugged individualism" reflected in values like a lifetime commitment to education, personal responsibility, hard work, and perseverance will not allow blacks to succeed. President Obama echoed this sentiment about meritocracy and individualism as well on December 6, 2011, when he mocked these ideas in his now infamous speech in Osawatomie, Kansas. In that speech, Mr. Obama called rugged individualism a "bumper sticker" in that "It doesn't work. It has never worked." Obama's remarks infuriated conservatives as they were taken as a direct assault on a prime cultural tenet of American exceptionalism. Unfortunately, the progressive Left has committed itself to the idea that advocating personal responsibility or promoting a strong work ethic are racist themes.[417] After all, progressives would say, if some blacks are failing then conservatives must be implying that they are not working hard enough to achieve success.

Author and columnist Shelby Steele (who is black) has written extensively on matters of race and has made important observations explaining why progressives profess the idea of white privilege so aggressively. Mr. Steele believes that the political Left is essentially anti-American in its ideology as they react skeptically to any implication that America is an exceptional nation. He says the Left prefers to blame a range of disparities between whites and other minorities on the damage done by American values, and specifically those of Western Civilization.[418] Steele points out that the Left's anti-Americanism is reflected as moral relativism, an ideology that says America offers itself as no better an example to the world than any other nation.[419] Steele sees the notion of relativism as one that permits progressives to make value judgments about America's character and actions, while at the same time avoiding such judgments about an individual's behavior and cultural values. This explains why progressives will often focus blame on white privilege, or racism in general, for the under-performance of minority groups rather that holding individuals personally responsible for their own actions and success. Conservatives, who oppose relativism, are viewed by progressives as their moral inferiors because they believe in personal accountability. This moral distinction frequently becomes clear in public policy. For example, conservatives oppose progressive solutions like affirmative action because far too often such policy translates into de facto reverse discrimination practices designed to provide unqualified minorities unearned advantages in academic admissions and hiring.

POLICY ARGUMENTS CONCERNING THE CREDIBILITY OF WHITE PRIVILEGE

Constitutional conservatives should counter progressive arguments about white privilege by turning this notion on its head and calling it what it is: *the soft bigotry of low expectations for blacks and other minorities.* The Constitution does not guarantee equality in all aspects of American life. Even if inequality exists, conservatives should remind progressives that a lifetime commitment of education, personal responsibility and perseverance are factors that weigh more heavily in terms of one's personal success than any form of privilege held by others. Conservatives should emphasize the ideal of "equal opportunity" not "equal outcomes," in their advocacy of public policy, economic advancement and social interactions.

Progressives have used white privilege as an all-encompassing hammer to bang away at differences in racial outcomes to keep their case for discrimination and victimization alive. They also choose to ignore cultural factors that explain racial disparities in social and economic outcomes, including out-of-wedlock birth rates now exceeding 70 percent for blacks.[420]

Commentator Ben Shapiro has pointed out that claims of white privilege always assume racism without evidence.[421] Careful examination of such claims show that Mr. Shapiro is correct. That is why the best way for conservatives to counter claims of white privilege is to counter them with factual evidence.

More importantly, detailed examination of facts pertaining to false claims of privilege can also serve as a cautionary tale to highlight why such claims can be so dangerous. For example, Dr. McIntosh has asserted that white people can be assured of purchasing housing in an area which they can afford, but blacks cannot.[422] One can reach back to the early 1990s to show how progressive groups like ACORN[423] and La Raza[424] have made similar claims. These groups believe that banks and other mortgage originators employ "redlining," a practice that makes it less likely that blacks and Hispanics will be approved for mortgage loans—solely based on race. To investigate such claims, the Federal Reserve Bank of Boston released a study in 1992 that analyzed lending data reported by banks under the Home Mortgage Disclosure Act or 1975. The study concluded the following for calendar year 1990:

> [We observe] substantially higher denial rates for black and Hispanic applicants than for white applicants. These minorities were two to three times as likely to be denied mortgage loans as whites. In fact, high-income minorities in Boston were more likely to be turned down than low income whites.[425]
> —Federal Reserve Bank of Boston, 1992

At first glance, these findings would indicate that whites enjoyed the privilege of higher mortgage loan approval rates solely based on their race. However, this study became the subject of much criticism in subsequent years, both in academia and the private sector, due to its flawed research methodology. For example, the study did not consider criteria such as the creditworthiness of applicants[426] or their eligibility for government-subsidized loans.[427] By eliminating crucial evaluation criteria from its methodology, the Boston Fed developed flawed analysis that led to inaccurate conclusions that were presented as fact. The findings of the Boston Fed Study would later be "refuted" by a 1995 study conducted by Raphael Bostic, a senior economist at the Federal Reserve's Division of Research and Statistics.[428]

The mainstream media disregarded legitimate criticism of the Boston Fed's 1992 study and promoted its conclusions about discrimination until the findings became national news. Seizing on a political opportunity created by sloppy journalism, James Johnson, CEO of Fannie Mae (Fannie) and former Walter Mondale presidential campaign manager, created a plan to expand Fannie's mission to better serve the housing needs of minorities. Johnson's lobbied Congress, along with ACORN and La Raza, to build political support for lowering mortgage loan underwriting standards. The success of such lobbying would allow Fannie, and later Freddie Mac, to expand their participation in the subprime mortgage market. Congress saw nothing but political benefits from the initiatives proposed by Johnson in offering constituents expanded access to home ownership. Participation by Congress virtually assured the success of Johnson's plan because they were the de facto regulators of Fannie/Freddie, and not the Office of Federal Housing Enterprise Oversight (OFHEO).

Johnson's plan was crystallized in May 1995 with the announcement of President Clinton's National Homeownership Strategy. For the next thirteen years, Fannie and Freddie would purchase ever more subprime mortgages for packaging and resale to investment banks and other investors.[429] Commercial banks were already motivated to participate as originators in the subprime markets to ensure compliance with the Community Reinvestment Act of 1977. And the Clinton administration got involved in 1999 when HUD Secretary Andrew Cuomo placed a quota on Fannie and Freddie requiring that 50 percent of all mortgages purchased from originators be subprime.[430] Of course, all of this was done while ignoring the systematic moral hazards that allowed market participants to make money by originating and/or processing a mortgage, but then passing the risky subprime instruments they processed on to the next link in the investment food chain. This poorly regulated incestuous relationship encouraged by Johnson and Congress between commercial banks, private mortgage originators, Fannie and Freddie, and Wall Street investment banks was at the core of what would eventually become the root-cause of the 2008 financial crisis.

Had progressives in Congress and the mainstream media been better informed about the facts and research methodology employed in the Boston Fed's housing study, and the risks posed by subprime mortgages, there is a good chance that the 2008 financial crisis could have been averted. However, both progressives and the media put their blinders on by assuming that blacks were victims and that whites were privileged in that they had an advantage when acquiring mortgage financing in the private marketplace. Therefore, one could say that the history of the 2008 financial crisis explains why unsubstantiated claims of white privilege not only reflect how progressives use the noble lie to achieve political advantage, but how social engineering can also place our entire nation and the economy at risk.

14

THE LEGALITY OF GAY MARRIAGE

I was reminded that it is my obligation not only as an elected official in a pluralistic society, but also as a Christian, to remain open to the possibility that my unwillingness to support gay marriage is misguided.[431]"

—Barack Obama, 2006, as U.S. senator writing in
The Audacity of Hope"

I believe marriage is between a man and a woman. I am not in favor of gay marriage.[432]

—Barack Obama, November 2, 2008,
while a Candidate for President

I've just concluded that for me personally it is important for me to go ahead and affirm that I think same-sex couples should be able to get married.[433]

—Barack Obama, May 9, 2012, as President
of the United States

On June 26, 2015, the Supreme Court of the United States (the "Court") handed down a 5–4 split decision in the *Obergefell v. Hodges* case, a decision that declared marriage to be a fundamental right that cannot be denied to same-sex couples.[434] As many as fourteen previous Court decisions had referred to the idea that a right to marry was fundamental.[435] However, the *Obergefell* decision was the first time the Court declared that such a right would apply as a matter of law to same-sex couples across all fifty states.

Justice Anthony Kennedy, who wrote the majority opinion in Obergefell, cited the Fourteenth Amendment as a basis for the Court's decision saying, "there is no lawful basis for a State to refuse to recognize a lawful same-sex marriage performed in another State on the ground of its same-sex character."[436] Kennedy also identified four "principles and traditions" he said demonstrate why same-sex marriage should be considered fundamental. These include:[437]

- The right of an individual to choose to marry is inherent in personal liberty;

- Marriage supports a two-person union unlike any other in its importance to committed individuals;

- Marriage safeguards children and families, thereby drawing meaning from related rights of childrearing, procreation and education; and

- Marriage is a keystone of the nation's social order.

Based on these principles and traditions, Kennedy presented the Court's justification for the decision with the following narrative:

Under the Due Process Clause of the Fourteenth Amendment, no State shall "deprive any person of life, liberty, or property, without due process of law" . . . these liberties extend to certain personal choices central to individual dignity and autonomy, including intimate choices that define personal identity and beliefs . . .

The identification and protection of fundamental rights is an enduring part of the judicial duty to interpret the Constitution. That responsibility, however, has not been reduced to any formula . . . Rather, it requires courts to exercise reasoned judgment in identifying interests of the person so fundamental that the State must accord them its respect... That process is guided by many of the same considerations relevant to analysis of other constitutional provisions that set forth broad principles rather than specific requirements. History and tradition guide and discipline this inquiry but do not set its outer boundaries. That method respects our history and learns from it without allowing the past alone to rule the present.

. . . analysis [of precedent] compels the conclusion that same-sex couples may exercise the right to marry. The four principles and traditions . . . demonstrate that the reasons marriage is fundamental under the Constitution apply with equal force to same-sex couples.[438]

—Justice Anthony Kennedy for the majority, *Obergefell v. Hodges* (2015)

Conservatives did not receive Kennedy's justification for *Obergefell* well because they interpreted it as a classic example of judicial activism. The most strident voices in this regard came from the Court itself, including that of Chief Justice John Roberts. Roberts wrote a blistering dissent to *Obergefell* that, for him, was uncharacteristic in its tone. He described the majority's declaration of a fundamental right to same-sex marriage "an act of will, not legal judgement."[439] Roberts went on to lecture the majority by delivering what amounted to be a refresher in basic jurisprudence.

This [Supreme] Court is not a legislature. Whether same-sex marriage is a good idea should be of no concern to us. Under the Constitution, judges have power to say what the law is, not what it should be. The people who ratified the Constitution authorized courts to exercise "neither force nor will but merely judgment."

Although the policy arguments for extending marriage to same-sex couples may be compelling, the legal arguments for requiring such an extension are not. The fundamental right to marry does not include a right to make a State change its definition of marriage. And a State's decision to maintain the meaning of marriage that has persisted in every culture throughout human history can hardly be called irrational. In short, our Constitution does not enact any one theory of marriage. The people of a State are free to expand marriage to include same-sex couples, or to retain the historic definition.

Today, however, the Court takes the extraordinary step of ordering every State to license and recognize same-sex marriage. Many people will rejoice at this decision, and I begrudge none their celebration. But for those who believe in a government of laws, not of men, the majority's approach is deeply disheartening. Supporters of same-sex marriage have achieved considerable success persuading their fellow citizens—through the democratic process—to adopt their view. That ends today. Five lawyers have closed the debate and enacted their own vision of marriage as a matter of constitutional law. Stealing this issue from the people will for many cast a cloud over same-sex marriage, making a dramatic social change that much more difficult to accept.[440]

—Chief Justice John Roberts, dissenting from *Obergefell v. Hodges* (2015)

When reading these arguments, one is reminded of an adage that aspiring lawyers are taught in first year law school. That adage goes like this: "If you can't argue the facts, argue the law; if you can't argue the law, argue the facts; if you can't argue the facts or the law, pound the table." In the *Obergefell* decision, the

THE LEGALITY OF GAY MARRIAGE

majority chose to argue both the facts (i.e., public policy) and the law. In terms of policy, the majority cites several benefits of traditional heterosexual marriage that they say should be assumed to apply to same-sex couples. The majority goes on to justify its decision by saying we must learn from "history and tradition," but not allow the past to rule the present. The Court presents this as an odd justification given thousands of years of experience that ordered societies have had with heterosexual marriage when compared to the relatively few years for same-sex couples. Even Justice William O. Douglas, considered one of the most liberal of all Supreme Court justices, cited historical "right of privacy older than the Bill of Rights" when defending traditional hetero-sexual marriage as a unique and fundamental right in *Griswold v. Connecticut.*[441]

However, in 2015, the Supreme Court was a progressive institution. That means the majority on the Court deciding *Obergefell* did not feel bound by the original meaning of the Constitution's text. Chief Justice Roberts rejected the majority's reasoning on *Obergefell* and used his dissent to chastise them for judicial activism, and to refocus them back to the legal side of argument. Roberts writes:

> The right [of same-sex marriage] it announces has no basis in the Constitution or this Court's precedent. The major-ity expressly disclaims judicial "caution" and omits even a pretense of humility, openly relying on its desire to remake society according to its own "new insight" into the "nature of injustice." As a result, the Court invalidates the marriage laws of more than half the States and orders the transformation of a social institution that has formed the basis of human society for millennia . . . Just who do we think we are? . . .
>
> Understand well what this dissent is about: It is not about whether, in my judgment, the institution of marriage should be changed to include same-sex couples. It is instead about whether, in our democratic republic, that decision should rest with the people acting through their elected representatives,

or with five [unelected] lawyers who happen to hold commissions authorizing them to resolve legal disputes according to law. The Constitution leaves no doubt about the answer.[442]

—Chief Justice Roberts, *Obergefell v. Hodges* dissent

Of course, Justice Roberts was saying the decision to legalize same-sex marriage should reside with the people acting through their elected representatives and not with the courts.

Constitutional conservatives should feel somewhat comforted to know that there are several sound reasons why *Obergefell* should be overturned. Arguably, the most important reason is to protect the integrity of our democratic republic by reinstituting proper checks and balances between branches of government. In his own dissent to *Obergefell*, the late Justice Antonin Scalia called attention to how an activist Court was a threat to American democracy.

The substance of today's decree is not of immense personal importance to me. The law can recognize as marriage whatever sexual attachments and living arrangements it wishes, and can accord them favorable civil consequences, from tax treatment to rights of inheritance. Those civil consequences—and the public approval that conferring the name of marriage evidences—can perhaps have adverse social effects, but no more adverse than the effects of many other controversial laws. So it is not of special importance to me what the law says about marriage. It is of overwhelming importance, however, who it is that rules me. Today's decree says that my Ruler, and the Ruler of 320 million Americans coast-to-coast, is a majority of the nine lawyers on the Supreme Court. The opinion in these cases is the furthest extension in fact—and the furthest extension one can even imagine—of the Court's claimed power to create "liberties" that the Constitution and its Amendments neglect to mention. This practice of constitutional revision by an unelected committee of nine, always accompanied (as it is today) by extravagant praise of liberty, robs the People of the most important liberty they asserted in the Declaration of

Independence and won in the Revolution of 1776: the freedom to govern themselves.[443]

—Justice Antonin Scalia, dissenting from *Obergefell v. Hodges* (2015)

Historians will note that in the aftermath of the Civil War when the Fourteenth Amendment was adopted, same-sex marriage did not have either legal legitimacy or social acceptance. In fact, the word *marriage* is not mentioned anywhere in the Constitution or its amendments. Therefore, it is clear the Court's majority pushed a progressive agenda and went beyond originalist thinking in *Obergefell*. But as columnist Jonah Goldberg has pointed out, progressivism is about "social engineering and social control."[444] Progressives believe they have a higher moral authority to act than even legal boundaries would permit. That's why progressives on the Roberts Court chose to exercise authority to enforce their social viewpoint on marriage. This is the essence of the noble lie as it applies to a progressive Supreme Court justice—taking an oath to uphold the Constitution and then ignoring that oath to impose their own vision of policy and rights.

When progressives gain power, they can be counted on to push legislation and impose programs of questionable constitutional legitimacy. For example, in 2010 President Obama and progressive Democrats brought us Obamacare. Obamacare legislation was never designed to stay within the boundaries constitutionally required of Congress to simply regulate interstate commerce. Instead, the Court upheld Obamacare even though it coercively imposed commerce by forcing some people to purchase insurance they did not need or want. Originalists would say these progressive actions by the Court ignored constraints imposed by the Constitution and reflects "tyranny-of-the-majority." The Founders would have objected to such abuse of power by the Court, having experienced it all too well at the hands of King George III of Britain.

The judiciary imposes its own special form of tyranny anytime it acts to enforce its own views instead of interpreting the law. When this happens, "judicial review" then becomes "judicial supremacy," a power not granted by the Constitution or legal precedent.[445] But what happens when the Court ignores the Constitution? Where do the people go to check the power of an activist Court? Some would argue that the power to interpret the Constitution is also vested in the president and Congress.[446] After all, elected officials in both branches have taken an oath to "preserve, protect and defend the Constitution of the United States" just as those serving on the Supreme Court have.[447] Therefore, when the Court rules in a manner that conflicts with the Constitution, some would say the president and Congress have a moral and legal obligation to ignore the Court's decision. With *Obergefell* now assumed to be the law of the land, both the president and Congress could adopt their own interpretation of the decision and exercise their own powers to defend traditional marriage.

Most legal scholars would say that for a president or Congress to ignore a Supreme Court decision would risk a constitutional crisis, as there might be no legal recourse for resolving such a conflict. But the concept of judicial supremacy is not without its detractors. One of these critics is Professor Michael S. Paulsen, a constitutional scholar at the University of St. Thomas. In *The Constitution: An Introduction*, Paulsen highlights several prominent Americans whose ideas conflict with the notion of judicial supremacy. One of these Americans was James Madison who in The Federalist No. 49 wrote the following:

> The several departments [of the Federal government] being perfectly co-ordinate by the terms of their common commission, none of them, it is evident, can pretend to an exclusive or superior right of settling the boundaries between their respective powers; and how are the encroachments of the stronger to be prevented, or the wrongs of the weaker to be redressed, without an appeal to the people themselves, who, as the grantors of the commissions, can alone declare its true meaning, and enforce its observance?[448]
>
> —James Madison, The Federalist No. 49

According to Paulsen, Madison's comments reflect his interpretation that the "co-ordinate" status of our three branches of government supports the idea that no one branch had a superior right to interpret the Constitution, and that constitutional supremacy (not Judicial supremacy) was reinforced by the separation of powers. Therefore, Madison's argument left room for the executive and legislative branches to form their own interpretations of the Constitution.[449]

Paulsen also points out that Abraham Lincoln was consistent in his own opposition to judicial supremacy, an issue that became a point of argument when he and Stephen Douglas debated the *Dred Scott* decision during the senatorial election of 1858.[450] Likewise, following the presidential election of 1860, Lincoln went on to criticize judicial supremacy in his First Inaugural Address.

> [T]he candid citizen must confess that if the policy of the Government upon vital questions affecting the whole people is to be irrevocably fixed by decisions of the Supreme Court, the instant they are made in ordinary litigation between parties in personal actions the people will have ceased to be their own rulers, having to that extent practically resigned their Government into the hands of that eminent tribunal.[451]
>
> —President Abraham Lincoln, First Inaugural Address

Given that enforcement is a power vested in the executive branch, the president could very well choose to ignore *Obergefell* or appoint an attorney general who would agree not to enforce it. Upon doing this, the president might then instruct the states to enforce the laws they see fit on same-sex marriage, effectively returning to the states the power that is rightfully theirs under the doctrine of federalism. Such action would be highly controversial, and there might even be bipartisan opposition to it. However, conservatives should at least understand that this is one strategy they have at their disposal to defend the institution of traditional marriage.

Of course, completely lost in any discussion about the *Obergefell* decision are the rights of children. Although the

Constitution does not explicitly mention rights that are unique to minors or the unborn, we know by natural law that all children are the by-products of heterosexual relationships. Further, our Declaration of Independence refers to the "Laws of Nature and Nature's God"[452] for a reason. It proclaims that "all men are created equal, that they are endowed by their Creator with certain unalienable Rights." These rights include natural fundamental rights that are explicitly stated in the Declaration and Constitution, and others that may not be explicitly stated in these documents. Most conservatives intuitively know that *the right to know one mother and one father* is one of these natural rights, even though it is not stated in our Founding Documents. We can say this because the Ninth Amendment to the Constitution reminds us that there may be other rights not enumerated in the Constitution that belong to the people. Despite this, the Supreme Court chose to execute the progressive playbook in *Obergefell* by subordinating the natural rights of children by favoring a voting constituency supporting same-sex marriage. Subordination of such rights reflects a common pattern among progressives serving in the judiciary. Given that children cannot vote or speak for themselves, the existence of such a pattern imposes a special obligation upon conservatives to defend the rights of children, both born and unborn.

A progressive's first concern is not the interest of children, but rather political power. They have no compunction about placing our most valuable societal asset, our children, into their progressive petri dish to experiment on them with alternate lifestyles. Therefore, conservatives have a moral obligation to see that public policy gives first consideration to the rights and interests of children when it concerns same-sex marriage.

POLICY ARGUMENTS CONCERNING THE LEGALITY OF GAY MARRIAGE

In response to the *Obergefell* decision, conservatives should mobilize political support to pass a constitutional amendment that would explicitly state that "every child from the moment of conception and born into this world has a natural right to know one mother and one father." Conservatives should also work to build public support for traditional marriage by educating voters about the potential risks posed to children when raised by same-sex couples.

While it may be undesirable to modify the Constitution for this purpose, the *Obergefell* decision does not leave much room for alternative strategies. Such an amendment would do two things. First, it would legally and explicitly acknowledge that children, born and unborn, have rights that need protection within family relationships. Secondly, an amendment would force the Court to reconsider *Obergefell* in a future case where the interests of the child would be considered and balanced against those of same-sex parents. The amendment might also be drafted to ensure such a decision would seek to protect a child's fundamental right to know one mother and one father in cases of adoption, and possibly foster care placement. Some would say that such an amendment would discriminate against same-sex couples. However, shouldn't it be obvious that in a moral society the interests of its children should be considered more important than adults? Most thoughtful Americans would answer this question unequivocally as yes.

However, conservatives should act cautiously about any strategy that involves amending the Constitution to address social relationships because such amendments can lead to unforeseen consequences. Justice Roberts highlighted an example of this in his *Obergefell* dissent by pointing out the short leap from same-sex marriage to polygamy:

> Although the majority randomly inserts the adjective "two" in various places, it offers no reason at all why the two-person element of the core definition of marriage may be preserved while the man-woman element may not. Indeed, from the standpoint of history and tradition, a leap from opposite-sex marriage to same-sex marriage is much greater than one from a two-person union to plural unions, which have deep roots in some cultures around the world. If the majority is willing

to take the big leap, it is hard to see how it can say no to the shorter one.[453]

—Chief Justice John Roberts, dissenting from *Obergefell v. Hodges*

HOW ARE CHILDREN AFFECTED BY GAY MARRIAGE?

While the majority in *Obergefell* provided a legal rationale for their decision, they did not consider how an alternative lifestyle involving gay marriage would affect the social well-being of children. Public policy advocates need to be just as concerned about the unintended social consequences of legal decisions as they are with the law itself. And when the courts choose not to defend the rights of children, policy makers need to step in and consider legal remedies to address these consequences. But are there real social consequences for children raised in households headed by same-sex couples?

The American Academy of Pediatrics[454] (AAP) and the American Psychological Association[455] (APA) have concluded that same-sex couples have an equivalent impact on the rearing of children as those being raised by biological or heterosexual couples. However, these conclusions are based on studies that included relatively small sample sizes and, therefore, cannot be deemed reliable.[456] We have previously been warned about such biases in social science research by the late Daniel Patrick Moynihan, the liberal Democratic senator from New York and one of America's most respected sociologists.

> Social science is rarely dispassionate, and social scientists are frequently caught up in the politics which their work necessarily involves. The social sciences are, and have always been, much involved with problem-solving and, while there is often much effort to disguise this, the assertion that a 'problem' exists is usually a political statement that implies a proposition as to who should do what for (or to) whom . . . Social scientists are

never more revealing of themselves than when challenging the objectivity of one another's work. In some fields, almost any study is assumed to have a more-or-less-discoverable political purpose. Moreover, there is a distinct social and political bias among social scientists. In all fairness, it should be said that this is a matter which social scientists are quick to acknowledge and have studied to some purposes. It all has to do, one suspects, with the orientation of the discipline toward the future: It attracts persons whose interests are in shaping the future rather than preserving the past. In any event, the pronounced "liberal" orientation of sociology, psychology, political science, and similar fields is well established.[457]

—Senator Daniel Patrick Moynihan, 1979

Given the liberal bias running through much of the available social science research, and the public pressure that can be brought by left-wing activists, it is no wonder that the progressive consensus on the Court was to endorse same-sex marriage. But we also know social science research methodology has inherent weaknesses because of the inability to create controlled environments for measurement that are more feasible with research conducted for the physical sciences. This concern was brought to the attention of the Court in another same-sex marriage case that predated *Obergefell* through an amicus brief submitted by the Institute for Marriage and Public Policy for *Hollingsworth v. Perry* (2013). This brief summarized the Institute's concerns as follows:

The Court's deep concern about the use of unreliable evidence in the context of physical causation should be magnified a thousand-fold in a case like this one. Unlike the tort case, this litigation raises elusive and contentious issues about the nature of homosexuality and the personal and social effects of alternative family structures. A decision constitutionalizing a right to same-sex marriage, moreover, would have social implications far beyond any that might arise from a mistake in a product liability case.

Academic studies of the issues raised in this case, like many others in the various fields of social science, are subject to severe constraints arising from limited data and from a dearth of the kind of controlled and replicable experiments that are characteristic of the physical sciences. This Court should not rely on the social science research that will undoubtedly be cited by Respondents and their amici.[458]

—Institute for Marriage and Public Policy, Amicus Brief submitted on behalf of petitioners, *Hollingsworth v. Perry*

Had the majority on the Court truly sought guidance on same-sex marriage from the social science community when deciding *Obergefell,* one would have expected them to have considered a study conducted by Dr. Mark Regnerus, Professor of Sociology at the University of Texas at Austin. In 2012, Dr. Regnerus published his New Family Structures Study that remains, as of this writing, the only study having used a large random-ized sample of adult children interviewed to measure differences in childrearing outcomes when comparing same-sex parents to heterosexual couples.[459] Contrary to other research, the Regnerus study concluded that differences do exist between children raised by these two parental groups. These differences included educa-tional attainment, employment history, likelihood of depression, and the need for public assistance as an adult.[460] Upon the study's release, supporters of same-sex marriage, both inside and outside the social sciences, were quick to criticize its research methodol-ogy and findings. However, such criticism was to be expected from political and academic circles that are dominated by the progressive Left.

Unfortunately, in the aftermath of *Obergefell,* passage of a constitutional amendment may be the best and only practical strategy available to protect the rights of children in family rela-tionships. Once such an amendment is passed, states could pass new legislation that seeks to protect a child's rights in the context of marital relationships, negating the need for further legislative intervention by Congress. States would remain free to establish "domestic partnerships" for same-sex couples that may look and feel like traditional marriage, but with priority in adoption rights being reserved for heterosexual couples.

Progressives will say that restricting traditional marriage to heterosexual couples is bigotry because it denies gay couples equal rights. But what rights are progressives denying to children? Prior to *Obergefell*, the fundamental right of a child to know one mother and one father might have trumped any state civil right to marriage. After *Obergefell*, Americans need to decide whether the rights and interests of children are truly more important than those seeking government endorsement of their alternate lifestyle.

15

THE DEBATE OVER EQUAL PAY FOR EQUAL WORK

Equal pay is not yet equal. A woman makes 77 cents on a dollar and women of color make 67 cents . . . We feel so passionately about this because we are not only running for office, but we each, in our own way, have lived it. We have seen it. We have understood the pain and the injustice that has come because of race, because of gender. And it's imperative that . . . we make it very clear that each of us will address these issues.[461]

—Hillary Clinton, Democratic Primary Debate,
January 21, 2008

Now we could fix this [problem of equal pay for women]. If Republicans would get on board, we in fact could fix this today but they won't. One Republican candidate dismissed equal pay as a "bogus issue." Another said Congress was "wasting time" worrying about it. One even said that efforts to guarantee fair pay reminded him of the Soviet Union. And to that I say: What century are they living in?[462]

—Hillary Clinton, Speech before the Democratic Women's
Council, Columbia, SC, May 27, 2015

—

213

On July 26, 2016, when the Democratic Party nominated Hillary Clinton as their candidate for president of the United States, the former first lady and secretary of state quickly became the face of progressive politics in America. Part of her appeal to progressives, and to a broader segment of the American people, is the fact that she is a woman. Regardless of one's political orientation, it is right that all Americans celebrate her achievement. For each time a woman achieves a social or political breakthrough as Mrs. Clinton has done, it sends a message that validates American exceptionalism.

However, Hillary Clinton is—first and foremost—a progressive woman. As such, she has used her position of national prominence to press the progressive agenda while emphasizing specific concerns that appeal to women, particularly those who believe they have been victimized. Case in point, the issue of equal pay for equal work. In 2005 as a senator from New York, Mrs. Clinton sponsored the Paycheck Fairness Act (PFA).[463] If this bill were to have become law it would have modified the Fair Labor Standards Act of 1938 to require employers to prove that wage discrepancies between men and women are based on legitimate criteria and not gender. The text of her bill sheds light on Mrs. Clinton's personal viewpoint on this issue as it states, "pay disparities can only be due to continued intentional discrimination or the lingering effects of past discrimination."[464] After all, a progressive politician cannot be seen suggesting that wage discrepancies might be attributable to criteria other than those victimizing women. But are these claims of discrimination legitimate, or does Mrs. Clinton's support for the PFA simply reflect one more example of the noble lie at work?

Unfortunately, Mrs. Clinton has a habit of employing the noble lie when it benefits her politically, including when she discusses the equal-pay issue. For example, in May 2015, the *Washington Post* Fact Checker investigated charges that Mrs. Clinton levied against several of her prominent Republican rivals for the presidency. One incident involved a Clinton spokesperson charging that Governor Scott Walker of Wisconsin had called the equal-pay issue "bogus." According to this spokesperson,

THE DEBATE OVER EQUAL PAY FOR EQUAL WORK

Governor Walker made this statement after he signed a repeal of his state's equal-pay law that he considered redundant to federal law. Similarly, a Clinton spokesperson charged that Senator Marco Rubio believed the issue of equal pay was wasting Congress's time because he opposed Mrs. Clinton's Paycheck Fairness Act. The *Washington Post* (WP) Fact Checker investigated these claims against Walker and Rubio and found them taken completely out of context. Their Fact Checker assigned Mrs. Clinton three (out of four) Pinocchios citing that, in both cases, Republicans had expressed their reason for opposition was that Democrat sponsored legislation in question would encourage litigation.[465]

Progressives like Mrs. Clinton, along with former President Obama and radical feminist groups, have been extraordinarily successful in convincing many American women that they are the victims of wage discrimination.[466] The most commonly cited piece of evidence that progressives use to defend their point of view is that women only make 77 cents for every dollar a man makes when doing the same job. This "raw wage gap" metric is sourced to a 2008 U.S. Bureau of Labor Statistics (BLS) report entitled "Highlights of Women's Earnings." The BLS updated this report in 2014 and subsequently revised the raw wage gap metric upward to 83 percent. According to the 2014 report, their analysis behind this 83 percent metric does not control for many bona fide factors in addition to outright discrimination that can explain the earnings differential. Such factors include chosen occupation, age, job skills, level of responsibility, work experience, educational attainment, and hours worked."[467]

The raw wage gap metric is calculated as an average of median usual weekly earnings for full-time wage and salaried workers. In other words, BLS adds up all the median weekly compensation for full-time male workers, and likewise for women, and then they divide by the number of workers in each respective group. This leaves a gap of 17 percent for 2014 (or 23 percent if using Mrs. Clinton's 77 metric from 2008) between the two groups, meaning a woman earns about 83 percent of what a man earns, on average. Therefore, this metric *does not* even attempt to measure equal pay for equal work. Instead, it presents a simple averaging of median compensation for the two groups—hardly a comparison that proves discrimination.

Mrs. Clinton has not bothered to update her rhetoric surrounding the raw wage gap since 2008, or to explain how her 77 percent metric is calculated because it is not in her political interest to do so. Even President Obama used the 77 percent metric in his 2014 State of the Union speech to highlight the pay gap issue, something administration officials were forced to backtrack on just three months later after being challenged by the press.[468] Progressives simply use this metric to promote a feeling of victimization within their political base, and particularly amongst women.

But when progressives raise concerns about equal pay for women, do they have a legitimate point? After all, the history of the twentieth century is replete with examples of American women being shut out of certain professions and being paid lower wages than men solely because of their gender. Fortunately, there is credible research available to help us better understand the truth about wage discrimination that will allow us to form effective public policy.

In January 2009, CONSAD Research Corporation released a study funded by the Bush administration's Department of Labor entitled *An Analysis of the Reasons for the Disparity in Wages Between Men and Women*. Considered by many to be one of the most thorough studies of its kind, CONSAD reviewed the results of more than fifty previous economic studies on gender wage gaps, including those most often cited by progressives. CONSAD considered bona fide factors such as the industry and occupations where persons were employed, level of experience, educational attainment and chosen field of study, career interruptions that included motherhood, employment benefits, and overtime work. Based on its analysis, CONSAD concluded the following:

> It is not possible to produce a reliable quantitative estimate of the aggregate portion of the raw gender wage gap for which the explanatory factors that have been identified account. Nevertheless, it can confidently be concluded that, collectively,

those factors account for a major portion and, possibly, almost all of the raw gender wage gap.[469]

—CONSAD, January 2009

If CONSAD's analysis is correct, only a small portion of the raw wage gap might be attributable to discrimination. They identified limitations in the availability of specific research data that made it impossible to measure with statistical reliability whether some, all or none is attributable to discrimination. Putting aside the influence of compensation benefits (e.g., health insurance) and overtime work, CONSAD estimated the adjusted raw wage gap to be somewhere between 4.8 and 7.1 percent.[470] However, the Bush administration's Labor Department noted the following about CONSAD's findings:

> Although additional research in this area is clearly needed, this study leads to the unambiguous conclusion that the differences in the compensation of men and women are the result of a multitude of factors and that *the raw wage gap should not be used as the basis to justify corrective action.* Indeed, there may be nothing to correct. The differences in raw wages may be almost entirely the result of the individual choices being made by both male and female workers.
>
> —Charles E. James, Deputy Assistant Secretary, U.S. Department of Labor (January 2009)

The CONSAD study clearly did not support the progressive narrative of continued wage discrimination against women. Therefore, in 2009 the incoming Obama administration apparently purged the study document from all federal government websites. Fortunately, the report is still available from other public sources and remains widely referenced by the media, interest groups, political analysts and think tanks to facilitate discussion on the equal-pay issue.

President Obama was not about to let CONSAD become the final word on equal pay for equal work. Immediately after taking office in January 2009, Mr. Obama revived the equal-pay issue by signing the Lilly Ledbetter Fair Pay Act of 2009. This Act modified the Civil Rights Act of 1964 to change the statute of limitations for women filing discrimination suits so that it resets each time a new paycheck reflecting discriminatory compensation is issued by an employer. Although signing of the Lilly Ledbetter Act garnered much media attention at the time, most analysts believed its actual impact on pay equity has been minimal. Therefore, progressive activists turned their attention back to Mrs. Clinton's PFA as their priority for legislative reform.

As the PFA languished for the next five years in congressional committee without Republican support, Mr. Obama finally decided he needed to do more. Therefore, on April 8, 2014, the president issued two directives specifically targeting federal contractors. The first was an executive order that sought to protect employees of contracting firms from disciplinary action should they choose to discuss compensation with their fellow workers.[471] The second was a Presidential Memorandum instructing the Department of Labor to require federal contractors to collect and submit wage, employment, and demographic data pertaining to their employees to the EEOC. Mr. Obama believed these two initiatives, taken together, would provide greater visibility into potential wage discrimination by contracting firms. More importantly, these directives established new Federal employment practices that mirrored the PFA, thereby establishing a model for possible future application to all private sector firms.

The Obama administration also joined with both progressive and feminist groups to advance the notion that women choose certain fields of study and lower paying professions due to social conditioning. In other words, they believe that women are victims of their own choices. For example, one can cite the following from an April 2015 Issue Brief published by the President's Council of Economic Advisors that suggests the need for social engineering:

But why do women earn less than men? Some people point to women's choices, some point to discrimination, and some people point to differences in men and women's experience and

education. There is no single answer, which is why we need to
make progress on a number of dimensions.[472]

—President's Council of Economic Advisors

In January 2016, President Obama undertook one final act
to eliminate the raw gender wage gap in lieu of passage of the
PFA. He put in place the same rule for all employers with 100
employees or more that he previously established for government
contractors, a rule requiring them to report wage, gender, race
and other demographic data to the EEOC. This rule, scheduled
for implementation in 2018, would have empowered the EEOC
to calculate a raw wage gap for private companies, presumably
to identify wage discrimination. However, with the election of
Donald Trump as President, the rule was not to be. On August
29, 2017, President Trump announced that he would suspend
this Obama era rule citing the fact that it would not produce the
results intended.[473] While progressive and feminist groups were
outraged at the decision, conservatives reminded us that women
have been empowered to make choices about their employment
that affect their compensation. For example, women often choose
in-kind benefits over compensation including better health insurance, flexible working hours, and more vacation time to be with
family.[474] Unfortunately, the progressive Left never consider these
factors in their thinking about pay equity because they believe
such choices by women are counterproductive to their efforts in
promoting victimization.

All reasonable people can agree with the Obama administration's concern about outright discrimination against women.
But why did Mr. Obama and his political allies see the need to
make progress for women by influencing their personal choices
about their occupations or fields of study? After all, haven't
women in America and throughout the Western world been
empowered to make their own social and economic choices that
affect their future?[475] Feminist organizations such as the National
Organization for Women (NOW) have suggested that women
are not free to make such choices because they are steered into
certain educational, career, and family roles because of sexist

cultural stereotypes.[476] By contrast, the American Association of University Women (AAUW) has acknowledged that women have a right to personal choice, but they believe outright discrimination against women still exists and more needs to be done to reduce the raw wage gap. The AAUW has suggested that "comparable worth"[477] evaluations based on the PFA could reduce the wage gap. These evaluations would replace market-based decisions about compensation with decisions by government bureaucrats who would engineer equal pay between jobs they consider of equal value.

The AAUW, NOW, and other women's groups continue to lobby Congress to support passage of the Paycheck Fairness Act. If passed, the PFA would effectively assume that employers are guilty of wage discrimination until they can prove their raw wage gap is legitimate based on statistical accounting. But the CONSAD study indicates that it is impossible to explain the raw wage gap using statistical measurement. Therefore, should the PFA become law, it would almost certainly increase litigation. One should note that such litigation would also feed one of the progressive Left's most important constituencies: trial lawyers. For these reasons, Republicans at the federal and state levels have consistently opposed such legislation. However, unless the modern-day Democratic Party turns away from its commitment to progressive leftism, the Paycheck Fairness Act will likely remain at the top of their agenda for quite some time.

The inability of the progressive left to accept that women can make independent choices affecting their own interests and earnings potential, including choosing motherhood over a career, is demeaning and misogynistic. Yet, they are the ones accusing Republicans, and conservatives in general, of waging a "war on women" because they defend an employer's right to make compensation decisions without undue oversight from government. This is the essence of what makes the Progressive movement so dangerous. Progressives will claim to celebrate diversity, but instead will demand conformity to their political ideology.[478] As Catholic Archbishop Charles Chaput once put it, "Evil preaches tolerance until it is dominant, and then it tries to silence good."[479]

Such intolerance is a hallmark of the progressive Left in America, and both men and women should be aware of this when offering their support at the ballot box.

POLICY ARGUMENTS CONCERNING THE DEBATE OVER EQUAL PAY FOR EQUAL WORK

Constitutional conservatives have historically defended "presumption of innocence" as a key principle of American jurisprudence, even though this principle is imbedded in the tradition of Anglo-American Common Law and not the Constitution. However, this principle should apply to commercial organizations as well. Therefore, conservatives should oppose the Paycheck Fairness Act that assumes employers are actively engaged in wage discrimination. Instead, conservatives should seek enforcement of existing law when a credible case of discrimination can be made against a specific employer. However, employers of a certain size should be required to collect and maintain detailed wage, employment status, and demographic data so that appropriate authorities can effectively investigate credible complaints of discrimination.

Progressives see more legislation and government bureaucracy as the answer to what they say is residual wage discrimination against women in the workplace. But as we have seen from the CONSAD study, it is unclear as to whether a residual 4.8 to 7.1 percent raw wage gap between genders is a result of discrimination, insufficient research data, or perhaps other bona fide factors not yet accounted for. In short, it could be that men and women simply choose to pursue happiness by setting different personal, educational, and career goals.[480]

At the federal level, progressives see passage of the Paycheck Fairness Act (PFA) as their best option for achieving their agenda on pay equity for women. However, the PFA will empower EEOC bureaucrats to place undue burdens on employers pertaining to the collection and reporting of detailed employee data, a practice that could lead to excessive litigation. For example, a progressive EEOC receiving such data might seek more control over private-sector hiring and compensation practices based on quotas or other considerations. If you do not believe this could happen, note that regulators at the Securities and Exchange Commission have previously considered a quota system at the board level for public companies based on their progressive diversity agenda.[481]

Given that the CONSAD study and other objective research cannot substantiate outright wage discrimination against women, it is unreasonable to expect employers to bear the burden of the PFA. Therefore, conservatives should reject this legislation until credible and comprehensive research can establish that gender-based wage discrimination exists at most companies across a broad range of industries. Progressives will say that data provided by the PFA is required to prove that such discrimination exists, but in practice this has not been the case. The Equal Pay Act of 1963 and Title VII of the Civil Rights Act of 1964 already prohibit wage discrimination for equal work.[482] Based on existing law, once a credible pay disparity has been established for an individual (or group of individuals) in a specific case, their employer then owns the burden of proving that discrimination does not exist based on bona fide factors other than gender.[483]

Conservatives should also note that there is an intuitive argument that can be made against the credibility of the raw wage gap metric suggesting that it does not make economic sense. Thomas Sowell, the economist and political philosopher, has made this point by asking an obvious question. That question is why an employer would pay a man as much as 30 percent more if they could hire an equally qualified woman for less?[484] Therefore, if such a raw wage gap does exist, it would create an incentive for employers to hire equally qualified women before men. Increased competition for female employees would, in turn, lead to increasing wages for women as employment markets adjust to increasing demand. This naturally occurring process in market dynamics would reduce any true gap in wages between men and women without instituting oppressive government regulation.

Given the private-sector business mandate of "doing more with less" it is unlikely that employers are paying men more than women for equal work in anything other than the most isolated of cases. When this occurs, women who believe they have been discriminated against already have viable legal options they can initiate to remediate the problem.

Finally, if progressives are so committed to eliminating the raw wage gap, one would think they would be more cautious about their own hiring practices. For example, in July 2014 the *Washington Post* (WP) reported that the Obama White House had yet to narrow its own raw wage gap between male and female employees that had existed since the president took office in January 2009. The WP said one of the reasons the wage gap remained at 13 percent during this five-year period was because more men in the administration held higher paying jobs. Obama administration officials defended the administration's pay practices by saying "men and women in equivalent roles earn equivalent salaries."[485] If this was true, then the administration obviously believed their own raw wage gap was not important. Maybe President Obama should have shown some leadership by telling other progressives to drop their social engineering efforts and begin respecting the choices women are making in the private sector. Now that would be truly progressive.

Men and women doing equal work should receive equal pay. However, developing public policy around the assumption that gender discrimination permeates the job market demonstrates its own version of bias and bigotry. Employers deserve the benefit of the doubt, just as we all deserve the presumption of innocence. However, should a gender-bias complaint be filed, employers of a certain size also need to be able to demonstrate that their decisions about compensation for equal work are based on legitimate criteria.

16

THE RIGHT OF WOMEN TO CHOOSE ABORTION

The unborn person doesn't have constitutional rights. Now, that doesn't mean that we don't do everything we possibly can, in the vast majority of instances to, you know, help a mother who is carrying a child and wants to make sure that child will be healthy, to have appropriate medical support. It doesn't mean that you don't do everything possible to try to fulfill your obligations. But it does not include sacrificing the woman's right to make decisions. And I think that's an important distinction, that under Roe v. Wade we've had enshrined under our Constitution.[486]

—Hillary Clinton, NBC's *Meet the Press*, April 3, 2016

The Supreme Court of the United States in its landmark 1973 *Roe v. Wade* decision declared that women have a right to choose abortion, a right that becomes more limited as an unborn child reaches the point of viability.[487] Justice Harry Blackmun, delivering the opinion for the Court in *Roe*, argued that women have a "qualified" right to abortion based on a fundamental right to privacy.

State criminal abortion laws, like those involved here, that except from criminality only a life-saving procedure on the mother's behalf without regard to the stage of her pregnancy and other interests involved violate the Due Process Clause of the Fourteenth Amendment, which protects against state action the right to privacy, including a woman's qualified right to terminate her pregnancy. Though the State cannot override that right, it has legitimate interests in protecting both the pregnant woman's health and the potentiality of human life, each of which interests grows and reaches a "compelling" point at various stages of the woman's approach to term.[488]

—*Roe v. Wade*, Syllabus, 410 US 113 (1973)

As decided by a 7–2 majority, *Roe v. Wade* was the Court's attempt to settle a contentious public issue that had not been resolved legislatively at the federal level. This settlement was inherently a compromise between what it saw as two conflicting fundamental rights: privacy and life.[489] The Court sought to balance between these rights by guaranteeing women a new unrestricted right to abortion in the first trimester of pregnancy, and only a limited right during the second trimester assuming a child had not reached the point of viability. The Court also determined that abortion rights would extend throughout a woman's pregnancy, even into the third trimester if the life and health of the mother were at risk. However, in handing down the Roe decision, the Court also set off a firestorm of criticism from conservatives for having overstepped its constitutional authority by acting as de facto legislators. Chief among these critics was Justice Byron White whose dissent from Roe described the Court's reasoning as "an exercise of raw judicial power."

With all due respect, I dissent. I find nothing in the language or history of the Constitution to support the Court's judgment. The Court simply fashions and announces a new constitutional right for pregnant mothers and, with scarcely any reason or authority for its action, invests that right with sufficient substance to override most existing state abortion statutes. The upshot is that the people and the legislatures of the 50 States are constitutionally disentitled to weigh the relative importance of the continued existence and development of the fetus, on the one hand, against a spectrum of possible impacts on the mother, on the other hand. As an exercise of raw judicial power, the Court perhaps has authority to do what it does today; but, in my view, its judgment is an improvident and extravagant exercise of the power of judicial review that the Constitution extends to this Court.[490]

—Justice Byron White, dissenting from *Roe v. Wade*

As a matter of originalist constitutional jurisprudence Justice White had *Roe* correct. However, an implicit but limited right to privacy has been imbedded in the Constitution since the nation's founding. For example, the Third Amendment protects the privacy of our homes by preventing government from using our property without permission to quarter troops; And the Fourth Amendment guarantees privacy of our person and possessions against unreasonable searches and seizures by government. Additionally, the Ninth Amendment recognizes there may be other fundamental rights that are not explicit within the Constitution's text but are retained by the people. These may include expanded privacy rights that are not yet defined. However, nowhere within the U.S. Constitution does it identify a generalized all-encompassing right to privacy. As a result, federal and state courts should recognize the need for restraint in how they interpret the scope of privacy rights as they apply to abortion and other concerns.

A Brief History of Privacy

In 1868, the door for expanding the Court's view of privacy rights was opened with the passage of the Fourteenth Amendment. Section 1 of this amendment declared that "No State shall make or enforce any law which shall abridge the privileges or immunities of citizens of the United States; nor shall any State deprive any person of life, liberty, or property, without due process of law."

The Fourteenth Amendment built upon the Fifth by empowering courts to protect two types of due process rights: procedural and substantive. Procedural due process required government to establish and follow proper procedures before depriving a citizen of life, liberty, or property. Substantive due process sought to prevent government from arbitrarily depriving citizens of rights that may or may not have been enumerated explicitly in the Constitution, but nonetheless were understood to be retained by the states or the people. Therefore, the Fourteenth Amendment added "substance" to due process by requiring that government have a legitimate justification before interfering in the private lives of its citizens.

The Supreme Court first invoked substantive due process for selected cases between 1897 to 1937, the period legal scholars have called the "Lochner" era.[491] During this period, the Court was focused on protecting the right of workers to contract-at-will with employers by striking down state minimum-wage laws, limitations on work hours, child-labor laws, and other laws affecting the employer-employee relationship."[492] But as the Great Depression dragged on into the late 1930s, the Court's attempts to protect right-to-contract undermined President Franklin D. Roosevelt's efforts to enact New Deal legislation. This era of economic rights finally ended when Justice Owen Roberts, a member of the pro-Lochner majority on the Court, feeling pressure from the Roosevelt administration, switched his vote in a state minimum-wage maximum-hour case.[493] This change of heart would undermine further attempts by the Supreme Court to incorporate broadly defined economic rights under the banner of liberty.[494]

During the first half of the twentieth century, one of the great debates among jurists was whether the framers of the Fourteenth Amendment sought to extend individual liberty by making the Bill of Rights applicable to state law.[495] Beginning in the Lochner era, the Supreme Court began acting on this debate by extending liberty protections into two related categories of rights. The first was incorporating individual liberty as defined by the Bill of Rights by making these rights applicable for the first time to state law.[496] The second was to invoke substantive due process as the basis for protecting fundamental rights and liberties from state intrusion even though they are not explicitly enumerated in the Constitution or the Bill of Rights.[497] Since Lochner and continuing to the present day, some progressive justices who have served on the Court have felt empowered by the Fourteenth Amendment to find new fundamental rights without being constrained to the text of the Constitution and its original meaning. This is the essence of judicial activism, and it is what has made substantive due process the most controversial aspect of modern-day American jurisprudence.[498]

The Supreme Court's acceptance of cases involving substantive due process accelerated during the 1960s with most of these centering on matters concerning a "right to privacy"[499] These privacy cases focused primarily on four aspects of individual liberty: parental rights concerning child rearing; procreation; family relationships; and private sexual activity.[500] The first case to address privacy specifically was *Griswold v. Connecticut*.[501] In this 1965 case, the Court overturned an 1879 Connecticut law called the Comstock Act that prohibited the use of birth control, even for married couples. Justice William O. Douglas, writing for the majority in Griswold, defended the decision and the Court's adoption of a fundamental right to privacy by saying the following:

> [Griswold v. Connecticut] concerns a [marital] relationship lying within the zone of privacy created by several fundamental constitutional guarantees. And it concerns a law which, in forbidding the use of contraceptives, rather than regulating their manufacture or sale, seeks to achieve its goals by means having a maximum destructive impact upon that relationship. Such a law cannot stand in light of the familiar principle, so often applied by this Court, that a governmental purpose to control or prevent activities constitutionally subject to state regulation may not be achieved by means which sweep unnecessarily broadly and thereby invade the area of protected freedoms.

> We deal with a right of privacy older than the Bill of Rights— older than our political parties, older than our school system.

Marriage is a coming together for better or for worse, hopefully enduring, and intimate to the degree of being sacred. It is an association that promotes a way of life, not causes; a harmony in living, not political faiths; a bilateral loyalty, not commercial or social projects. Yet it is an association for as noble a purpose as any involved in our prior decisions.[502]

—Justice William O. Douglas, writing for the majority, *Griswold v. Connecticut*

Conservatives criticized the *Griswold* decision as just another case of judicial activism, like those when the Court had invoked substantive due process during the Lochner era. What is important to note about this criticism, however, is that it had nothing to do with the intent of the Comstock Act. In fact, Justice Hugo Black, who dissented from *Griswold*, described Comstock as "every bit as offensive to me as it is to my Brethren of the majority."[503] Instead, conservatives both on and off the Court were rightly concerned with "living constitutionalism," as the majority had justified its opinion based on a fundamental right of privacy not explicitly found in the Constitution's text. With its decision in *Griswold*, the Court established a precedent for a broad-based right of privacy that would open the door eight years later to the controversial decision that legalized abortion: *Roe v. Wade*.

THE EVOLUTION FROM PRIVACY TO LIBERTY

In the aftermath of *Roe*, there were attempts by subsequent justices and progressive legal scholars to bolster the credibility of the decision by advocating that its constitutional basis was grounded in "liberty" and not "privacy." After all, the Fourteenth Amendment explicitly referenced liberty as requiring due process protections while the word privacy does not appear anywhere in the Constitution or its amendments. Chief among these advocates was Justice John Paul Stevens who argued that substantive due process did not originate in explicit text of law but as a notion of liberty in natural law.[504] Later courts would almost universally cite liberty instead of privacy as the basis for protecting unwarranted government intrusions when applying substantive due process.[505] However, progressive justices would also use such arguments to expand the boundaries of liberty without regard to their obligations to interpret the law. Therefore, it is this transition to liberty-based substantive due process that has been used by subsequent courts to expand the progressive social agenda, including most recently gay marriage.

This is not to say that all conservatives oppose the idea that liberty justifies protecting certain rights from unwarranted intrusions by government. Former Chief Justice William Rehnquist, a conservative, once noted that fundamental rights and liberties recognized under due process should only be protected if they are "deeply rooted in this Nation's history and tradition" or there is a "careful description" of the right observed in the Constitution's text.[506] Justice Scalia has articulated a point of view similar to Rehnquist, but he emphasized that any such claim on liberty should be "so deeply imbedded within society's traditions as to be a fundamental right."[507] This standard creates a very narrow window within which a conservative justice can mold an interpretive decision on liberty. Therefore, conservatives have remained largely opposed to any attempts by the Court to invoke privacy or liberty-based substantive due process because they see these as attempts to legislate and not interpret the law.

A Conservative Change of Heart?

Conservative support for a broad-based right-to-privacy took an interesting turn in May 2016 when the Heritage Foundation's Daily Signal posted an opinion piece entitled "Our Constitutional Right to Privacy Is Missing from Bathroom Debate."[508] Matt Sharp, an attorney for Alliance Defending Freedom (ADF), wrote the piece in response to President Obama's May 2016 directive concerning Title IX of the Educational Amendments of 1972 and its application to transgender students. This directive notified public schools that they must allow transgender students to use the bathrooms that match their chosen gender identity or risk losing federal aid. Mr. Sharp presented a credible argument about the risks posed to young women should schools allow trans-gendered men to change or shower in women's facilities. Sharp's legal reasoning defended a right-to-privacy as being essential to protecting young women he believed were highly vulnerable to such intrusions. Progressive blogs and media pundits were quick to point out the contradiction with Heritage's historical position that condemned the idea of a broad-based right-to-privacy.[509] Yet, here was Heritage using an expanded interpretation of privacy rights to defend the idea of bodily privacy guaranteeing women access to restricted bathroom accommodations.

The transgender issue raised by President Obama's directive and the personal risks to women posed by such a policy highlight why conservatives need to recognize expanded privacy rights in American jurisprudence. The key is for conservatives to find a constitutionally consistent way of recognizing these rights when common sense dictates they should apply in public policy. There are several ways to do this. The most obvious way would be to pass a constitutional amendment that would explicitly delineate the boundaries of privacy (or liberty). The states could also lever-age the political framework provided by the Ninth and Tenth Amendments to acknowledge privacy protections. This strategy turns the tables on progressives in the judiciary, but ultimately the Supreme Court would weigh in to confirm or invalidate how these rights might be applied. Future presidents could also oppose decisions that they believe reflect judicial supremacy by withholding the power of enforcement. Finally, Congress could use its constitutional authority to change the number of sitting justices on the Supreme Court, an action that is not without precedent,[510] thereby influencing how the Court might decide future cases affecting privacy rights.

POLICY ARGUMENTS CONCERNING THE RIGHT OF WOMEN TO CHOOSE ABORTION

Conservatives who want to avoid a contradiction on privacy rights such as that posed by Mr. Sharp's publication need to consider two things. First, they need to accept and acknowledge that a fundamental right-to-privacy exists, whether enumerated in the Constitution or not, to provide common sense protections from unwarranted government intrusion. Second, they need to acknowledge that on matters involving abortion there needs to be a balance drawn between privacy (or liberty) and life when implementing public policy. This is not to say that conservatives need to accept that abortion in certain circumstances, or any circumstances, is a moral option. However, the law and our Constitution are secular instruments that at times reflect inherent contradictions between fundamental rights. That means conservatives also need to acknowledge that legal decisions that resolve such contradictions are not always aligned with Judeo-Christian values.

In American jurisprudence, when a contradiction between fundamental rights exists, the moral obligation is not to choose one right over another, or to sidestep the Constitution by invoking biblical principles of morality. Instead, we need to find a constructive way to balance between conflicting fundamental rights in public policy. People of good conscience can disagree about where to draw that balance on a particular policy concern. Nonetheless, a balance must be drawn in public policy to resolve a contradiction between rights as constructively as possible.

Under the leadership of Hillary Clinton and Barack Obama, the progressive Left has rejected balance and adopted an absolutist position on the abortion issue. That is why the 2016 Democratic Party Platform included an explicit call to abandon what has been a forty-year bipartisan compromise that outlawed government funding of elective abortions: The Hyde Amendment.[511] Progressives believe the moral high ground involves providing the poor with equal access to elective abortion services. This reflects a major shift from the position former president Jimmy Carter articulated in a 1977 news conference when he reminded us that "there are many things in life that are not fair, that wealthy people can afford and poor people can't."[512] Mr. Carter went on to point out that the federal government did not need to take action to equalize access to abortion when morality is a consideration.[513] But progressives have a completely different view of morality

233

than conservative Americans or even mainstream Democrats, one that is not linked to Judeo-Christian traditions and ethics. Their morality includes undermining the rights of unborn children in favor of adults who can vote, even when that unborn child is viable and can live outside a mother's womb.

Constitutional conservatives should also look to the public consensus on abortion to identify a viable and realistic public policy agenda that will save unborn lives: that being the outlawing of late-term abortions after 20 weeks of gestation.[514] Congress has already acted to pass the Partial-Birth Abortion Ban Act of 2003, a law that outlawed the practice of surgical late-term abortions except when the mother's life is at serious risk.[515] More recently, House Republicans passed legislation in May 2015 called the Pain Capable Unborn Child Protection Act. This Act called for a ban on abortion after 20 weeks of pregnancy except in case of rape, incest, or when the life of the mother is at risk.[516] President Obama had threatened to veto any legislation containing a 20-week abortion ban while he was in office. As a result, the Senate version of this bill never made it out of committee and it never became law. However, these initiatives reflect an attempt by conservatives to balance privacy and life in a manner that is consistent with *Roe*, albeit with a more refined framework of abortion restrictions.

Hillary Clinton has adopted the progressive position on abortion by saying that the unborn have no rights and that women should have the right to terminate a pregnancy at any time and for any reason. Given her position, it is not hyperbole to point out that we treat animals the same way in American society as Mrs. Clinton suggests we should treat a viable unborn child. After all, federal and state law governing animal care requires their humane treatment when they are alive, but we do not recognize that animals share any of what we know as "rights" as they apply to human-persons. That is why when animal shelters cannot find a home for dog or cat they are often euthanized out of economic necessity. Progressives are now seeking to establish this same standard of treatment for the unborn in secular law while requiring every taxpayer to pay for such abortions on demand. This is something that conservatives and even traditional mainstream Americans should find revolting and should reject outright.

What Mrs. Clinton and other progressive advocates of unrestricted abortion refuse to acknowledge concerning the unborn is that the *Roe* decision recognizes that the states have a compelling interest in protecting the "potentiality of human life" when regulating abortion.[517] The phrase "potentiality of human life" indicates that "personhood" may not yet have been achieved in a legal sense, but that states have a compelling interest in protecting the "natural" rights of the unborn. This compelling interest is not without historical precedent. Sir William Blackstone, in his commentary on English Common Law, observed that the unborn inherit a right to life from nature at the time they begin to stir in the mother's womb.[518] Blackstone's commentaries were known to have influenced the Founders' understanding of rights when they drafted the Declaration of Independence and the Constitution. Therefore, just as we look to the Federalist Papers to understand the original intent of the Constitution's text, Blackstone's writings provide us with insight as to what the Founders understood about a right to life and other fundamental rights that would be applicable to the unborn under the Ninth Amendment.[519]

Hillary Clinton and other progressives will continue to insist that an unborn child has no rights and that abortion law must only reflect the rights and interests of the mother. Their absolutist position has little to do with abortion or equal opportunity; instead, it is about expanding political power. Progressives believe they gain political advantage with women by emphasizing choice and ignoring personal responsibility. By rejecting bipartisan compromise and by specifically defending an absolutist position supporting elective late-term abortions, the Democratic Party is now advocating what former Democratic Senator Patrick Moynihan once described as infanticide.[520]

It is important to note that judicial absolutism always has unintended consequences, even for conservatives. For example, some conservatives believe that a right to life should be considered paramount in American jurisprudence, thereby weighing the protection of life in absolute terms to prevent women from ever obtaining an abortion for any reason. In a world where this absolutist view of a right to life applies in all aspects of the law and public policy, creative lawyers could force any of us to become blood or bone marrow donors to save a life—this despite violating our personal privacy. After all, neither procedure carries with it excessive health risks. Likewise, they could also force any of us to become organ donors after our death to save the lives of others—this despite any religious or family objections. There are likely dozens of unintended consequences that could be identified from holding any fundamental right as paramount relative to others. That's why a constructive balance between privacy and life should be the goal when developing the laws that govern abortion.

Since 1973, when *Roe v. Wade* was decided by the Supreme Court, abortion has done more to divide Americans into political camps on the left and right than any other issue. We can find common ground here, but it will require rejecting absolutism and expanding our understanding of privacy rights. We can start down this road by first seeking a federal ban on late-term abortions unless the life and health of the mother are at serious risk.

CONCLUSION

America is a unique and exceptional nation. Our uniqueness and exceptionalism is embodied in the ideas and ideals that were cast into our Declaration of Independence, Constitution, and Bill of Rights more than two hundred years ago. We are not reminded enough of this in our daily lives, but these ideas and ideals are eternal and remain as steadfast as human nature itself. It is only when we stray from these ideas and ideals, as progressives would have us do, that America finds itself divided and failing to achieve its true potential as a nation.

Ideas are defined as conceptions of the mind. Ideals, on the other hand, reflect a standard of perfection that we strive for but have not yet achieved. America is not perfect. But the Framers provided us with the framework and tools that would allow America to improve as a nation and move forward to set an example for the rest of the world to follow. It is this example and the ideas upon which our nation has been founded that make us exceptional, as the international human rights activist Bono has reminded us:

> It's not a right/left issue. It's a right/wrong issue, and America has constantly been on the side of what's right. Because when it comes down to it, this is about keeping faith with the idea of America. Because America's an idea, isn't it? I mean, Ireland's a great country, but it's not an idea. Great Britain's a great country, it's not an idea. That's how we see you around the world, as one of the greatest ideas in human history, right up

there with the Renaissance, right up there with crop rotation and the Beatles' White Album.

The idea, the American idea—it's an idea—the idea is that you and me are created equal, and will ensure that an economic recession need not become an equality recession. The idea that life is not meant to be endured but enjoyed. The idea that if we have dignity, if we have justice then leave it to us, and we'll do the rest. This country was the first to claw its way out of darkness and put that on paper. And God love you for it, because these aren't just American ideas anymore. There's no copyright on them. You brought them into the world. It's a wide world now. I know Americans say they have a bit of the world in them, and you do, the family tree has lots of branches. But the thing is, the world has a bit of America in it, too. These truths, your truths, they're self-evident in us.[521]

—Bono, Speech at Georgetown University, July 3, 2014

If America as an idea is going to achieve its ideal, we need to do more to educate both ourselves and future generations about what has made America exceptional. That education starts with understanding the principles of republican democracy embodied in the Declaration of Independence and Constitution. George Mason once reminded us that "no free government, nor the blessings of liberty, can be preserved to any people, but by a firm adherence to justice, moderation, temperance, frugality and virtue; by frequent recurrence to fundamental principles; and by the recognition by all citizens that they have duties as well as rights."[522] Unfortunately, modern-day America has failed to heed Mason's admonition.

As civics and economics education has taken a back seat in our public schools, at least one generation of Americans has begun to express sympathy for a new set of ideas being pushed by the progressive Left. For example, progressives have sought to replace the idea of equal rights and equal opportunity with equal economic outcomes enforced by coercive taxation policies and wealth redistribution. Progressives have also undermined the rule of law to push their social justice agenda by attacking our First Amendment right to freedom of religion and by undermining the rights of children, both born and unborn. These are destructive trends that can only end in a diminished America that is less prosperous and less free.

Fortunately, we as Americans have it within our capability to push back on this progressive agenda that seeks to undermine our constitutional republic. This starts with each one of us acquiring a competent education about our Constitution to understand what makes it unique, even when compared to similar documents drafted for democracies around the world. We must be willing to open our eyes to the dangers posed by those seeking to undermine the Constitution and the rights that are guaranteed to every American. However, for every constitutional right we enjoy we also have a corresponding responsibility. The most fundamental responsibility we have as Americans is to defend the Constitution when it is under political assault. That is why this book was written, to help give the reader the information needed to defend the Constitution in the court of public opinion.

But we need to do more. Any citizen wanting to take further action and become politically involved to defend our Constitution has several courses of action they can take. Here are six actionable steps that should be considered:

- **Join the Article V Convention of the States Movement.** A Convention of the States, as authorized by Article V of the Constitution, bypasses the political authorization (or obstruction) of Congress and allows the states to propose constitutional amendments. However, it is important to note that an Article V Convention of the States is not the same thing as a constitutional convention. One cannot rewrite the Constitution at an Article V Convention. Instead, any amendments approved at an Article V Convention must then be approved by three-fourths of the state legislatures just like any amendment that originates in Congress. Therefore, an Article V Convention empowers the states to restrain an out-of-control federal government by proposing amendments to reestablish its proper balance of power in its relation to the states. Such amendments might address the need for term limits for members of Congress, require a balanced budget, limit the power of lobbyists, and impose restraints on the Supreme Court that eliminate judicial supremacy. If you want to change the way Washington, DC works, an Article V Convention of the States can make this happen.

- **Promote Civic and Economic Education through Your Local School Board.** Promoting the need for mandatory education in civics and economics in public schools may be the most important thing the average citizen can do to preserve our liberty and the Founders' vision of the American Dream. George Washington once noted that the primary objective of education for our youth should be in promoting the science of government. That's because Washington knew that an educated populace that understood the Constitution and the proper role of government would resist the tyranny of a large centralized state. We have already seen how today's high school students are graduating with unnecessarily high illiteracy rates in civics and economics. This suggests that we have graduated at least one generation of Americans not properly prepared to be citizens. Education in civics and economics will empower the next generation of citizens to determine the fiscal and operational viability of promises made by politicians, whether they be progressive or not. Making education in civics and economics mandatory disciplines for every high school graduate can create such empowerment and help guard our nation against progressive influence.

- **Provide Financial Support to a Civic Educational Institution.** Many people may resist the idea of donating money to a cause. However, there is no better way to demonstrate your support for the Constitution than to donate to an organization that is focused primarily on civic education. One such organization is Hillsdale College that offers free online public courses on the Constitution along with a free monthly newsletter on relevant topical issues. Other organizations like the Cato Institute and the Heritage Foundation operate as think tanks and provide a wealth of free public research materials that speak to the defense of the Constitution and "first principles" of republican government. By supporting these and other similar institutions, one can facilitate better public understanding of the constitutional principles upon which our nation was founded.

- **Sponsor a Trip to the National Constitution Center.** One of the great historical treasures of America in the city of Philadelphia is the National Constitution Center (NCC). The NCC was established by Congress as an institution to disseminate information on a nonpartisan basis to increase awareness and understanding of the Constitution among the American people. This institution offers a wealth of free special event programming that includes the participation of notable journalists, constitutional scholars, and public officials offering their insights on topics subject to public debate. Consider encouraging your church, local schools, or affiliated civic groups to visit the NCC and to take advantage of their educational programs, as well as the free resources they make available online at ConstitutionCenter.org.

- **Run for Public Office.** Choosing to run for public office is an enormous personal commitment of time, as well as money, so this action may not be for everyone. However, for those motivated to get personally involved in challenging progressive attempts to undermine the Constitution, you have no better option. If you choose to run, be advised that you will need a great deal of preparation on the issues to effectively debate your progressive counterparts. This book can be a great starting point for updating your understanding of public policy, so be sure to read it early in your campaign and reference it often. Even if you disagree with some the ideas presented herein, this book will give you a better understanding of how progressives think and what motivates their activism.

- **Tell People about This Book.** The book you now hold in your hands may be the best tool available to you for learning how to counter progressive ideology. Getting a copy of this book into the hands of young people, especially those in high school or who are about to leave for college, may be your best investment in building a unified America. That's because today's young people are hungry for ideas but often lack the analytical framework with which to challenge the social and economic policies espoused by the progressive Left. This book will give them that framework and prepare them to defend the Constitution from the damage being done by those trying to undermine it.

The Founders' idea of America has not been lost. However, for many Americans it has simply been confused with the notion that America can only progress if it moves beyond the constitutional principles upon which our nation was founded.[523] This notion was reflected in President Obama's 2008 election call to "fundamentally transform America," and in Hillary Clinton's call to "turn our progressive platform into real change for America." Such progressive leadership may be well intentioned, but their movement's end game is to establish a radically different vision for our nation that rallies around the state as opposed to the Constitution. The Framers understood the potential risk posed by such left-wing populism, so they drafted the Constitution that would serve as a bulwark against fundamental change from transient majorities. These two visions for the nation, that of progressive Left and that handed down to us by the American Founders, are fundamentally incompatible. Therefore, there can be no political compromise with progressivism; we must exorcise it if America is to remain a free and exceptional nation.

James Madison once reminded us that "knowledge will forever govern ignorance; and a people who mean to be their own governors must arm themselves with the power which knowledge gives." Therefore, let us all arm ourselves with a common understanding of the Declaration of Independence and Constitution and pass this same understanding on to our children and grandchildren as well. It is that collective understanding that remains the best way—the only way—to unify our divided nation.

ACKNOWLEDGMENTS

Taking on a project like *Conquering the Political Divide* is not an effort that can be accomplished by any single person. Therefore, I owe a debt of gratitude to many individuals for their contributions of support, advice, knowledge sharing, and work effort that have combined to produce a higher quality and more influential work product.

Chief among those to whom I owe a debt is my wonderful wife, Katherine. Her support for the inordinate amount of time I committed to my 2012 campaign for Congress, and to the writing of this book, has been a gift of faith and love. She also served as my moral and editorial conscience for every word in this text. This book would not exist if it were not for her.

I have also benefited from the contributions of friends and colleagues whose early review of my draft manuscript provided me with expanded perspectives on its content and conclusions. First, my thanks to Michael Richmond, whose legal training and knowledge of early American political history were essential to ensuring this book remains consistent with Constitutional jurisprudence. Thanks also to my colleague and business partner at Risk Masters International, Allan Cytryn, who provided important input on how conservative arguments could be made more influential to those susceptible to the influence of the progressive Left. Likewise, to Mark Elberg, who contributed his insights on how individuals politically left-of-center would receive my arguments that support originalist interpretation of the Constitution. Also, to Tim Mathews, my friend and a long-time business associate, who digested every word of my manuscript and provided critical input that helped add clarity and consistency in the story this book is designed to tell.

I would like to offer a special thank you to Congressman Dick Zimmer of New Jersey who not only provided excellent feedback on my manuscript, but who was also one of the first political professionals to advise me on the opportunities and challenges of running for national office.

I would be remiss if I did not extend my thanks to two individuals who inspired my lifelong desire to understand the critical disciplines of economics and civics that played such a key role in influencing the political theory contained in this manuscript. The first is Marc A. Miles, PhD, my former economics professor at Rutgers University, for inspiring my interest in economic matters and for helping me to understand that public policy can have unintended consequences in the long run. The other is the late Mortimer J. Adler, PhD, whose landmark book *We Hold These Truths* became the spark that set me on a path toward becoming a life-long student of civics and the U.S. Constitution.

I would also like to express my appreciation to Mary Hollingsworth and her team of professionals at Creative Enterprises Studio (CES) for their tireless due diligence in the editing of my manuscript. I would especially like to recognize Rhonda Lowry, CES Copy Editor and Permissions/Research Editor, for her patience and coaching as we worked together to obtain all required copyright permissions and to ensure compliance with professional writing standards.

I cannot forget Beth Leoni, graphics designer extraordinaire, who competed for and won the right to provide the artwork for my book cover. Her patience and creativity in crafting just the right visual message was confirmed by the wonderful feedback we both received from many of my future readers.

Finally, I would like to extend my gratitude to Kary Oberbrunner and David Branderhorst, founding partners of Author Academy Elite. Kary's guidance and coaching during the final stages of drafting this book, along with the education David has provided on the business end of authorship, has been of immeasurable benefit to me personally and professionally. I'll always be indebted to them for introducing me to my new profession of author.

ABOUT THE AUTHOR

Eric A. Beck is an entrepreneur, author, activist and a former candidate for the U.S. House of Representatives from New Jersey. Eric is founder and Editor-In-Chief of Free Nation Media LLC, a communications and policy analysis firm established to defend American exceptionalism and the principles that embody America's unique form of Constitutional government. His passion for public affairs stems from his desire to pass on a better future to his children and grandchildren, and to yours. Eric holds a Master's in Business Administration from the Rutgers Business School and is a lifetime student of economics and civics. He and his wife Kathy have two grown children and currently reside in Greenville, South Carolina.

NOTES

Foreword

[1]   Mortimer J. Adler, *We Hold These Truths* (New York: McMillian Publishing, 1987), ix–x.

[2]   Thomas Jefferson, Extract from Thomas Jefferson to William C. Jarvis, *Thomas Jefferson Foundation*, http://tjrs. monticello.org/letter/382, Retrieved: September 26, 2017.

Introduction – Why America is a Divided Nation

[3]   Robert P. Sutton, *Federalism* (Westport: Greenwood Press, 2002), 5.

[4]   Declaration of Independence (US 1776).

[5]   Barack Obama, *The Audacity of Hope: Thoughts on Reclaiming the American Dream*, (New York: Crown Publishers 2006), 10.

[6]   The American Presidency Project, Barack Obama Speech at Wesleyan College Commencement, May 25, 2008, http://www.presidency.ucsb.edu/ws/?pid=77361, Retrieved: July 24, 2017.

[7]   Obama White House Archives, *Remarks by the President on the Economy in Osawatomie, Kansas*, December 6, 2011, https://obamawhitehouse.archives.gov/the-press-office/2011/12/06/remarks-president-economy-osawatomie-kansas, Retrieved: July 24, 2017.

[8]   Ibid.

9   Obama White House Archives, *Remarks by the President at a Campaign Event in Roanoke*, Virginia, July 13, 2012, https://obamawhitehouse.archives.gov/the-press-office/2012/07/13/remarks-president-campaign-event-roanoke-virginia, Retrieved: July 24, 2017.

10   Ben Smith, "Obama on Small-Town Pa.: Clinging to Religion, Guns, Xenophobia," *Politico*, April 11, 2008, http://www.politico.com/blogs/ben-smith/2008/04/obama-on-small-town-pa-clinging-to-religion-guns-xenophobia-007737, Retrieved: October 26, 2016.

Chapter 1: The Founders' Vision of the American Dream

11   James Madison, et al., *The Federalist Papers – The Famous Papers on the Principles of American Government*, ed. Benjamin F. Wright (New York: Barnes & Noble Books, 1961), 328.

12   The term "Framers" is generally understood as those individuals who craft the Constitution, while the term "Founders" or "Founding Fathers" is used to identify those who participated in the fight for independence and founding of the United States as a nation.

13   Thomas G. West, "First Principles Series - The Economic Principles of America's Founders: Property Rights, Free Markets, and Sound Money," *Heritage Foundation*, No. 32., (2010), http://thf_media.s3.amazonaws.com/2010/pdf/fp0032.pdf, Retrieved: November 2, 2016.

14   Madison, *The Federalist Papers*, 417.

15   Ibid., 51.

16   Susan James, *Spinoza on Philosophy, Religion and Politics: The Theologico-Political Treatise*, (New York: Oxford University Press, 2012), 281.

17   Madison, *The Federalist*, xii.

18 Michael F. Ford, "Civic Illiteracy: A Threat to the American Dream," *Xavier University: Center for the Study of the American Dream*, para. 6 (April 26, 2012), http://xuamericandream.blogspot.com : Retrieved: November 3, 2016.

19 Intercollegiate Studies Institute – American Civic Literacy Program, "ENLIGHTENED CITIZENSHIP: HOW CIVIC KNOWLEDGE TRUMPS A COLLEGE DEGREE IN PROMOTING ACTIVE CIVIC ENGAGEMENT" (2011), www.americancivicliteracy.org/2011/conclusion.html, Retrieved: November 3, 2016.

20 Ibid.

21 Ibid.

22 June Marie Freund, "Economic Literacy: Measuring the Economic Human Capital of Arkansas K-12 Teachers" (2015), Theses and Dissertations 1237, http://scholarworks.uark.edu/etd/1237, Retrieved: November 3, 2016.

23 William Walstad and Ken Rebeck, "Assessing the Economic Understanding of U.S. High School Students" (2001) 456, *CBA Faculty Publications*, Paper 37, http://digitalcommons.unl.edu/cgi/viewcontent.cgi?article=1036&context=cbafacpub, Retrieved: November 3, 2016.

24 National Council on Economic Education, What American Teens & Adults Know About Economics," *The Harris Poll*, April 26, 2006, http://www.councilforeconed.org/cel/WhatAmericansKnowAboutEconomics_042605-3.pdf, Retrieved: November 3, 2016.

25 National Center for Education Statistics – U.S. Department of Education, "The Nation's Report Card – Economics 2012 – National Assessment of Educational Progress at Grade 12" (2012), http://nces.ed.gov/nationsreportcard/subject/publications/main2012/pdf/2013453.pdf, Retrieved: November 3, 2016.

26 National Assessment Governing Board, "Overall Grade 12 Scores on The Nation's Report Card in Economics Are Flat" (2013), https://www.nagb.org/newsroom/naep-releases/2012-economics.html, Retrieved: November 3, 2016.

27 Ibid.

28 National Council on Economic Education, The Harris Poll, "What American Teens & Adults Know About Economics," *The Harris Poll*, (April 2006), 44, http://www.councilforeconed.org/cel/WhatAmericansKnowAboutEconomics_042605-3.pdf, Retrieved: November 3, 2016.

29 MacKenzie Weinger, "Study: 8 in 10 Pols Lack Econ Studies," *Politico* (August 23, 2011), http://www.politico.com/story/2011/08/study-8-in-10-pols-lack-econ-studies-061929, Retrieved: November 3, 2016.

Chapter 2: Progressive Transformation of the American Dream

30 Ronald J. Pestritto, "The Progressives and their Attack on America's Founding," April 16, 2009, http://www.glennbeck.com/content/articles/article/198/23936/#II?utm_source=glennbeck&utm_medium=contentcopy_link, Retrieved: November 11, 2016.

31 Conservative Political Action Committee Conference, *C-SPAN*, Washington, DC, February 18, 2010, https://www.c-span.org/video/?292148-21/george-will-remarks, Retrieved: November 4, 2016.

32 Frank Bruni, "A Wordsmith That Shapes Bush's Prose," *New York Times*, April 3, 2001, http://www.nytimes.com/2001/04/03/us/a-wordsmith-who-shapes-bush-s-prose.html, Retrieved: November 4, 2016.

33 The American Presidency Project, "Jimmy Carter: The President's News Conference," July 12, 1977. Online

by Gerhard Peters and John T. Woolley, *The American Presidency Project.* http://www.presidency.ucsb.edu/ws/?pid=7786.

34 Jonah Goldberg, "Politics and the Symptoms of a Sick Culture," *National Review* (July 6, 2012), http://www.nationalreview.com/article/304819/politics-and-symptoms-sick-culture-jonah-goldberg, Retrieved: November 4, 2016.

35 The O'Reilly Factor, *Fox News Channel*, New York, July 2, 2013, https://www.youtube.com/watch?v=DXnKnPRUzZY, Retrieved: November 4, 2016, Retrieved: July 25, 2017.

36 ProjectKnow, "Alcoholism Statistics in the U.S." (2016), http://www.projectknow.com/research/drug-addiction-statistics-alcoholism-statistics, Retrieved: November 4, 2016.

37 National Institute of Drug Abuse, "Nationwide Trends" (June 2015), https://www.drugabuse.gov/publications/drugfacts/nationwide-trends, Retrieved: July 25, 2017.

38 Erica York, "Table 6. Total Income Tax Shares, 1980–2015," *The Tax Foundation*, January 17, 2018, https://taxfoundation.org/summary-federal-income-tax-data-2017, Retrieved: October 23, 2018.

39 The Kauffman Foundation, "Three Things Entrepreneurs Do" (2013), http://www.youtube.com/watch?v=M7VZIbeUrSU, Retrieved: November 4, 2016.

40 Amity Shlaes, *The Forgotten Man* (New York: Harper Collins, 2007), 132.

41 New York Times, "Through the Eyes of Lord Keynes," May 29, 1983, http://www.nytimes.com/1983/05/29/business/through-the-eyes-of-lord-keynes.html, Retrieved: November 4, 2016.

42 Matthew Spalding, *We Still Hold These Truths* (Wilmington: ISI Books, 2010), 209.

43 Woodrow Wilson, *Constitutional Government in the United States* (New York: Columbia University Press, 1917), 22, https://archive.org/stream/ constitutionalg00wilsgoog#page/n34/mode/2up/search/ atmosphere+is+opinion, Retrieved: November 4, 2016.

44 Woodrow Wilson, "Socialism and Democracy" 1887, *Hillsdale College*, https://online.hillsdale.edu/document. doc?id=278, Retrieved: November 5, 2016.

45 Los Angeles Times, "On the Record," March 2, 2000, http://articles.latimes.com/2000/mar/02/news/ss-4678, Retrieved: May 12, 2017.

46 Natalie Gewargis, "McCain to Attack Obama for Public Radio Comments From 2001," *ABC News*, October 8, 2008, http://blogs.abcnews.com/politicalpunch/2008/10/ mccain-to-attac.html, Retrieved: July 25, 2017.

47 Obergefell v. Hodges 576 U.S. ___ (2015).

48 Adler, *We Hold These Truths*, 118.

49 Ibid.

50 Josh Gerstein, "SCOTUS Strikes Appointments," *Politico*, June 26, 2014, http://www.politico.com/story/2014/06/ supreme-court-recess-appointments-108347, Retrieved: November 5, 2016.

51 Janet Napolitano, "Memorandum: Exercising Prosecutorial Discretion with Respect to Individuals Who Came to the United States as Children," *U.S. Department of Homeland Security*, June 15, 2012, https://www.dhs.gov/xlibrary/ assets/s1-exercising-prosecutorial-discretion-individuals-wh o-came-to-us-as-children.pdf, Retrieved: November 6, 2016.

52 Juliet Eilperin and Amy Goldstein, "White House Delays Health Insurance Mandate for Medium-Size Employers Until 2016," *Washington Post*, February 10, 2014, https://

www.washingtonpost.com/national/health-science/
white-house-delays-health-insurance-mandat
e-for-medium-sized-employers-until-2016/2014/02/10/
ade6b344-9279-11e3-84e1-27626c5ef5fb_story.html,
Retrieved: November 6, 2016.

53 "Religious freedom and contraception," *Chicago Tribune*, February
3, 2013, http://articles.chicagotribune.com/2013-02-03/
opinion/ct-edit-contraceptive-0203-jm-20130203_1_firs
t-amendment-obama-administration-coverage, Retrieved:
November 6, 2016.

54 Brian Montopoli, "Obama administration Will
No Longer Defend DOMA," *CBS News*, February
24, 2011, http://www.cbsnews.com/news/
obama-administration-will-no-longer-defend-doma,
Retrieved: November 6, 2016.

55 Robert Rector, "How Obama Has Gutted Welfare
Reform," *Washington Post*, September 6, 2012,
https://www.washingtonpost.com/opinions/
how-obama-has-gutted-welfore-reform/2012/09/0
6/885b0092-f835-11e1-8b93-c4f4ab1c8d13_story.html,
Retrieved: November 6, 2016.

56 Antonin Scalia, "Constitutional Interpretation the
Old Fashioned Way," Speech to the Woodrow Wilson
International Center for Scholars in Washington, D.C.,
March 14, 2005, http://www.bc.edu/content/dam/files/
centers/boisi/pdf/Symposia/Symposia%202010-2011/
Constitutional_Interpretation_Scalia.pdf, Retrieved:
November 6, 2016.

57 Adler, *We Hold These Truths*, 48.

58 Ibid., 47.

59 Declaration of Independence (1776).

60 Adler, *We Hold These Truths*, 48.

61   The Supreme Court's decision in Obergefell v. Hodges declared marriage to be a fundamental right, but the author among other conservatives believe this case was wrongly decided.

62   National Coalition to Stop the HHS Mandate, "About President Obama's HHS Mandate," http:// standupforreligiousfreedom.com/mandate, Retrieved: November 8, 2016.

63   Cliff Kincaid, "Catholic Church Rejects Surrender Terms from Obama," *Accuracy in Media*, January 30, 2012, http://www.aim.org/aim-column/ catholic-church-rejects-surrender-terms-from-obama, Retrieved: November 8, 2016.

64   Donald Wuerl, Charles Colson and Meir Y. Soloveichik, United We Stand on Religious Freedom, *Wall Street Journal*, February 10, 2012, http://online.wsj.com/article/ SB10001424052970204136404577211601075404714. html?mod=djemEditorialPage_h

65   Ariane de Vogue, "Back to the Lower Court," *CNN*, May 16, 2016, http://www.cnn.com/2016/05/16/politics/ supreme-court-obamacare-contraceptive-mandate, Retrieved: November 6, 2016.

66   Anne Hendershott, "NLRB Make Inroads at Catholic Colleges," *The Catholic World Report*, February 12, 2015, http://www.catholicworldreport.com/Item/3690/ nlrb_makes_inroads_at_catholic_colleges.aspx, Retrieved: November 7, 2016.

67   Doug Donovan, "Obama to Renew Call to Limit Charitable Deduction," *The Chronicle of Philanthropy*, April 8, 2013, https://www.philanthropy.com/article/ Obama-to-Renew-Call-to-Limit/155033, Retrieved: November 7, 2016.

68   Dennis Prager, *Still the Best Hope* (New York: HarperCollins Publishers, 2012), 42.

69 Ibid, 41.

70 Ibid, 41.

71 Karl Marx, *A Criticism of the Hegelian Philosophy of Right* (1844).

72 Michael Brown, "The Battle for Your Child's Future," *Charisma Magazine*," June 27, 2013, http://www.charismamag.com/life/culture/18151-the-battle-is-for-your-child-s-future, Retrieved: November 7, 2016.

73 Lydia Saad, "Americans' Abortion Views Steady Amid Gosnell Trial," *Gallup*, May 13, 2013, http://www.gallup.com/poll/162374/americans-abortion-views-steady-amid-gosnell-trial.aspx, Retrieved: November 8, 2016.

74 National Right to Life, "State Homicide Laws That Recognize Unborn Victims," May 24, 2104, http://www.nrlc.org/federal/unbornvictims/statehomicidelaws092302, State Homicide Laws That Recognize Unborn Victims, Retrieved: November 7, 2016.

75 Adam Liptak, "Supreme Court Ruling Makes Same-Sex Marriage a Right Nationwide," *New York Times*, June 26, 2015, http://www.nytimes.com/2015/06/27/us/supreme-court-same-sex-marriage.html?_r=0, Retrieved: November 7, 2016.

Chapter 3: The Morality of Free Markets

76 Walter Williams, "On Liberty's Moral Superiority," *Acton Institute* Vol. 4, No. 6 (2010), https://acton.org/pub/religion-liberty/volume-4-number-6/libertys-moral-superiority, Retrieved: September 24, 2018.

77 Nolan Hicks and Carl Campanile, "Most Voters Stayed Home for Stunning Alexandria Ocasio-Cortez Win," *New York Post*, June 28, 2018, https://nypost.

com/2018/06/28/most-voters-stayed-home-for-stunnin g-alexandria-ocasio-cortez-win, Retrieved: August 3, 2018.

78   Melanie Zanona and Vicki Needham, "GOP Braces for Trump's $1T Infrastructure Push," *The Hill*, November 17, 2016, http://thehill.com/business-a-lobbyin g/306490-gop-braces-for-trumps-1t-infrastructure-push, Retrieved: November 19, 2016.

79   Brian M. Reidl, "Why Government Spending Does Not Stimulate Economic Growth," *Heritage Foundation*, November 12, 2008, http:// www.heritage.org/research/reports/2008/11/ why-government-spending-does-not-stimulat e-economic-growth, Retrieved: November 19, 2016.

80   Dinesh D'Souza, "An Alternative View to Obamacare," Socrates Club Debate, Oregon University, October 8, 2012, http://www.youtube.com/watch?v=rEM4NKXK-iA, Retrieved: November 19, 2016.

81   Conner D. Wolf, "$15 Minimum Wage Advocates Rally with Bernie," *The Daily Caller*, January 18, 2016, http://dailycaller.com/2016/01/18/ sanders-rallies-for-15-minimum-wage/, Retrieved: November 19, 2016.

82   Bernie Sanders, "Issues: A Living Wage" (2016), https:// berniesanders.com/issues/a-living-wage, Retrieved: July 25, 2017.

83   Michael Saltzman, "The Fight For $15 is a Job Killer," *Employment Policies Institute*, April 2013, https://www. epionline.org/oped/the-fight-for-15-is-a-job-killer, Retrieved: November 20, 2016.

84   "Cronyism" is a form of corruption practiced by some government officials who seek to provide special benefits to their political allies, whether they be individuals, companies or political organizations. Often cronyism takes the form of hiring unqualified individuals for government

positions, distributing public funds for political (not public) benefit, or employing public pressure in ways that might be considered a conflict-of-interest.

85 Mark J. Perry, "The Fixed Pie Fallacy," *American Enterprise Institute*, December 23, 2006, http://www.aei.org/publication/the-fixed-pie-fallacy, Retrieved: December 22, 2016.

86 The Kaufmann Foundation, "Entrepreneurs Do Three Things," http://alltopstartups.com/2011/12/02/kauffman-foundation-3-things-entrepreneurs-do, Retrieved: December 27, 2016.

87 Elizabeth Warren, Andover Massachusetts, September 21, 2011, https://www.youtube.com/watch?v=htX2usfqMEs, Retrieved: December 22, 2016.

88 The Annie F. Casey Foundation, "2015 Kids Count Data Book," July 21, 2015, 6, http://www.aecf.org/m/resourcedoc/aecf-2015kidscountdatabook-2015.pdf, Retrieved: December 23, 2016.

89 Brooks Jackson, "Obama's Numbers April 2016 Update," *FactCheck.org*, April 6, 2016, http://www.factcheck.org/2016/04/obamas-numbers-april-2016-update, Retrieved: December 23, 2016.

90 Drew Desilver, "At 42 Months and Counting, Current job 'recovery' is slowest since Truman was President," *Pew Research Center*, September 25, 2013, http://www.pewresearch.org/fact-tank/2013/09/25/at-42-months-and-counting-current-job-recovery-is-slowest-since-truman-was-president, Retrieved: December 23, 2016.

91 Terrence P. Jeffery, "U.S. Has Record 10th Straight Year Without 3% Growth in GDP," *CNSnews.org*, February 26, 2016, https://www.cnsnews.com/news/article/terence-p-jeffrey/us-has-record-10th-straight-year-without-3-growth-gdp, Retrieved: December 23, 2016.

92   Dave Boyer, "Obama Reverts to 2008 Plan: Blame Bush," *The Washington Times*, April 19, 2012, http://www.washingtontimes.com/news/2012/apr/19/obama-reverts-to-2008-plan-blame-bush, Retrieved: December 27, 2016.

93   Paul Krugman, "In Defense of Obama," *Rolling Stone*, October 8, 2014, http://www.rollingstone.com/politics/news/in-defense-of-obama-20141008, Retrieved: December 23, 2016.

94   Jason DeParley, "Two Classes, Separated by 'I Do'," *New York Times*, July 14 2012, http://www.nytimes.com/2012/07/15/us/two-classes-in-america-divided-by-i-do.html?_r=3&pagewanted=all, Retrieved: December 29 2012.

95   Shea Gunther, "Seven Places Where You Can Get Free Online Education," February 23, 2012, http://www.mnn.com/money/personal-finance/stories/7-places-where-you-can-get-a-free-online-education, Retrieved: December 29, 2016.

96   Career Education Colleges and Universities (CECU), "Shortage of Skills: Construction & Skilled Trades," *CECU*, July 8, 2016, http://www.career.org/news/shortage-of-skills-construction-skilled-trades, Retrieved: December 29, 2016.

97   Tom Coburn, "Duplication Nation" 2015, http://coburn.library.okstate.edu/duplication-nation.html, Retrieved: December 29, 2016.

Chapter 4: The Root Cause of the 2008 Financial Crisis

98   Stephen Labaton, "New Agency Proposed to Oversee Freddie Mac and Fannie Mae," *New York Times*, September 11, 2003, http://www.nytimes.com/2003/09/11/business/new-agency-proposed-to-oversee-freddie-mac-and-fannie-mae.html, Retrieved: December 31, 2016.

99 Adam Hersh, Michael Ettlinger, and Kalen Pruss, "The Consequences of Conservative Economic Policy," *Center for American Progress*, October 20, 2010, https://www.americanprogress.org/issues/economy/reports/2010/10/20/8521/the-consequences-of-conservative-economic-policy, Retrieved: December 31, 2016.

100 Gretchen Morgenson and Joshua Rosner, *Reckless Endangerment* (New York: Times Books, 2011), 116.

101 Charles W. Calomiris and Peter J. Wallison, "Blame Fannie Mae and Congress for the Credit Mess," *Wall Street Journal*, September 23, 2008, http://online.wsj.com/article/SB122212948811465427.html#printMode, Retrieved: July 25, 2017.

102 Lindsay Renick Mayer, "Update: Fannie Mae and Freddie Mac Invest in Lawmakers", *Center for Responsive Politics*, September 11, 2008, http://www.opensecrets.org/news/2008/09/update-fannie-mae-and-freddie.html, Retrieved: July 25, 2017.

103 Glenn Kessler, "The Fact Checker: Obama's claim that the Bush tax cuts led to the economic crisis," *Washington Post*, October 10, 2012, https://www.washingtonpost.com/blogs/fact-checker/post/obamas-claim-that-the-bush-tax-cuts-led-to-the-economic-crisis/2012/09/30/06e8f578-0a6e-11e2-afff-d6c7f20a83bf_blog.html?utm_term=.0141017eaa56, Retrieved: December 31, 2016.

104 Ibid.

105 United States, "The Financial Crisis Inquiry Report," (Washington: GPO, 2011), xv–xxviii, https://www.gpo.gov/fdsys/pkg/GPO-FCIC/pdf/GPO-FCIC.pdf, Retrieved: December 31, 2016.

106 Ibid., 414.

107 Ibid., 443.

[108] Ibid., 444.

[109] United States, White House Press Release, "Fact Sheet: Making Homeownership More Accessible and Sustainable," January 7, 2015, https://www. whitehouse.gov/the-press-office/2015/01/07/ fact-sheet-making-homeownership-more-accessibl e-and-sustainable, Retrieved: January 7, 2017.

[110] Edward Pinto, "Building Toward Another Mortgage Meltdown," *Wall Street Journal*, January 28, 2015, http://www.wsj.com/articles/ edward-pinto-building-toward-another-mortgag e-meltdown-1422489618, Retrieved: January 7, 2017.

[111] Les Christie, "The 3% Down Payment Mortgage Makes a Comeback," *CNNmoney.com*, December 9, 2014, http://money.cnn.com/2014/12/08/real_ estate/3-down-payment-mortgage, Retrieved: January 7, 2016.

[112] United States, Office of the Comptroller of the Currency, "2015 Survey of Credit Underwriting Practices" 3, December 2015, https://www.occ.gov/publications/ publications-by-type/survey-credit-underwriting-practices- report/pub-survey-cred-under-2015.pdf, Retrieved: January 7, 2017.

[113] Fannie Mae, "HomeReady® Mortgage Built for Today's Home Buyers" (June 2017), https://www.fanniemae.com/ content/fact_sheet/homeready-overview.pdf, Retrieved: July 26, 2017.

[114] Paul Sperry, "Obama is Setting Us Up for Another Housing Crash," *New York Post*, March 12, 2016, http:// nypost.com/2016/03/12/obama-is-setting-us-up-fo r-another-housing-crash, Retrieved: January 8, 2017.

[115] United States, Department of the Treasury, Antonio Weiss and Karen Dynan, "Housing Finance Reform: Access and Affordability in Focus," October

26, 2016, https://medium.com/@USTreasury/ housing-finance-reform-access-and-affordabilit y-in-focus-d559541a4cdc#.k19tiio17, Retrieved: January 8, 2017.

[116] Eric Goldschein, "The Complete History Of U.S. Real Estate Bubbles Since 1800," *BusinessInsider.com*, January 12, 2012, http://www.businessinsider.com/ the-economic-crash-repeated-every-generation-1800-2012- 1?op=1/#nk-lending-picked-back-up-after-the-1849-go ld-rush-putting-credit-back-into-expansion-mode-4, Retrieved: January 8, 2017.

[117] U.S. Constitution, Article 1, Section 8, Clause 1.

[118] John. C. Eastman, "Enough is Enough: Why General Welfare Limits Spending," *Heritage Foundation*, Report #4, http://www.heritage.org/research/reports/2011/01/ enough-is-enough-why-general-welfare-limits-spending, Retrieved: January 29, 2017.

[119] Ibid.

[120] Steven M. Davidoff, "A Partnership Solution for Investment Banks," *New York Times*, August 20, 2008, https://dealbook.nytimes.com/2008/08/20/a-partnership -solution-for-investment-banks/?_r=0, Retrieved: January 29 2017.

[121] Sylvan Lane, "Trump: We're keeping some of Dodd-Frank," *The Hill*, April 11, 2017, http:// thehill.com/policy/finance/328313-trump-were-k eeping-some-of-dodd-frank, Retrieved: July 1, 2017.

[122] Alan Rappeport and Matthew Goldstein, "Trump Administration Says Financial Watchdog Agency Should Be Defanged," *New York Times*, June 12, 2017, https://www.nytimes.com/2017/06/12/business/ banking-regulations-consumer-financial-protection.html, Retrieved: July 1, 2017.

Chapter 5: The Value of Supply-Side Economics

123 William Greider, "The Education of David Stockman," *The Atlantic*, December 1981, https://www.theatlantic. com/magazine/archive/1981/12/the-education-of-david-stockman/305760, Retrieved: February 4, 2017.

124 Aaron Blake, "The first Trump-Clinton Presidential Debate Transcript, Annotated," *Washington Post*, September 26, 2016, https://www.washingtonpost.com/news/the-fix/ wp/2016/09/26/the-first-trump-clinton-presidential-debat e-transcript-annotated, Retrieved: February 4, 2017.

125 Robert Reich, "Why the Three Biggest Economic Lessons Were Forgotten," February 11, 2014, http://robertreich. org/post/76339971895, Retrieved: July 26, 2017.

126 Museum of the Moving Image - The Living Room Candidate, "Trickle Down," Ross Perot Campaign Commercial (1992), http://www.livingroomcandidate.org/ commercials/1992/trickle-down, Retrieved: July 26, 2017.

127 Paul Krugman, *The Return of Depression Economics* (New York: W.W. Norton, 2009), 182.

128 Arthur B. Laffer, Stephen Moore and Peter J. Tanous, *The End of Prosperity* (New York: Simon & Schuster, 2008), 36.

129 One must differentiate FDR's recovery policies from his relief and reform policies. Some of the latter were successful, such as his efforts to stabilize the banking system.

130 Veronique de Rugy, "1920s Income Tax Cuts Sparked Economic Growth and Raised Federal Revenues," *Cato Institute*, March 4, 2003, https://www.cato.org/ publications/commentary/1920s-income-tax-cuts-spar ked-economic-growth-raised-federal-revenues, Retrieved: February 9, 2017.

131 Thomas Sowell, *Trickle Down Theory and Tax Cuts for the Rich* (Stanford: Hoover Institution Press, 2012), 13.

[132] Ibid.

[133] Milton Friedman and Rose Friedman, *Free to Choose: A Personal Statement* (New York: Harcourt, 1979), 13.

[134] John F. Kennedy, "The Case for Tax Cuts," Speech to the Economic Club of New York, December 14, 1962, https://archive.org/details/JfkTheCaseForTaxCuts, Retrieved: February 5, 2017.

[135] Brian Domitrovic, "The Laffer Curve Files: JFK's Advisor Said Tax Cuts Raise Revenue," *Forbes*, August 23, 2011, http://www.forbes.com/sites/briandomitrovic/2011/08/23/the-laffer-curve-files-jfks-advisor-said-tax-cuts-raise-revenue, Retrieved: February 5, 2017.

[136] Robert Reich, "Why We Should Raise Taxes on the Super-Rich and Lower Them on the Middle Class," February 15, 2011, http://robertreich.org/post/3317811319, Retrieved: February 5, 2017.

[137] Daniel Mitchell, "How Taxes Reduce Savings," *Heritage Foundation*, July 22, 1999, http://www.heritage.org/taxes/report/how-taxes-reduce-savings, Retrieved: June 5, 2017.

[138] Brian Domitrovic, "The Left's Dubious History of Income Inequality," *The Laffer Center*, July 2012, 9, http://www.laffercenter.com/wp-content/uploads/2012/07/2012-07-TheLeftsDubiousHistoryofIncomeInequality-Domitrovic-LafferCenter.pdf

[139] Zachary Pleat, "The Main Problem With Jobs Growth Is Lack Of Demand, Not Taxes," *Media Matters for America*, June 8, 2012, http://mediamatters.org/research/2012/06/08/the-main-problem-with-jobs-growth-is-lack-of-de/185857, Retrieved: February 5, 2012.

[140] The Conference Board, Consumer Confidence Survey, https://www.conference-board.org/data/consumerconfidence.cfm, Retrieved: June 5, 2017.

141 Ewing Marion Kaufmann Foundation, "Three Things Entrepreneurs Do," http://www.kauffman.org/multimedia/sketchbook/kauffman-sketchbook-three-things, Retrieved: June 5, 2017.

142 ABC News, "Transcript: Obama and Clinton Debate," April 16, 2008, http://abcnews.go.com/Politics/DemocraticDebate/story?id=4670271&page=1&singlePage=true, Retrieved: November 21, 2013.

143 Business people understand this same concept in terms of raising or lowering prices for a product or service that they offer to customers. One can maximize profits earned by selling a product or service at the optimal market price. Set the price too high and volume or sales will decrease effecting overall profitability. Set the price too low and you may not earn enough on each sale to maximize profit. Likewise, the effect of raising or lowering tax rates above or below the optimal rate will earn government a sub-optimal level of tax revenue.

144 The Laffer Center at the Pacific Research Institute, "Laffer Curve," http://www.laffercenter.com/supply-side-economics/laffer-curve, Retrieved: August 29, 2013.

145 NewsMax, "Transcript: President Obama's Twitter Town Hall," July 7, 2011, http://www.newsmax.com/TheWire/obama-twitter-transcript-town/2011/07/07/id/402840, Retrieved: February 5, 2017.

146 Steve Case, "Steve Case: The Complete History Of The Internet's Boom, Bust, Boom Cycle," *Business Insider*, http://www.businessinsider.com/what-factors-led-to-the-bursting-of-the-internet-bubble-of-the-late-90s-2011-1#ixzz2d78TDYj8, Retrieved: July 26, 2017.

147 United States, Office of Management and Budget, "Fiscal Year 2017 Historical Tables, Budget of the U.S. Government," Table 1.1—Summary of Receipts,

Outlays and Surpluses or Deficits: 1789–2021, https://
www.gpo.gov/fdsys/pkg/BUDGET-2017-TAB/pdf/
BUDGET-2017-TAB.pdf, Retrieved: July 13, 2018.

148 Charles Kadlec, "The Dangerous Myth About the Bill
Clinton Tax Increase," *Forbes*, July 16, 2012, http://
www.forbes.com/sites/charleskadlec/2012/07/16/
the-dangerous-myth-about-the-bill-clinton-tax-increase/
print/

149 Sowell, "'Trickle Down Theory' and 'Tax Cuts for the
Rich'," 14.

150 George Will, Fox News – Special Report, October 3,
2014, http://www.realclearpolitics.com/video/2014/10/03/
george_will_obama_is_practicing_trickle-down_economics.
html#!, Retrieved: February 11, 2017.

151 Ibid.

152 Selin Kesebir, "When Economic Growth Doesn't
Make Countries Happier," *Harvard Business
Review*, April 25, 2016, https://hbr.org/2016/04/
when-economic-growth-doesnt-make-countries-happier,
Retrieved: June 5, 2017.

Chapter 6: The Myth of Economic Stimulus

153 Heather Boushey and Michael Ettlinger,
"Government Spending Can Create Jobs—and It
Has," *The Center for American Progress*, September
8, 2011, https://www.americanprogress.org/
issues/economy/reports/2011/09/08/10257/
government-spending-can-create-jobs-and-it-has,
Retrieved: February 25, 2017.

154 ABC News, "This Week Transcript: VP-Elect Joe Biden,
December 21, 2008, http://abcnews.go.com/ThisWeek/sto
ry?id=6499340&page=1&singlePage=true, Retrieved: July
26, 2017.

155 David Harsanyi, "Obama's Imaginary Consensus," *Real Clear Politics*, April 16, 2009, https://www.realclearpolitics. com/articles/2009/12/18/all_the_presidents_ mendactiy_99605.htm, Retrieved: July 20, 2018.

156 Angie Drobnic Holan, "Some Economists Disagree with Obama," *Politifact.com*, http://www.politifact.com/ truth-o-meter/statements/2009/jan/30/barack-obama/ some-economists-disagree-obama, Retrieved: February 12, 2017.

157 Cato Institute, "With All Due Respect Mr. President, That Is Not True" (2009), https://object.cato.org/sites/cato. org/files/pubs/pdf/cato_stimulus.pdf, Retrieved: February 12, 2017

158 CBS News, "Transcript: Obama's Speech to Congress," February 24, 2009, http://www.cbsnews.com/news/ transcript-obamas-speech-to-congress, Retrieved: February 12, 2017.

159 David Leonhardt, "Judging Stimulus by Jobs Data Reveals Success," *New York Times*, February 16, 2010, http://www. nytimes.com/2010/02/17/business/economy/17leonhardt. html?_r=0, Retrieved: February 12, 2017.

160 United States, "Estimated Impact of the American Recovery and Reinvestment Act on Employment and Economic Output from January 2010 and March 2010" 2, Congressional Budget Office, May 2010, https://www. cbo.gov/sites/default/files/111th-congress-2009-2010/ reports/05-25-arra_0.pdf, Retrieved: July 26, 2017.

161 Ibid.

162 Arthur Laffer, "We Are All Keynesians Now," *Tennessee's Business*, Vol. 18, No. 3, May 2009, 15, https://core.ac.uk/ download/pdf/6940171.pdf, Retrieved: July 26, 2017.

163 Ibid, 16.

164 Peter Schweizer, *Throw Them All Out* (New York: Houghton Mifflin Harcourt; 2011), 90.

165 Shawn Tully, "How Obama Got Keynes Wrong," *CNN Money*, February 5, 2010, http://archive.fortune.com/2010/02/04/news/economy/meltzer_keynes.fortune/index.htm, Retrieved: May 18, 2017.

166 Ibid.

167 Ibid.

168 Peter Lancett, "The Wealth Tax Act," *Ehow.com*, http://www.ehow.com/info_7862125_wealth-tax-act.html, Retrieved: July 26, 2017.

169 Amity Shlaes, *The Forgotten Man* (New York: Harper Collins, 2007), 269.

170 History Channel, "The Second New Deal" (2017), http://www.history.com/topics/new-deal, Retrieved: July 26, 2017.

171 Jim Powell, "How FDR's New Deal Harmed Millions of Poor People," *Cato Institute*, December 29, 2003, https://www.cato.org/publications/commentary/how-fdrs-new-deal-harmed-millions-poor-people, Retrieved: July 26, 2017.

172 United States, Department of Commerce, Bureau of Economic Analysis, "National Income and Product Accounts – Table 1.1.5 Gross Domestic Product," July 13, 2013, https://www.bea.gov/national/nipaweb/TablePrint.asp?FirstYear=1929&LastYear=1949&Freq=Year&SelectedTable=5&ViewSeries=NO&Java=no&MaxValue=13939&MaxChars=8&Request3Place=N&3Place=N&FromView=YES&Legal=&Land=, Retrieved May 12, 2017.

173 Paul Krugman, "That '30s Feeling," *New York Times*, June 18, 2010, http://dealbook.nytimes.com/2010/06/18/krugman-that-30s-feeling/?_r=0, Retrieved: May 12, 2017.

174 United States, Department of Commerce, Bureau of Economic Analysis, "National Income and Product Accounts – Table 1.1.5 Gross Domestic Product."

175 Frederick W. Smith, "One Simple Way to Create Jobs," *Wall Street Journal*, February 5, 2010, https://www.wsj.com/articles/SB10001424052748704259304575043560442180360, Retrieved: February 12, 2017.

176 The Institute for Policy Innovation, "Tax Cuts Are Better," https://www.ipi.org/ipi_issues/detail/tax-cuts-are-better, Retrieved: July 20, 2018.

177 Ibid.

178 Evan I. Schwartz, "Is Renewable Energy a Good Investment?" *MIT Technology Review*, January 6, 2011, https://www.technologyreview.com/s/422295/is-renewable-energy-a-good-investment, Retrieved: May 18, 2017.

179 United States, Department of Transportation, "Transportation Policy Studies – Forum Proceedings," https://www.fhwa.dot.gov/policy/otps/060320a/forum.cfm, Retrieved: July 26, 2017.

180 Mike Lillis, "Report: Majority of Congress With No Education in Business," *The Hill*, August 23, 2011, http://thehill.com/homenews/news/177897-report-three-fourths-of-congress-has-no-education-in-business-economics, Retrieved: February 26, 2017.

Chapter 7: The Politics of Inequality

181 Brett LoGiurato, "Obama Blasts Republicans In Major Economic Speech: 'You Can't Just Be Against' Everything I Propose," *Business Insider*, July 23, 2013, http://www.businessinsider.com/obama-speech-economy-knox-college-full-text-2013-7, Retrieved: May 13, 2017.

182 United States, Office of Management and Budget, "A New Era of Responsibility: Renewing America's Promise," February 26, 2009, 9, https://www.doi.gov/sites/doi.gov/files/migrated/budget/appropriations/2010/upload/A_New_Era_of_Responsibility2.pdf, Retrieved: July 26, 2017.

183 Organization for Economic Cooperation and Development (OECD), "Divided We Stand - Why Inequality Keeps Rising," 2011, 22, http://www.oecd.org/els/soc/dividedwestandwhyinequalitykeepsrising.htm, Retrieved: May 12, 2017.

184 Emannual Saez, "Striking it Richer: The Evolution of Top Incomes in the United States," *UC Berkeley*, September 3, 2013, http://eml.berkeley.edu/~saez/saez-UStopincomes-2012.pdf, Retrieved: February 28, 2017.

185 U.S. Office of Management and Budget, "A New Era of Responsibility: Renewing America's Promise," 11, https://www.gpo.gov/fdsys/pkg/BUDGET-2010-BUD/pdf/BUDGET-2010-BUD.pdf, Retrieved: October 10, 2018.

186 Richard V. Burkhauser, Jeff Larrimore, and Kosali I. Simon, "A Second Opinion on the Economic Health of the American Middle Class," *National Bureau of Economic Research*, Working Paper No. 17164, June 2011, http://www.nber.org/papers/w17164, Retrieved: July 26, 2017.

187 The Tax Policy Center defines a "Tax Unit" is an individual or a married couple who file a joint tax return that also incorporates dependents. It is important to note that a tax unit can be different from a family or a household. For example, two persons who are not legally married but are living together might be considered one household, even though they would file separate tax returns. Therefore, the Tax Policy Center concludes that the number of tax units will tend to be larger than the number of families or households. See http://www.taxpolicycenter.org/numbers/

displayatab.cfm?DocID=1535#q6 as referenced on
November 9, 2013.

188 The U.S. Census Bureau defines "Household Income" to
include cash income received by persons 15 years old and
over (exclusive of certain money receipts such as capital
gains) before payments for personal income taxes, social
security, union dues, Medicare deductions, etc. Therefore,
money income does not reflect the fact that some families
receive part of their income in the form of noncash
benefits, such as food stamps, health benefits, rent-free
housing, payments for retirement programs, and goods
produced and consumed. See www.census.gov/cps/about/
cpsdef.html for additional information.

189 United States, Congressional Budget Office (CBO),
"Trends in the Distribution of Household between 1979
and 2007, Publication #4031, October 2011, Notes
and Definitions, http://www.cbo.gov/sites/default/files/
cbofiles/attachments/10-25-HouseholdIncome.pdf,
Retrieved: July 26, 2017.

190 The CBO defines size adjusted household income by
dividing income by the square root of a household's size.
Further, they define a household as the people who share a
housing unit without regard to their relationships.

191 Burkhauser, et. al., "A Second Opinion on the Economic
Health of the Middle Class," 10.

192 Brian Domitrovic, "The Left's Dubious History of
Income Inequality," *The Laffer Center for Supply-Side
Economics* (2012): 4, http://www.laffercenter.com/
wp-content/uploads/2012/07/2012-07-TheLeftsDubiou
sHistoryofIncomeInequality-Domitrovic-LafferCenter.pdf,
Retrieved: March 6, 2017.

193 Ibid.

194 Joseph Rosenberg, "Measuring Income for
Distributional Analysis," *Tax Policy Center* (July 25,

2013): 6, http://www.taxpolicycenter.org/publications/
measuring-income-distributional-analysis, Retrieved: July
26, 2017.

195 Chuck Schumer, "A Better Deal for American Workers," *New York
Times*, July 24, 2017, https://www.nytimes.com/2017/07/24/
opinion/chuck-schumer-employment-democrats.html,
Retrieved: July 26, 2017.

196 Carl Schramm, "Three Things Entrepreneurs Do,"
Kauffman Foundation for Entrepreneurship, http://
www1.kauffman.org/KauffmanMultimedia.
aspx?VideoId=1148130737001, As viewed November
11, 2013.

197 Rea Hederman, Guinevere Nell and William Beach,
"Economic Effects of Increasing the Tax Rates on
Capital Gains and Dividends," *Heritage Foundation*,
April 15, 2008, http://www.heritage.org/taxes/
report/economic-effects-increasing-the-tax-rate
s-capital-gains-and-dividends, Retrieved: July 3, 2017.

198 Richard Fry, "Four takeaways from Tuesday's
Census income and poverty release," *Pew
Research Center*, September 18, 2013, http://
www.pewresearch.org/fact-tank/2013/09/18/
four-takeaways-from-tuesdays-census-incom
e-and-poverty-release, Retrieved: October 10, 2018.

199 Ibid, 25.

200 Burkhauser, Richard V., Larrimore, Jeff, and Simon, Kosali
I. (2012), A "Second Opinion" on the Economic Health
of the American Middle Class, *National Tax Journal*, 65:1,
34, http://www.nber.org/papers/w17164.pdf, Retrieved:
May 18, 2017.

201 Mark J. Perry, "Yes, the middle-class has been
disappearing, but they haven't fallen into the lower
class, they've risen into the upper class," *Carpe Diem
Blog*, July 12, 2013, http://www.aei.org/publication/

yes-the-middle-class-has-been-disappearing-but-they-have
nt-fallen-into-the-lower-class-theyve-risen-into-the-upp
er-class, Retrieved: February 28, 2017.

202 Steven Nelson, "Census Bureau Links Poverty With
Out-of-Wedlock Births," *U.S. News and World Report*,
May 6, 2013, https://www.usnews.com/news/newsgram/
articles/2013/05/06/census-bureau-links-poverty-with-
out-of-wedlock-births, Retrieved: March 6, 2017.

203 National Council on Drug Abuse, "Drug Talk," http://ncda.
org.jm/index.php/publications/drug-talk/66-poverty-a-drug-
abuse, Retrieved: March 6, 2017.

204 Betsy Mikel, "Mark Cuban Says This Will
Soon Be the Most Sought-After Job Skill," *Inc.
com*, February 21, 2017, http://www.inc.com/
betsy-mikel/mark-cuban-says-this-will-soo
n-be-the-most-sought-after-job-skill.html, Retrieved:
February 28, 2017.

205 Thomas Friedman, "More Than Ever, It's What
You Can Do, Not What You Know," ADN.com,
May 30, 2013, https://www.adn.com/commentary/
article/thomas-friedman-more-ever-its-wha
t-you-can-do-not-what-you-know/2013/05/31, Retrieved:
March 5, 2017.

206 Ibid.

207 John Haltiwanger, Ron Jarmin, Javier Miranda,
"Business Dyanamics Statistics Briefing: Where Have
All the Young Firms Gone?," *Kauffman Foundation for
Entrepreneurship*, May 2012, 2., http://www.kauffman.
org/what-we-do/research/business-dynamics-statistics/
business-dynamics-statistics-briefing-where-hav
e-all-the-young-firms-gone, Retrieved: May 12, 2017.

208 The Kauffman Foundation, "Three Things Entrepreneurs
Do" (2013).

209 The Kauffman Foundation, "The Case for the Startup
Act,"May 23, 2012, http://www.kauffman.org/
what-we-do/resources/policy/the-startup-act, Retrieved:
May 12, 2017.

210 Robert Fairlie, Arnobio Morelix, Inara Tareque, "2017
Kauffman Index of Startup Activity – National Trends,"
Ewing Marion Kauffman Foundation, (May 2017): 22,
file:///C:/Users/Eric%20Beck/AppData/Local/Packages/
Microsoft.MicrosoftEdge_8wekyb3d8bbwe/TempState/
Downloads/2017_Kauffman_Index_Startup_Activity_
National_Report_Final%20(1).pdf, Retrieved: September
9, 2017.

211 Fox News Radio, President Obama's "You
Didn't Build That," Roanoke, Virginia, July 26,
2012, http://radio.foxnews.com/2012/07/26/
president-obamas-you-didnt-build-that-transcript,
Retrieved: July 26, 2017.

212 Jim Tankersley, "The 100% Economy: Why the U.S.
Needs a Strong Middle Class to Thrive, *The Atlantic*,
May 18 2012, https://www.theatlantic.com/business/
archive/2012/05/the-100-economy-why-the-u
s-needs-a-strong-middle-class-to-thrive/257385, Retrieved:
May 12, 2017.

213 Calvin Coolidge, Calvin Coolidge Presidential Foundation,
https://coolidgefoundation.org/quote/quotations-t,
Retrieved: September 25, 2017

Chapter 8: The Progressive View of Morality and Health Care

214 Paul Ryan, Politico Interview, March 23, 2010, http://
www.politico.com/news/stories/0310/34844_Page2.
html?utm_source=huffingtonpost.com&utm_
medium=referral&utm_campaign=pubexchange_article,
Retrieved: March 28, 2017

215 Bill McKibben, "Together, We Save the Planet," *The Nation*, March 9, 2009, https://www.thenation.com/ article/together-we-save-planet, Retrieved: May 18, 2017.

216 Ruy Teixeira and John Halpin, "The Origins and Evolution of Progressive Economics," *Center for American Progress* (March 2011): 1, https://www.americanprogress. org/issues/democracy/reports/2011/03/14/9311/ the-origins-and-evolution-of-progressive-economics, Retrieved: March 9, 2017.

217 Angie Drobnic Holan, "Lie of the Year: 'If You Like Your Health Care Plan, You Can Keep It'," *PolitiFact*, December 12, 2013, http://www.politifact.com/ truth-o-meter/article/2013/dec/12/lie-year-if-you-like-you r-health-care-plan-keep-it, Retrieved: July 26, 2017.

218 United States, Federal Register, Volume 75, Number 116 (June 17, 2010): 34553, https://www.gpo.gov/fdsys/pkg/ FR-2010-06-17/pdf/2010-14488.pdf, Retrieved: August 17, 2018.

219 Ibid.

220 Charles Krauthammer, Fox News: Special Report Interview, November 25, 2013, http:// video.foxnews.com/v/2867164204001/ can-president-obama-shore-up-his-base

221 Plato's definition of a "noble lie" as presented in *The Republic* may help to explain why President Obama did not keep many of his promises about the benefits of Obamacare. As articulated by Socrates, the noble lie is one told by elite philosopher-kings to preserve the health and harmony of a city's social structure. In this context, Socrates is reflecting the need for specific class structure that includes educated elites who may lie to preserve the best interests of society-as-a-whole. Therefore, elites might resort to the noble lie periodically to build public support for a common agenda benefit the "city" as it is referred to

by Plato. In effect, President Obama resorted to the same tactic when he lied about how American's could keep the health insurance plans that currently had.

222 Ibid.

223 Barack Obama, Remarks at Health Care Town Hall, Bristol, Virginia, *FactCheck.org*, June 5, 2008, http://www.factcheck.org/2008/06/obamas-inflated-health-savings, Retrieved: December 22, 2013.

224 Avik Roy, November 4, 2013, "49-State Analysis: Obamacare To Increase Individual-Market Premiums by Average Of 41%," *Forbes*, November 4, 2013, https://www.forbes.com/sites/theapothecary/2013/11/04/49-state-ana lysis-obamacare-to-increase-individual-market-premiums -by-avg-of-41-subsidies-flow-to-elderly/#6dc564487f6b, Retrieved: July 26, 2017.

225 Reed Abelson and Margot Sanger-Katz, "A Quick Guide to Rising Obamacare Rates," *New York Times*, October 25, 2017, https://www.nytimes.com/2016/10/26/upshot/ rising-obamacare-rates-what-you-need-to-know.html?_r=0, Retrieved: March 9, 2017.

226 Angie Drobnic Holan, "Smokers, Tanning Aficionados, the Happily Uninsured: More Taxes Coming At Ya", *PolitiFact*, September 12, 2008, http://www.politifact. com/truth-o-meter/promises/obameter/promise/515/ no-family-making-less-250000-will-see-any-form-tax, Retrieved: December 22, 2013.

227 Alyene Senger, "Obamacare's Impact on Today's and Tomorrow's Taxpayers: An Update," *Heritage Foundation*, August 21, 2013, http:// www.heritage.org/health-care-reform/report/ obamacares-impact-todays-and-tomorrows-taxpayers- update?_ga=2.188901486.456579829.1499097093- 1853481365.1498921747, Retrieved: July 3, 2017.

228 ABC News, "Text of President Obama's
Address to Congress," September 9, 2009,
http://abcnews.go.com/Politics/HealthCare/
transcript-president-obama-address-joint-congres
s-health-care/story?id=8527252, Retrieved: July 26, 2017.

229 United States, Government Accountability Office,
"PPACA and the Long-Term Fiscal Outlook," Report
#GAO-13-281, January 2013, 17, https://www.gao.gov/
products/GAO-13-281, Retrieved: July 26, 2017.

230 The White House, "Remarks by the President on the
Affordable Care Act and the Government Shutdown,"
October 1, 2013, https://obamawhitehouse.
archives.gov/the-press-office/2013/10/01/
remarks-president-affordable-care-act-an
d-government-shutdown, Retrieved: December 23, 2013.

231 Alyene Senger, "Ten Broken Obamacare Promises,"
Heritage Foundation – Issue Brief No. 4112, December 18,
2013, 2, http://thf_media.s3.amazonaws.com/2013/pdf/
IB4112.pdf, Retrieved: July 26, 2017.

232 Ali Meyer, "Insurer Participation in Obamacare Exchanges
Declined 27% Since Law Took Effect," *Washington Free
Beacon*, May 18, 2016, http://freebeacon.com/issues/
insurer-participation-obamacare-exchanges-declined-2
7-since-aca-took-effect, Retrieved: March 9, 2017.

233 ABC News, "Text of President Obama's Address to
Congress," September 9, 2009.

234 United States, Department of Health and Human Services,
Richard S. Foster, "Estimated Financial Effects of the
Patient Protection and Affordable Care Act," April 22,
2010, https://www.cms.gov/Research-Statistics-Data-and-
Systems/Research/ActuarialStudies/downloads/
ppaca_2010-04-22.pdf, Retrieved: July 26, 2017.

235 Avik Roy, "The Obamacare Exchange Scorecard:
Around 100,000 Enrollees and Five Million

Cancellations," *Forbes*, November 12, 2013, http://
www.forbes.com/sites/theapothecary/2013/11/12/
the-obamacare-exchange-scorecard-around-10000
0-enrollees-and-five-million-cancellations, Retrieved: July
26, 2017.

[236] Ruy Teixeira and John Halpin, "The Origins and
Evolution of Progressive Economics," *Center for American
Progress* (March 2011): 9, https://www.americanprogress.
org/wp-content/uploads/issues/2011/03/pdf/progressive_
economics.pdf, Retrieved: July 27, 2017.

[237] "Richard Ely Facts," http://biography.yourdictionary.com/
richard-ely?direct_search_result=yes, Retrieved: August
6, 2018.

[238] Jonah Goldberg, "Richard Ely's Golden Calf," *National
Review*, 34, December 30, 2009, http://c3.nrostatic.
com/sites/default/files/article_jonah_ely_05152015.pdf,
Retrieved: July 27, 2017.

[239] Richard Ely, *The Social Aspects of Christianity* (New York:
Thomas P. Crowell & Company, 1889), 92.

[240] Goldberg, "*Richard Ely's Golden Calf,*" 34.

[241] Richard Ely, *The World War and Leadership in a Democracy*
(New York: Macmillan Co., 1918), 115.

[242] Ibid.

[243] "Statism" reflects the idea of elevating state (government)
control over political and economic affairs as the expense
of individual rights. Examples include Socialism, Marxism,
Communism, and other forms of totalitarian regimes.

[244] Richard Ely, *Recent American Socialism. Johns Hopkins
University Studies in Historical and Political Science*
(Baltimore: John Murphy & Co, 1885), 73.

[245] Richard Ely, *An Introduction to Political Economy* (New
York: Chautauqua Press, 1889), 92.

246 Richard Ely, *Social Law of Service* (New York: Eaton and Mains, 1896), 162–173.

247 Richard Ely, "Fraternalism vs. Paternalism in Government," *Century Magazine,* New Series Vol XXXIII (1898), 780–781.

248 Jonah Goldberg, "Richard Ely's Golden Calf," 34.

249 American Presidency Project, "Special Message to the Congress Presenting a 21-Point Program for the Reconversion Period", September 6, 1945, http://www.presidency.ucsb.edu/ws/?pid=12359, Retrieved: August 7, 2017.

250 Charlotte Twight, "Medicare's Origin: The Economics and Politics of Dependency," *Cato Journal*, Vol. 16, No. 3, 315, https://object.cato.org/sites/cato.org/files/serials/files/cato-journal/1997/1/cj16n3-3.pdf, Retrieved: July 27, 2017.

251 Ibid.

252 Ibid.

253 Dennis Kucinich, "A New Movement – Healthcare is a Civil Right," *OpEdNews*, September 9, 2009, https://www.opednews.com/articles/A-New-Movement-Health-Car-by-Dennis-Kucinich-090909-152.html, Retrieved: May 18, 2017.

254 Adler, *We Hold These Truths*, 115.

255 Adler, *We Hold These Truths*, 120–121.

256 Abraham Lincoln, fragment on government (July 1, 1854)—*The Collected Works of Abraham Lincoln,* ed. Roy P. Basler, vol. 2, 220–21 (1953).

257 The 2018 Annual Report of the Board of Trustees of the Federal Old-Age and Survivors Insurance and Federal Disability Insurance Trust Funds, June 5, 2018, 71,

https://www.ssa.gov/oact/tr/2018/tr2018.pdf, Retrieved: July 22, 2018.

258 2018 Annual Report of the Boards of Trustees of the Federal Hospital Insurance and Federal Supplementary Medical Insurance Trust Funds, June 5, 2016, 207, https://www.cms.gov/Research-Statistics-Data-and-Systems/Statistics-Trends-and-Reports/ReportsTrustFunds/Downloads/TR2018.pdf, Retrieved: July 22, 2018.

259 Mark Hendrickson, "Did You Really Pay For Your Medicare Benefits?," *Forbes*, March 3, 2013, http://www.forbes.com/sites/markhendrickson/2013/03/07/did-you-really-pay-for-your-medicare-benefits, Retrieved: March 18, 2017.

260 Dennis Prager, "Ten Ways Progressive Policies Harm Society's Moral Character," *DennisPrager.com*, July 19, 2011, http://www.dennisprager.com/ten-ways-progressive-policies-harm-society s-moral-character, Retrieved: March 11, 2017.

261 Ibid.

Chapter 9: The Medicare Health Insurance Scam

262 Clayton Christiansen, "Smart Ideas for Fixing Healthcare," *BigThink.com*, http://bigthink.com/videos/smart-ideas-for-fixing-healthcare, Retrieved: March 18, 2017.

263 Twight, "Medicare's Origin: The Economics and Politics of Dependency," 319–320.

264 Jennifer Agiesta, "Health Care Reform Circa 1965: Polling on Medicare," Washington Post, 2010, http://voices.washingtonpost.com/behind-the-numbers/2009/07/health_care_reform_circa_1965.html, Retrieved: July 27, 2017.

265 Pete G. Peterson Foundation, "Census Bureau Report on Poverty and Health Insurance Coverage," October 25,

2010, http://pgpf.org/Issues/Health-Care/2010/10/25/ Census-Bureau-Report-on-Poverty-an d-Health-Insurance-Coverage, Retrieved: July 27, 2017.

266 Twight, "Medicare's Origin: The Economics and Politics of Dependency," 321.

267 Ibid., 324–325.

268 Avik Roy, "Fact-Checking the Obama Campaign's Defense of its $716 Billion Cut to Medicare," *Forbes*, August 16, 2012, https://www. forbes.com/sites/theapothecary/2012/08/16/ fact-checking-the-obama-campaigns-defens e-of-its-716-billion-cut-to-medicare/#21eb39fe385f, Retrieved: May 12, 2017.

269 Twight, "Medicare's Origin: The Economics and Politics of Dependency," 328.

270 Catherine Richert, "Dean claims Social Security and Medicare were passed without Republican support," *PolitiFact*, August 28, 2009, http://www.politifact.com/ truth-o-meter/statements/2009/aug/28/howard-dean/ dean-claims-social-security-and-medicare-were-pass, Retrieved: July 27, 2017.

271 Jack Wooldridge, "Federal Health Estimates – 300% Wrong," *Nation's Business*, Vol. 52, No. 11, (November 1964): 32, http://digital.hagley.org/ Nationbiz_196411#page/1/mode/1up, Retrieved: July 27, 2017.

272 Wooldridge, "Federal Health Estimates – 300% Wrong," *Nation's Business*, 112.

273 Ibid, 114.

274 Arthur Laffer, Donna Arnuin and Wayne Winegarden, The Prognosis for National Health Insurance: A Pennsylvania Perspective," *Commonwealth Foundation for Public Policy Alternatives*, (August 19, 2009): 1.,

https://www.commonwealthfoundation.org/issues/
detail/the-prognosis-for-national-health-insuranc
e-a-pennsylvania-perspective, Retrieved: March 23, 2017.

275 Centers for Medicare and Medicaid Services,
     National Health Expenditure Accounts, https://
     www.cms.gov/Research-Statistics-Data-and-Systems/
     Statistics-Trends-and-Reports/NationalHealthExpendData/
     NationalHealthAccountsHistorical.html, Retrieved: March
     23, 2017.

276 Bradley Sawyer and Cynthia Cox, "Total Health
     Expenditures as Percent of GDP by Public vs. Private
     Spending," *Peterson-Kaiser Health System Tracker*, 2016,
     https://www.healthsystemtracker.org/chart-collection/
     health-spending-u-s-compare-countries/#item-start,
     Retrieved: July 24, 2018.

277 Ibid.

278 Andrew Foy and Brenton Stransky, "Understanding
     the Cause of Health Care Inflation," *AmericanThinker.
     com*, September 15, 2009, http://www.americanthinker.
     com/2009/09/understanding_the_cause_of_hea.html,
     Retrieved: July 27, 2017.

279 U.S. Department of Labor - Bureau of Labor Statistics,
     "Health Care – Spotlight on Statistics: Chart Data,"
     https://www.bls.gov/spotlight/2009/health_care/data.
     htm#chart_cpi, Retrieved: March 25, 2017

280 Ibid.

281 Ibid.

282 Ibid.

283 Organization for Economic Cooperation and
     Development, "OECD Health Statistics 2015," https://
     www.oecd.org/unitedstates/Country-Note-UNITED%20
     STATES-OECD-Health-Statistics-2015.pdf, Retrieved:
     March 26, 2017.

284 Andrew Foy and Brenton Stransky, "Understanding the Cause of Health Care Inflation," *American Thinker.com*, September 15, 2009, http://www.americanthinker.com/2009/09/understanding_the_cause_of_hea.html, Retrieved: July 27, 2017.

285 Robert J. Myers, "How Bad Were the Original Actuarial Estimates for Medicare's Hospital Insurance Program," *The Actuary* (February 1994): 6, http://www.forhealthfreedom.org/BackgroundResearchData/OriginalMedicareCostProjections.pdf, Retrieved: July 27, 2017.

286 Ibid.

287 Ibid, 7.

288 "2016 Annual Report of the Boards of Trustees of the Federal Hospital Insurance and Federal Supplementary Medical Insurance Trust Funds," 214.

289 Karoun Demirjian, "Reid Says Obamacare a Step Toward a Single-Payer System," *The Las Vegas Sun*, August 10, 2013, http://www.lasvegassun.com/news/2013/aug/10/reid-says-obamacare-just-step-toward-eventual-sing, Retrieved: December 29, 2013.

290 Paul Krugman, "The Big Kludge," *New York Times*, October 28, 2013, http://www.nytimes.com/2013/10/28/opinion/krugman-the-big-kludge.html?mtrref=www.google.com&gwh=DD6255CD15C3E7F961B04113DB14A3F5&gwt=pay&assetType=opinion, Retrieved: March 22, 2017.

291 Sarah Kliff, "Everything You Every Wanted to Know About Canadian Healthcare in One Post," *Washington Post*, July 1, 2012, http://www.washingtonpost.com/blogs/wonkblog/wp/2012/07/01/everything-you-ever-wanted-to-know-about-canadian-health-care-in-one-post, Retrieved: March 26, 2017.

292 CTV News, "Canada ranked last among OECD countries in health care wait times," January 20, 2014, http://www. ctvnews.ca/health/canada-ranked-last-among-oecd-countrie s-in-health-care-wait-times-1.1647061, Retrieved: March 26, 2017.

293 Bacchus Barua, "Waiting Your Turn: Wait Times for Health Care in Canada, 2017 Report" Studies in Health Care Policy, *Fraser Institute*, December 7, 2017, https://www.fraserinstitute. org/sites/default/files/waiting-your-turn-2017-execsummary. pdf, Retrieved: July 23, 2018.

294 Clifford Krauss, "Canada's Supreme Court Chips Away at National Health Care," *New York Times*, June 9, 2005, http://www.nytimes.com/2005/06/09/international/ americas/09cnd-canada.html?_r=0, Retrieved: July 27, 2017.

295 Chaoulli *c.* Quebec (p.g.), 2005 SCC 35 (CANLII), 795, 860, http://www.canlii.org/en/ca/scc/ doc/2005/2005scc35/2005scc35.pdf, Retrieved: July 27, 2017.

296 Jacques Chaoulli, "A Seismic Shift: How Canada's Supreme Court Sparked a Patient's Rights Revolution," *CATO Institute*, Policy Analysis No. 568 (May 8, 2006): 6, http://www.cato.org/publications/ policy-analysis/seismic-shift-how-canadas-supreme-cour t-sparked-patients-rights-revolution, Retrieved: July 27, 2017.

297 Fox News, "Canadian Health Officials: Our Universal Health Care Is 'Sick', Private Insurance Should Be Welcomed," August 17, 2009, http://www.foxnews.com/story/2009/08/17/ canadian-health-officials-our-universal-healt h-care-is-sick-private-insurance, Retrieved: July 27, 2017.

298 Ibid.

299 Yankick Labrie, "The Chaoulli Decision and Health Care Reform: A Missed Opportunity?" *Montreal Economic Institute*, June 2015, http://www.iedm.org/files/lepoint0415_en.pdf, Retrieved: July 24, 2018.

300 Michael Tanner, "The Grass is Not Always Greener – A Look at National Healthcare Systems Around the World," *CATO Institute*, Policy Analysis No. 613, 1, March 18, 2008, http://www.cato.org/publications/policy-analysis/grass-is-not-always-greener-loo k-national-health-care-systems-around-world, Retrieved: March 23, 2017.

301 Michael E. Porter and Elizabeth Olmsted Teisberg, *Refining Health Care: Creating Value-Based Competition on Results* (Boston: Harvard Business School Press, 2006), 89.

302 Quote by Daniel Patrick Moynihan found in *Congressional Record*, Vol. 146, Part 17 (Washington, DC: United States Government Printing Office, 2000), 25616.

303 Bob Bryan, "Healthcare spending in the U.S. just did something that rarely happens outside a recession," *Business Insider*, December 3, 2016, http://www.businessinsider.com/healthcare-spending-as-percent-of-gd p-recession-2016-12, Retrieved: March 25, 2017.

Chapter 10: The Case for Real Health Care Reform

304 Newsweek Staff, "Ted Kennedy and Health Care Reform," *Newsweek*, July 17, 2009, http://www.newsweek.com/ted-kennedy-and-health-care-reform-82011, Retrieved: May 8, 2017.

305 CNN, "'Talk to Neighbors, Spread the Facts on Health Care, says Obama", August 19, 2009, http://www.cnn.com/2009/POLITICS/08/19/obama.health.care/index.html, Retrieved: March 28, 2017.

306 Jonathan Cohn, "Maybe the GOP Establishment Should Have Embraced John Kasich Sooner," *Huffington Post*,

March 15, 2016, http://www.huffingtonpost.com/entry/
kasich-ohio-primaries_us_56e8c609e4b0860f99daf032,
Retrieved: March 28, 2017.

[307] Katherine Baicker, Sarah L. Taubman, Heidi L. Allen,
et al, "The Oregon Experiment — Effects of Medicaid
on Clinical Outcomes," *The New England Journal of
Medicine*, 1713, May 2, 2013, http://www.nejm.org/
doi/full/10.1056/NEJMsa1212321, Retrieved: March
28, 2017.

[308] Ibid., 1719.

[309] Damien J. LaPar, Castigliano M Bhamidipati, Carlos M.
Mery, et al, "Primary Payer Status Affects Mortality for
Major Surgical Operations," *Annals of Surgery* 252, No.
3, 544-551, https://www.ncbi.nlm.nih.gov/pmc/articles/
PMC3071622/pdf/nihms279555.pdf, Retrieved: March
28, 2017.

[310] Jonathan Gruber and David Rodriguez, "How Much
Uncompensated Care Do Doctors Provide?" *National
Bureau of Economic Research*, Working Paper 13585
(November 2007), 16, http://www.nber.org/papers/
w13585.pdf, Retrieved: March 28, 2017.

[311] Peter J. Cunningham and Ann S. O'Mally, "Do
Reimbursement Delays Discourage Medicaid Participation
by Physicians?" *Health Affairs* 28, No. 1 (2009): w17-w18,
November 18, 2008, http://content.healthaffairs.org/
content/28/1/w17.full.pdf+html, Retrieved: March 29,
2017.

[312] Edmund Haislmaier, "Obamacare's Enrollment
Increase: Mainly Due to Medicaid Expansion,"
Heritage Foundation, October 22, 2014, http://
www.heritage.org/health-care-reform/report/
obamacares-enrollment-increase-mainly-due-medicaid-
expansion, Retrieved: March 29, 2017.

[313] Ibid.

314 Jiaquan Xu, M.D., Sherry L. Murphy, B.S., Kenneth D. Kochanek, M.A., and Elizabeth Arias, Ph.D., "Mortality in the United States, 2015," *NCHS Data Brief*, No. 267, December 2016, https://www.cdc.gov/nchs/data/databriefs/db267.pdf, Retrieved: March 29, 2017.

315 Hillary for America, "Hillary Clinton's Commitment: Universal, Quality, Affordable Health Care for Everyone in America," https://www.hillaryclinton.com/briefing/factsheets/2016/07/09/hillary-clintons-commitment-universal-quality-affordabl e-health-care-for-everyone-in-america, Retrieved: July 27, 2017.

316 Gregory Korte, "Obama offers prescription for Affordable Care Act Growing Pains," *USA Today*, October 20, 2016, http://www.usatoday.com/story/news/politics/2016/10/20/obama-offers-prescription-affordable-care-ac t-growing-pains/92466252, Retrieved: March 29, 2017.

317 United Press International, "Obama Asks Clergy's Help in Pushing Reform," August 19, 2009, http://www.upi.com/Obama-asks-clergys-help-in-pushing-reform/56711250683093, Retrieved: March 29, 2017.

318 Centers for Medicare and Medicaid Services, "Emergency Medical Treatment & Labor Act (EMTALA)," March 26, 2012, https://www.cms.gov/Regulations-and-Guidance/Legislation/EMTALA, Retrieved: July 27, 2017.

319 Public Health Program, Open Society Foundations, https://www.opensocietyfoundations.org/about/programs/public-health-program, Retrieved: August 6, 2018.

320 Karoun Demirjian, "Reid Says Obamacare a Step Toward a Single-Payer System," *Las Vegas Sun*, August 10, 2013, http://www.lasvegassun.com/news/2013/aug/10/reid-says-obamacare-just-step-toward-eventual-sing, Retrieved: December 29, 2013.

321 Porter, et. al., *Refining Health Care: Creating Value-Based Competition on Results*, 3.

322 Paul Krugman, "Why markets can't cure healthcare," *New York Times*, July 25, 2009, https://krugman.blogs.nytimes.com/2009/07/25/why-markets-cant-cure-healthcare/comment-page-34/?_r=0, Retrieved: April 2, 2017.

323 Ibid.

324 "Third-party-payment" describes the arrangement where an insurance company shields the consumer from bearing the full cost of a service they are insured for. Third-party-payment arrangements thereby create an incentive to consume more service.

325 Richard Amerling, "NO: The Problems Are Due to Payments from Third Parties," *Wall Street Journal*, March 22, 2015, https://www.wsj.com/articles/should-the-u-s-move-away-from-fee-for-service-medicine-1427079653, Retrieved: July 4, 2017.

326 The Commonwealth Fund, "US Spends More on Health Care Than Other High-Income Nations But Has Lower Life Expectancy, Worse Health," October 8, 2015, http://www.commonwealthfund.org/publications/press-releases/2015/oct/us-spends-more-on-health-care-than-other-nations, Retrieved: April 19, 2017.

327 Avik Roy, "A Conservative Case for Universal Coverage," *Washington Examiner*, January 17, 2014, http://www.washingtonexaminer.com/a-conservative-case-for-universal-coverage/article/2542091, Retrieved: May 7, 2017.

328 Roger Aronoff, "A Doctor in the Senate: Interview with Sen. Tom Coburn," *Accuracy in Media*, July 30, 2012, http://www.aim.org/aim-report/a-doctor-in-the-senate-interview-with-sen-tom-coburn, Retrieved: April 3, 2017.

329 2018 Annual Report of the Boards of Trustees of the Federal Hospital Insurance and Federal Supplementary

Medical Insurance Trust Funds (June 5, 2016): 25, https://www.cms.gov/Research-Statistics-Data-and-Systems/Statistics-Trends-and-Reports/ReportsTrustFunds/Downloads/TR2018.pdf, Retrieved: August 6, 2018.

330 Laurel White, "Wisconsin Republicans Eye Possible Federal Move to Medicaid Block Grants," *Wisconsin Public Radio*, November 22, 2016, https://www.wpr.org/wisconsin-republicans-eye-possible-federal-move-medicaid-block-grants, Retrieved: April 4, 2017.

331 Jeannie O'Sullivan, "Governor Christie: Need for Health Clinics is Extraordinary," *Burlington County Times*, August 9, 2011, http://www.burlingtoncountytimes.com/news/local/gov-christie-need-for-health-clinics-is-extraordinary/article_be155d2e-2b78-5645-bd64-9d11b11a9135.html, Retrieved: April 23, 2017.

332 Avik Roy, "How Paul Ryan's Obamacare Replacement Could Trap Millions in Poverty – And How to Fix It," *Forbes*, March 11, 2017, https://www.forbes.com/sites/theapothecary/2017/03/11/how-paul-ryans-obamacare-replacement-would-trap-millions-in-poverty-and-how-to-fix-it/#eed887841682, Retrieved: April 8, 2017.

333 Scott Wallace and Elizabeth Teisberg, "Implementing Value-Based Health Care Delivery in Nebraska," *Nebraska Medicine*, Volume 13, Number 2, (Summer 2014): 2, https://www.nebmed.org/uploadedFiles/Nebmed/News/Pdfs/Value%20Based%20Health%20Care%20Delivery.pdf, Retrieved: April 8, 2017.

334 Michael E. Porter and Elizabeth Olmsted Teisberg, *Refining Health Care: Creating Value-Based Competition on Results* (2006), 6.

335 Presentation by Michael Porter at Harvard Business School, Institute for Strategy and Competitiveness, "Faculty Perspectives on Healthcare," March 7, 2012,

http://www.hbs.edu/healthcare/pdf/2012%2003%20 07%20SUT%20HCI%20presentation.pdf

336 Robert Book, "How to Cover Everyone with Pre-Existing Conditions Without the System Collapsing," *Forbes*, November 13, 2016, https://www.forbes.com/sites/ theapothecary/2016/11/13/how-to-cover-everyone-with-pr e-existing-conditions-without -the-system-collapsing/#7b15eb74792d, Retrieved: April 18, 2017.

337 Editorial Board, "In Defense of the Freedom Caucus," *National Review*, March 31, 2017, http://www.nationalreview.com/article/446306/ freedom-caucus-republican-health-care-bil l-defeat-not-all-freedom-caucus, Retrieved: April 18, 2017.

338 An "age-band" rating is used by health insurance companies to establish premium pricing for older customers versus younger. For example, an age-band of "5:1" indicates that older customers can be charged up to five times the premium of a younger customer, recognizing that older customers will consume more healthcare than younger.

339 Robert Book, "Primer: Medicare Risk Adjustment," *American Action Forum*, February 11, 2015, https://www.americanactionforum.org/research/ primer-medicare-risk-adjustment, Retrieved: April 18, 2017.

340 James C. Capretta and Tom Miller, "How to Cover Pre-Existing Conditions," *National Affairs*, No. 31, Spring 2017, http://www.nationalaffairs.com/publications/detail/ how-to-cover-pre-existing-conditions, Retrieved: April 19, 2017.

341 Paul Roderick Gregory, "Obama's Pre-Existing Conditions Whopper," *Forbes*, October 8, 2013, https://www. forbes.com/sites/paulroderickgregory/2013/10/08/

lying-with-statistics-obamas-pre-existin
g-conditions-crisis/#1efbc4957d50, Retrieved: April
27, 2017.

342 Gary Claxton, et. al., "Pre-existing Conditions and Medical
Underwriting in the Individual Insurance Market Prior to
the ACA," *Henry J. Kaiser Family Foundation*, December
12, 2016, http://kff.org/health-reform/issue-brief/
pre-existing-conditions-and-medical-underwritin
g-in-the-individual-insurance-market-prior-to-the-aca,
Retrieved: May 6, 2017.

343 James C. Capretta and Tom Miller, "How to Cover
Pre-Existing Conditions," *National Affairs*, No. 31, Spring
2017, http://www.nationalaffairs.com/publications/detail/
how-to-cover-pre-existing-conditions, Retrieved: April
19, 2017.

344 United States, Committee on Energy and Commerce
Congressional Memorandum, Reps. Henry Waxman and
Bart Stupak, October 12, 2010, http://thehill.com/images/
stories/blogs/memo1.pdf, Retrieved: May 6, 2017.

345 Louise Norris, "Health Insurance and High-Risk Pools,"
HealthInsurance.org, November 14, 2016, https://www.
healthinsurance.org/affordable-care-act/risk-pools,
Retrieved: May 6, 2017.

346 United States, Center for Medicare and Medicaid Services,
"Covering People with Pre-Existing Conditions: Report
on the Implementation and Operation of the Pre-Existing
Condition Insurance Plan Program," Executive Summary,
January 31, 2013, https://www.cms.gov/CCIIO/Resources/
Files/Downloads/pcip_annual_report_01312013.pdf,
Retrieved: May 6, 2017.

347 Aviva Aron-Dine, "$8 Billion Comes Nowhere
Close to Meeting Republican Commitments
to People with Pre-Existing Conditions,"
CNBC.com, May 4, 2017, http://www.cnbc.

com/2017/05/04/health-care-reform-8-billion-won
t-cut-it-for-pre-existing-conditions-commentary.html,
Retrieved: May 6, 2017.

348 United States, Congressional Budget Office, "The Federal
Budget in 2016: An Infographic, February 8, 2017,"
https://www.cbo.gov/publication/52408, Retrieved: May
6, 2017.

349 Paul Roderick Gregory, "Obama's Pre-Existing Conditions
Whopper," *Forbes*, October 8, 2013, https://www.
forbes.com/sites/paulroderickgregory/2013/10/08/
lying-with-statistics-obamas-pre-existin
g-conditions-crisis/#1efbc4957d50, Retrieved: April
27, 2017.

350 Robert Pear and Thomas Kaplan, "House Republicans
Unveil Plan to Replace Health Law," *New York Times*,
March 6, 2017, https://www.nytimes.com/2017/03/06/
us/politics/affordable-care-act-obamacare-health.html,
Retrieved: July 30, 2017.

351 Quinnipiac University Poll, "U.S. Voters Oppose GOP
Health Plan 3-1, Quinnipiac University National Poll
Finds; Big Opposition to Cuts to Medicaid, Planned
Parenthood," March 23, 2017, https://poll.qu.edu/
national/release-detail?ReleaseID=2443, Retrieved: April
3, 2017.

352 Federal Debt Clock, http://www.usgovernmentdebt.us,
Retrieved: July 27, 2017.

353 Margot Sanger-Katz, "What Changed in the Health Repeal
Plan to Win Over the Freedom Caucus, *New York Times*,
April 26, 2017, https://www.nytimes.com/2017/04/26/
upshot/what-changed-in-the-health-repea
l-plan-to-win-over-the-freedom-caucus.html?action=click
&contentCollection=Politics&module=RelatedCoverage
&region=EndOfArticle&pgtype=article, Retrieved: April
27, 2017.

354 Joseph Antos and James Capretta, "The Senate Health Care Bill," *Health Affairs Blog*, June 23, 2017, http://healthaffairs.org/blog/2017/06/23/the-senate-health-care-bill, Retrieved: July 31, 2017.

355 Lynda Ramsey, "GOP Healthcare Disaster: 'Skinny Repeal' Dies as McCain Votes No," *Business Insider*, July 28, 2017, http://www.businessinsider.com/senate-republican-skinny-repeal-health-care-bill-vote-count-mccain-2017-7, Retrieved: July 31, 2017.

Chapter 11: The Treatment of Young Black Men by Police

356 Democracy Now, "Dehumanizing the Black Lives of America: Michael Eric Dyson on Ferguson, Police Brutality and Race," December 1, 2014, http://www.democracynow.org/2014/12/1/dehumanizing_the_black_lives_of_america, Retrieved: July 28, 2017.

357 United States, Department of Justice, Remarks to Justice Department, February 18, 2009, https://www.justice.gov/opa/speech/attorney-general-eric-holder-department-justice-african-american-history-month-program, Retrieved: July 28, 2017.

358 NBC News, "Meet the Press Transcript," November 30, 2014, http://www.nbcnews.com/meet-the-press/meet-press-transcript-november-30-2014-n258491, Retrieved: July 28, 2017.

359 Centers for Disease Control and Prevention, National Center for Health Statistics, Compressed Mortality File 1999–2016 on CDC WONDER Online Database, released June 2017, Data are from the Compressed Mortality File 1999-2016 Series 20 No. 2U, 2016, as compiled from data provided by the 57 vital statistics jurisdictions through the Vital Statistics Cooperative Program, http://wonder.cdc.gov/cmf-icd10.html, Retrieved: July 26, 2018.

360 Federal Bureau of Investigation, Crime in the United States 2013, Expanded Homicide Data Table 3, https://ucr.fbi.gov/crime-in-the-u.s/2013/crime-in-the-u.s.-2013/offenses-known-to-law-enforcement/expanded-homicide/expanded_homicide_data_table_3_murder_offenders_by_age_sex_and_race_2013.xls, Retrieved: July 26, 2018.

361 Bill O'Reilly, "Talking Points Memo," *Fox News*, December 1, 2014, http://www.foxnews.com/transcript/2014/12/02/bill-oreilly-what-ferguson-protesters-accomplished.html, Retrieved: September 25, 2017.

362 John R. Lott, Jr., "Dangerous Distortions About Cops Shooting Black Men," *Daily News*, December 2, 2014, http://www.nydailynews.com/opinion/john-lott-dangerous-distortions-cops-shootin g-black-men-article-1.2030545, Retrieved: May 13, 2017.

363 Ibid.

364 Michelle Ye Hee Lee, "The Viral Claim that a Black Person is Killed by Police Every 28 Hours," *Washington Post*, December 24, 2014, https://www.washingtonpost.com/news/fact-checker/wp/2014/12/24/the-viral-claim-that-a-black-person-is-killed-by-polic e-every-28-hours/?utm_term=.9c9368a5ff6b, Retrieved: July 28, 2017.

365 On July 19, 2018, the New York City Police Department announced that, barring objections from the U.S. Department of Justice, they would proceed with an internal administrative trial against the officer who used a choke hold on Eric Garner. Charges brought against the officer may result in either his suspension or dismissal from the NYPD.

366 YouTube, "Bill O'Reilly's Response to No Indictment on NYPD Chokehold Eric Garner Case," December 3, 2014, https://www.youtube.com/watch?v=4f9uCidkzzw, Retrieved: September 25, 2017.

367 The Huffington Post, "Obama Trayvon Martin Speech Transcript: President Comments On George Zimmerman Verdict," July 19, 2013, http://www.huffingtonpost.com/2013/07/19/obama-trayvon-martin-speech-transcript_n_3624884.html, Retrieved: July 28, 2017.

368 Jason L. Riley, "Race Relations and Law Enforcement", *Imprimis*, Vol. 44 No. 1, January 2015, 7. Reprinted by permission from *Imprimis*, a publication of Hillsdale College.

369 Ibid.

370 Jason L. Riley, "The Other Ferguson Tragedy," *Wall Street Journal*, November 25, 2014, http://www.wsj.com/articles/jason-riley-the-other-ferguson-tragedy-1416961287, Retrieved: July 28, 2017.

371 Ibid.

372 Larry Elder, "Racial Cop Stories That Didn't Make the Cut," *RealClearPolitics.com*, December 18, 2014, http://www.realclearpolitics.com/articles/2014/12/18/racial_cop_stories_that_didnt_make_the_cut_125004.html, Retrieved: July 28, 2017.

373 Ibid.

374 Lois James, Stephen M. James, and Bryan J. Vila, "The Reverse Racism Effect: Are Cops More Hesitant to Shoot Black Than White Suspects?" *American Society of Criminology*, Volume 15, Issue 2 (2016), https://assets.documentcloud.org/documents/2813702/The-Reverse-Racism-Effect.pdf, Retrieved: September 25, 2017.

375 Roland G. Fryer, Jr., "An Empirical Analysis of Racial Differences in Police Use of Force," *National Bureau of Economic Research*, Working Paper 22399, July 2016, http://www.nber.org/papers/w22399.pdf, Retrieved July 23, 2016, Retrieved: July 28, 2017.

376 Quoctrung Bui and Amanda Cox, "Surprising New Evidence Shows Bias in Police Use of Force but Not in Shootings," *New York Times*, July 11, 2016, http://www.nytimes.com/2016/07/12/upshot/surprising-new-evidence-shows-bias-in-police-use-of-force-but-not-in-shootings.html?_r=0, Retrieved: July 23, 2016.

377 Green B, Horel T, Papachristos AV. (2017). Modeling Contagion Through Social Networks to Explain and Predict Gunshot Violence in Chicago, 2006 to 2014. *JAMA Internal Medicine* Published online January 03, 2017. doi:10.1001/jamainternmed.2016.8245, Retrieved: July 30, 2018.

378 Ibid.

379 Bill O'Reilly, Shocking Violence in Chicago," *Fox News Channel*, April 15, 2016, http://video.foxnews.com/v/4848033175001/shocking-violence-in-chicago/?playlist_id=2781265840001#sp=show-clips, Retrieved: July 28, 2017.

Chapter 12: The Treatment of Blacks by the Justice System

380 CNN, Transcript: Democratic Presidential Candidates Debate in South Carolina, January 21, 2008, http://www.cnn.com/2008/POLITICS/01/21/debate.transcript3/index.html, Retrieved: July 11, 2018.

381 Newt Gingrich and Pat Nolan, "Prison Reform: A Smart Way for States to Save Money and Lives," *Washington Post*, January 7, 2011, http://www.washingtonpost.com/wp-dyn/content/article/2011/01/06/AR2011010604386.html, Retrieved: July 11, 2018.

382 Ibid., 15.

383 Joseph D. Osel, "Black Out: Michelle Alexander's Operational Whitewash – The New Jim Crow Reviewed," *International Journal of Radical Critique*, Vol. 01 No. 01,

April 7, 2012, http://www.radicalcritique.org/2012/03/black-out-michelle-alexanders.html, Retrieved: July 28, 2017.

384 Greg Thomas, "Why Some Like 'The New Jim Crow" So Much," *iMixWhatiLike*, April 26, 2012, https://imixwhatilike.org/2012/04/26/whysomelikethenewjimcrowsomuch, Retrieved: July 28, 2017.

385 Alexander, *The New Jim Crow*, 220.

386 Ibid.

387 United States, Department of Health and Human Services, "Results from the 2013 National Survey on Drug Use and Health," 26, http://www.samhsa.gov/data/sites/default/files/NSDUHresultsPDFWHTML2013/Web/NSDUHresults2013.pdf, Retrieved: July 28, 2017.

388 Ojmarrh Mitchell and Michael S. Caudy, "Examining Racial Disparities in Drug Arrests," *Justice Quarterly*, 4, January 22, 2013, https://www.gmuace.org/documents/publications/2013/examining.pdf, Retrieved: July 28, 2017.

389 Barry Latzer, "The Myth of Mass Incarceration," *Wall Street Journal*, 2. February 22, 2016, http://www.wsj.com/articles/the-myth-of-mass-incarceration-1456184736, Retrieved: July 28, 2017.

390 Healther Mac Donald, "Obama's Tragic Let 'em Out Fantasy," *Wall Street Journal*, October 23, 2015, http://www.wsj.com/articles/obamas-tragic-let-em-out-fantasy-1445639113, Retrieved: July 28, 2017.

391 Ibid.

392 Ibid.

393 Alexander, *The New Jim Crow*, 223.

394 E. Ann Carson and Daniela Golinelli, *Prisoners in 2012: Trends in Admissions and Releases 1991–2012*, Bureau of Justice Statistics Program, 1978–2012, September 2, 2014), 5, https://www.bjs.gov/content/pub/pdf/p12tar9112.pdf, Retrieved: July 28, 2017.

395 Ibid.

396 Sam Taxy, Julie Samuels, and William Adams, *Drug Offenders in Federal Prison: Estimates of Characteristics Based on Linked Data,* U.S. Department of Justice, October 2015, 2, https://www.bjs.gov/content/pub/pdf/dofp12.pdf, Retrieved: July 28, 2017.

397 "Restorative Justice" is an alternative to punishment by incarceration that engages both the victims of a crime and the offenders to repair the harm caused, and to encourage offenders to take responsibility for their actions. Restorative actions may include community service, apologizing to the victims and compensating them for damages. The long-term goal of restorative justice is to avoid recidivism by the offender.

398 Amy Craddock, James J. Collins, and Anita Timrots, *Fact Sheet: Drug-Related Crime,* U.S. Department of Justice , September 1994, 3, https://www.bjs.gov/content/pub/pdf/DRRC.PDF, Retrieved: July 28, 2017.

399 Brian Mann, "Timeline: Black America's surprising 40-year support for the Drug War," *PrisonTime.org,* August 12, 2013, http://prisontime.org/2013/08/12/timeline-black-support-for-the-war-on-drugs, Retrieved: July 28, 2017.

400 Ibid.

401 For more information see: http://www.RightonCrime.com.

402 Lyndon B. Johnson, "Remarks at University of Michigan," May 22, 1964. Online by Gerhard Peters and John T. Woolley, *The American Presidency Project.* http://www.

presidency.ucsb.edu/ws/?pid=26262, Retrieved: July 28, 2017.

403 Office of Policy Planning and Research, United States, Department of Labor, "The Negro Family: The Case for National Action," March 1965, i, http://web.stanford. edu/~mrosenfe/Moynihan's%20The%20Negro%20Family. pdf, Retrieved: July 28, 2017.

404 Ibid., 5–12.

405 Jason L. Riley, "Still Right on the Black Family After All These Years," *Wall Street Journal*, February 11, 2015, http://www.wsj.com/articles/jason-l-riley-still-right-o n-the-black-family-after-all-these-years-1423613625, Retrieved: July 28, 2017.

406 George A. Akerlof and Janet L. Yellen, "An Analysis of Out-Of-Wedlock Births in the United States," *Brookings*, August 1, 1996, http://www.brookings.edu/research/ papers/1996/08/childrenfamilies-akerlof, Retrieved: July 28, 2017.

407 Brady E. Hamilton, Joyce A Martin, Michelle J.K. Osterman, Sally C. Curtin, and T.J. Mathews, *Births: Final Data for* 2014, National Vital Statistics Report, Vol. 64 No. 12,Hyattsville, MD: National Center for Health Statistics, 2015, 41, http://www.cdc.gov/nchs/data/nvsr/ nvsr64/nvsr64_12.pdf, Retrieved: July 28, 2017.

408 Alisha B. Parks, "The Effects of Family Structure on Juvenile Delinquency," *East Tennessee State University*, December 2013, 10 (also see Comanor and Phillips 2002), http://dc.etsu.edu/cgi/viewcontent. cgi?article=3380&context=etd, Retrieved: July 28, 2017.

409 Alexia Cooper and Erica L. Smith, *Homicide Trends in the United States, 1980–2008,* U.S. Department of Justice, November 2011, 12, http://www.bjs.gov/content/pub/pdf/ htus8008.pdf, Retrieved: July 28, 2017.

410 Lauren Camera, "Achievement Gap Between White and Black Students Still Gaping," *U.S. News & World Report*, January 13, 2016, http://www. usnews.com/news/blogs/data-mine/2016/01/13/ achievement-gap-between-white-and-blac k-students-still-gaping, Retrieved: July 28, 2017.

411 United States, Department of Education - National Center for Education Statistics, "Table 1. Public High School 4-Year Adjusted Cohort Graduation Rate, http://nces.ed.gov/ccd/tables/ ACGR_RE_and_characteristics_2013-14.asp, Retrieved: July 28, 2017.

Chapter 13: The Credibility of White Privilege

412 Tim Wise, "The Pathology of Privilege - Racism, White Denial & the Costs of Inequality," *Media Education Foundation*, 2008, http://www.mediaed.org/transcripts/ Tim-Wise-On-White-Privilege-Transcript.pdf, Retrieved: July 28, 2017.

413 Peggy McIntosh, "White Privilege: Unpacking the Invisible Knapsack," *Wellesley Centers for Women*, 1989, http://nationalseedproject.org/images/documents/ Knapsack_plus_Notes-Peggy_McIntosh.pdf, Retrieved: July 18, 2016.

414 Tim Wise, *White Like Me: Reflections on Race from a Privileged Son* (Berkeley: Soft Skull Press, 2011), 36.

415 Luke 12:48.

416 Wise, "*White Like Me: Reflections on Race from a Privileged Son*," 92.

417 Shelby Steele, "Conservatism and Counterculture," *National Review*, March 2, 2015, http://www. nationalreview.com/node/414644/print Retrieved: July 19, 2016.

418 Ibid.

419 Steele, "Conservatism and Counterculture," March
2, 2015.

420 Joyce A. Martin, M.P.H., Brady E. Hamilton, Ph.D.,
Michelle J.K. Osterman, M.H.S., Anne K. Driscoll, Ph.D.,
and T.J. Mathews, M.S., *Births – Final Data for 2015*,
National Vital Statistics Report, DHHS Publication Vol.
66, No. 1, Hyattsville, MD: National Center for Health
Statistics, 2017, https://www.cdc.gov/nchs/data/nvsr/
nvsr66/nvsr66_01.pdf, Retrieved: October 13, 2018.

421 YouTube, "Ben Shapiro Destroys the Concept of White
Privilege," *University of Missouri*, November 19, 2015,
http://www.amara.org/en/videos/dHzRvSqWVbgk/
en/1468115, Retrieved: June 5, 2017.

422 Peggy McIntosh, "White Privilege: Unpacking the Invisible
Knapsack."

423 Gregory Seay, "Group Wants Probe of Allstate
in Redlining," *Hartford Courant*, September 3,
1993, http://articles.courant.com/1993-09-03/
business/0000005213_1_acorn-allstate-redlining,
Retrieved: May 13, 2017.

424 Neal R. Pierce, "A Quiet Attempt to Bring
Back Redlining," *Baltimore Sun*, July 16, 1991,
http://articles.baltimoresun.com/1991-07-16/
news/1991197039_1_community-reinvestment-act-
nation-banks-failing-banks, Retrieved: May 13, 2017.

425 Alicia H. Munnell, Lynn E. Browne, James McEneaney
and Geoffrey M. B. Tootell, "Mortgage Lending in Boston:
Interpreting HMDA Data," *Federal Reserve Bank of Boston*,
Working Paper No. 92-7, October 1992, 1, https://
www.bostonfed.org/economic/wp/wp1992/wp92_7.pdf,
Retrieved: July 28, 2017.

426 Gretchen Morgenson and Joshua Rosner, *Reckless
Endangerment* (New York: Henry Hold and Company,
2011), 35.

427 Peter Passell, "Race, Mortgages and Statistics; The Unending Debate Over a Study of Lending Bias," *New York Times*, May 10, 1996, http://www.nytimes.com/1996/05/10/business/race-mortgages-and-statistics-the-unendin g-debate-over-a-study-of-lending-bias.html Retrieved: July 21, 2016.

428 Raphael Bostic, "The Role of Race in Mortgage Lending: Revisiting the Boston Fed Study," United States Federal Reserve Board of Governors, December 1996, https://www.federalreserve.gov/pubs/feds/1997/199702/199702pap.pdf, Retrieved: July 21, 2016.

429 Edward Pinto, "From the American Dream to … Bailout America: How the Government Loosened Credit Standards and Led to the Mortgage Meltdown," *American Enterprise Institute*, https://www.aei.org/wp-content/uploads/2014/10/pinto-bailout-america-timeline-government-mortgage-complex_1305029805.pdf, Retrieved: July 21, 2016.

430 Morgenson, et. al., *Reckless Endangerment*, 116.

Chapter 14: The Legality of Gay Marriage

431 Obama, *The Audacity of Hope*, 223.

432 Mackenzie Weinger, "Evolve: Obama Gay Marriage Quotes," *Politico*, May 9, 2012, http://politi.co/ILbRf3, Retrieved: June 5, 2017.

433 Rick Klein, "Obama: 'I Think Same-Sex Couples Should Be Able to Get Married'," *ABC News Interview*, http://abcnews.go.com/blogs/politics/2012/05/obama-comes-out-i-think-same-sex-couples-should-be-abl e-to-get-married, Retrieved: June 5, 2017.

434 Obergefell v. Hodges, 576 U.S. 22 (2015), Opinion of the Court, https://www.supremecourt.gov/

opinions/14pdf/14-556_3204.pdf, Retrieved: July 29, 2016.

435 American Foundation for Equal Rights, "14 Supreme Court Cases: Marriage is a Fundamental Right," July 19, 2012, http://afer.org/blog/14-suprem e-court-cases-marriage-is-a-fundamental-right/, Retrieved: July 29, 2016.

436 Obergefell v. Hodges, 576 U.S. 28 (2015).

437 Obergefell v. Hodges, 576 U.S. 12 (2015).

438 Obergefell v. Hodges, 576 U.S. 10-12 (2015).

439 Obergefell v. Hodges, 576 U.S. 2-3 (2015), Roberts Dissenting.

440 Ibid.

441 Griswold v. Connecticut, 381 U.S. 486 (1965).

442 Obergefell v. Hodges, 576 U.S. 3 (2015), Roberts Dissenting.

443 Obergefell v. Hodges, 576 U.S. 1-2 (2015), Scalia Dissenting.

444 *Hillary's America*, D'Souza Media, Dir. Dinesh D'Souza, Producer: Gerald R. Molen, Released: May 15, 2016.

445 Marbury v. Madison, 5 U.S. 137 (1803).

446 Damon Root, "Can the President Lawfully Ignore a Supreme Court Decision?", *Reason.com*, June 4, 2015, http://reason.com/blog/2015/06/04/ can-the-president-lawfully-ignore-a-supr, Retrieved: August 2, 2016.

447 United States Constitution, Article 2, Section 1.

448 James Madison, "Federalist No. 49," *The Constitution Society*, http://www.constitution.org/fed/federa49.htm, Retrieved: August 8, 2016.

449 Michael S. Paulsen, *The Constitution: An Introduction* (New York: Basic Books, 2015), 271.

450 Ibid, 180–182.

451 Abraham Lincoln, First Inaugural Address, March 4, 1861, http://www.nationalcenter.org/LincolnFirstInaugural.html, Retrieved: August 8, 2016.

452 United States National Archives, "America's Founding Documents," http://www.archives.gov/exhibits/charters/declaration_transcript.html, Retrieved: August 5, 2016.

453 Obergefell v. Hodges, 576 U.S. 20 (2015), Roberts Dissenting.

454 American Academy of Pediatrics, "Press Release: American Academy of Pediatrics Supports Same Gender Civil Marriage," March 21, 2013, https://www.aap.org/en-us/about-the-aap/aap-press-room/pages/American-Academy-of-Pediatrics-Supports-Same-Gender-Civil-Marriage.aspx, Retrieved: July 28, 2017.

455 American Psychological Association, "Press Release: American Psychological Association Reiterates Support for Same-Sex Marriage," August 11, 2010, http://www.apa.org/news/press/releases/2010/08/support-same-sex-marriage.aspx, Retrieved: August 3, 2016.

456 Nelson Lund, "A Social Experiment Without Science Behind It," *Wall Street Journal*, March 26, 2013, http://www.wsj.com/articles/SB10001424127887324557804578376671175549596, Retrieved: August 3, 2016.

457 Daniel Patrick Moynihan, "Social Science and the Courts," *National Affairs*, 54 (Winter) 1979, 19–20, http://www.nationalaffairs.com/storage/app/uploads/public/58e/1a4/c81/58e1a4c8108d9827178919.pdf. Retrieved September 2, 2017.

458 Hollingsworth v. Perry, (570 U.S. __ 2013), "Brief for the Institute for Marriage and Public Policy" (as Amicus

Curiae), 5–7, https://supreme.justia.com/cases/federal/us/570/12-144, Retrieved: July 28, 2017.

459 Mark Regnerus, "New Family Structures Study," University of Texas at Austin, *Social Science Research* Vol, 41, Issue 4 (July 2012), 752-770, http://www.sciencedirect.com/science/article/pii/S0049089X12000610, Retrieved: July 28, 2017.

460 Ibid.

Chapter 15: The Debate Over Equal Pay for Equal Work

461 Alanna Vaglanos, "The Hillary Clinton Guide to Being an Empowered Woman," *The Huffington Post*, March 4, 2014, http://www.huffingtonpost.com/2014/03/04/hillary-clinton-quotes-lisa-rogak_n_4770130.html, Retrieved: July 4, 2017.

462 Glenn Kessler, "Hillary Clinton Cites GOP Quotes on Equal Pay Legislation Out of Context," *Washington Post*, May 29, 2015, https://www.washingtonpost.com/news/fact-checker/wp/2015/05/29/hillary-clinton-cites-gop-quotes-on-equal-pay-legislation-out-of-context/?utm_term=.886b463a01a5, Retrieved: July 4, 2017.

463 S. 841, 109th Cong (2005), "Paycheck Fairness Act."

464 GovTrack, "Paycheck Fairness Act (2005), Section 2, Findings, Paragraph 2, https://www.govtrack.us/congress/bills/109/s841/text.

465 Glenn Kessler, "Hillary Clinton cites GOP quotes on equal-pay legislation out of context," *Washington Post*, https://www.washingtonpost.com/news/fact-checker/wp/2015/05/29/hillary-clinton-cites-gop-quotes-on-equal-pay-legislation-out-of-context/, Retrieved: August 12, 2016.

466 Karen Agness, "Don't Buy into the Gender Pay Gap Myth," *Forbes*, April 12, 2016, http://www.forbes.com/

sites/karinagness/2016/04/12/dont-buy-into-the-gender-pa
y-gap-myth/#6ba10cb14766, Retrieved: August 12, 2016.

467   United States, Department of Labor - Bureau of Labor Statistics,
"BLS Reports: Highlights of Women's Earnings in 2014," 71,
https://www.bls.gov/opub/reports/womens-earnings/archive/
highlights-of-womens-earnings-in-2014.pdf, Retrieved:
August 1, 2018.

468   Chuck Ross, "Report: Obama Official Apologizes for
Misleading Rhetoric on Pay Wage Gap," *The Daily
Caller*, April 8, 2014, http://dailycaller.com/2014/04/08/
report-obama-official-apologizes-for-misleadin
g-rhetoric-on-gender-pay-gap/, Retrieved: August
15, 2016.

469   CONSAD Research Corporation, "An Analysis of Reasons
for the Disparity in Wages Between Men and Women,"
15, https://www.shrm.org/hr-today/public-policy/
hr-public-policy-issues/Documents/Gender%20Wage%20
Gap%20Final%20Report.pdf, Retrieved: August 15, 2016

470   Ibid, 35.

471   United States, Federal Register, Vol. 79, No. 70, Friday,
Executive Order 13665 of April 8, 2014, Non-Retaliation
for Disclosure of Compensation Information, https://www.
gpo.gov/fdsys/pkg/FR-2014-04-11/pdf/2014-08426.pdf,
Retrieved: August 16, 2016.

472   Council of Economic Advisers Issue Brief, "Gender Pay
Gap: Recent Trends and Explanations,". 2, April 2015,
https://www.whitehouse.gov/sites/default/files/docs/equal_
pay_issue_brief_final.pdf, Retrieved: August 16, 2016.

473   Clare O'Connor, "Trump Halting Equal Pay
Measure 'A Blatant Attack on Women,' Activist
Says," *Forbes*, August 30, 2017, https://www.
forbes.com/sites/clareoconnor/2017/08/30/
trump-halting-equal-pay-measure-

a-blatant-attack-on-women-activists-say/#3ee0fc4f395b, Retrieved: August 7, 2018.

474 Romina Boccia, "Trump's Reversal of Obama Pay Gap Rule is Good News for Women, Minorities," *Heritage Foundation*, August 31, 2017, https://www.heritage. org/economic-and-property-rights/commentary/ trumps-reversal-obama-pay-gap-rule-good-news-women, Retrieved: August 7, 2018.

475 Christina Sommers, Transcript: "Feminism vs. Truth," https://www.prageru.com/courses/political-science/ myth-gender-wage-gap, Retrieved: August 16, 2016.

476 Christina Hoff Sommers, "Wage Gap Myth Exposed — By Feminists," *The Huffington Post*, Updated January 23, 2104, http://www.huffingtonpost.com/ christina-hoff-sommers/wage-gap_b_2073804.html, Retrieved: 8/17/2016.

477 "Comparable Worth" can be defined as men and women being compensated equally for work requiring comparable skills, education and responsibilities as determined by a government bureaucrat instead of labor markets.

478 Mark Judge, "Assimilate! How Modern Liberalism is Destroying Individuality," *National Review Online*, August 11, 2016, http://www.nationalreview.com/article/438855/ modern-liberals-america-are-creating-monoculture, Retrieved: August 17, 2016.

479 Father Johannes Jacobse, "Tolerance In Not a Christian Virtue," *American Orthodox Institute*, January 15, 2013, http://www.aoiusa.org/tolerance-is-not-a-christian-virtue, Retrieved: August 20, 2016.

480 Christina Sommers, "No, Women Don't Make Less Money Than Men," *The Daily Beast*, February 1, 2014, http://www.thedailybeast.com/articles/2014/02/01/ no-women-don-t-make-less-money-than-men.html, Retrieved: August 18, 2016.

481 Mike Gonzalez, "The Diversity Police Raid the Boardroom," *Wall Street Journal*, August 17, 2016, http://www.wsj.com/articles/the-diversity-police-raid-the-boardroom-1471473464, Retrieved: August 18, 2016.

482 Gwen Moran, "Here's What It Takes to Sue for Gender Pay Discrimination – And Win," *Fortune*, April 12, 2016, http://fortune.com/2016/04/12/how-to-sue-for-gender-pay-discrimination/, Retrieved: August 18, 2016.

483 Ibid.

484 Thomas Sowell, "Statistical Frauds on the Left," *National Review Online*, April 15, 2014, http://www.nationalreview.com/article/375767/statistical-frauds-left-thomas-sowell, Retrieved: August 18, 2016.

485 Zachary A. Goldfarb, "Male-Female Pay Gap Remains Entrenched at White House," *Washington Post*, July 1, 2014, https://www.washingtonpost.com/politics/male-female-pay-gap-remains-entrenched-at-white-house/2014/07/01/dbc6c088-0155-11e4-8fd0-3a663dfa68ac_story.html, Retrieved: August 18, 2016.

Chapter 16: The Right of Women to Choose Abortion

486 CNSnews.com, "Hillary Clinton: 'The Unborn Person Doesn't Have Constitutional Rights," *Media Research Center*, April 3, 2016, http://www.cnsnews.com/news/article/cnsnewscom-staff/hillary-clinton-unborn-person-doesnt-have-constitutional-rights, Retrieved: May 13, 2017.

487 SCOTUS' opinion in Roe v. Wade 410 U.S. 113 (1973) permitted an exception to the restriction on abortion concerning viability and in situations where the life or health of the mother is at stake.

488 Roe v. Wade, 410 U.S. 113, Opinion of the Court, https://www.law.cornell.edu/supremecourt/text/410/113#writing-USSC_CR_0410_0113_ZO, Retrieved: September 6, 2016.

489 Laurence H. Tribe, *Abortion the Clash of Absolutes* (New York: W.W. Norton & Company, 1990), 78.

490 Doe v. Bolton, 410 U.S. 221-222 (1973), dissent also applicable to Roe v. Wade, https://supreme.justia.com/cases/federal/us/410/179/case.html, Retrieved: September 7, 2016.

491 The "Lochner Era" was so named for the case Lockner v. New York (198 U.S. 45 (1905).

492 Tribe, *Abortion the Clash of Absolutes*, 84–85.

493 West Coast Hotel v. Parrish 300 U.S. 379 (1937).

494 Tribe, *Abortion the Clash of Absolutes*, 86.

495 Richard L. Aynes, "On Misreading John Bingham and the Fourteenth Amendment," 103 Yale Law Journal 57 (1993), https://works.bepress.com/richard_aynes/21, Retrieved: July 4, 2017.

496 Tribe, *Abortion the Clash of Absolutes*, 86–87.

497 LawBrain, "Substantive Due Process," http://lawbrain.com/wiki/Substantive_Due_Process, Retrieved: September 13, 2016.

498 Erwin Chemerinsky, "Substantive Due Process," *Touro Law Review*, Vol 15, 1501-1534 (1999), http://scholarship.law.duke.edu/cgi/viewcontent.cgi?article=1638&context=faculty_scholarship, Retrieved: September 8, 2016.

499 William R. Musgrove, "Substantive Due Process: A History of Liberty in the Due Process Clause," *University of St. Thomas Journal of Law and Public Policy*, Vol. 2, Issue 1, Spring 2008, 131.

500 Ibid.

501 *Griswold v. Connecticut,* 381 U.S. 479 (1965).

502 Griswold v. Connecticut 381 U.S. 479 (1965), https://www.law.cornell.edu/supremecourt/ text/381/479#writing-ZS, Retrieved: September 15, 2016.

503 Griswold v. Connecticut 381 U.S. 527 (1965).

504 Jamal Green, "The So-Called Right to Privacy," *UC Davis Law Review*, Volume 43 (2010), 734, http://lawreview. law.ucdavis.edu/issues/43/3/liberty/43-3_Greene.pdf, Retrieved: October 6, 2016.

505 Green, "The So-Called Right to Privacy," 725.

506 Washington v. Glucksberg, 117 S. Ct. 2258

507 Michael v. Gerald, 491 U.S. 110.

508 Matt Sharp, "Our Constitutional Right to Privacy Is Missing From Bathroom Debate," *Daily Signal*, May 17, 2016, http://dailysignal. com/2016/05/17/our-constitutional-right-to-privacy-i s-missing-from-bathroom-debate, May 17, 2016, Retrieved: October 9, 2016.

509 Ian Millhiser, "The Stunning, Hilarious Hypocrisy of the Christian Right's Top Legal Team," *Think Progress*, June 30, 2016, https://thinkprogress. org/the-stunning-hilarious-hypocrisy-of-th e-christian-rights-top-legal-team-b13bbd6beaa9#. qhsh7zxps, Retrieved: October 10, 2016.

510 The Judicial Circuits Act of 1866 was passed by Congress and signed into law by President Andrew Johnson. The Act nullified the pending appointment of Henry Stanberry to the Supreme Court while Johnson was under threat of impeachment. The Act would lead to a gradual reduction in the number of sitting Justices from ten to seven.

511 2016 Democratic Party Platform, July 21, 2016, 37, https://www.demconvention.com/wp-content/

uploads/2016/07/Democratic-Party-Platform-7.2
1.16-no-lines.pdf, Retrieved: September 4, 2016.

512 The American Presidency Project, The President's News
Conference, July 12, 1977, http://www.presidency.ucsb.
edu/ws/?pid=7786, Retrieved: July 29, 2017.

513 Ibid.

514 Lydia Saad, "Americans' Abortion Views
Steady Amid Gosnell Trial," *Gallup*, May 10,
2013, http://www.gallup.com/poll/162374/
americans-abortion-views-steady-amid-gosnell-trial.aspx,
Retrieved: October 12, 2016.

515 United States, "Government Printing Office – Partial Birth
Abortion Ban Act of 2003," 18 USC 1531, November
5, 2003, https://www.congress.gov/108/plaws/publ105/
PLAW-108publ105.pdf, Retrieved: October 12, 2016

516 Congress.gov, "H.R.36 - Pain-Capable Unborn Child
Protection Act," 114th Congress, https://www.congress.
gov/bill/114th-congress/house-bill/36?q=%7B%22search%
22%3A%5B%22Pain+Capable+Unborn+Child+Protectio
n+Act%22%5D%7D&resultIndex=2, Retrieved: October
12, 2016.

517 Roe v. Wade 410 U.S. 113 (1973), Syllabus,
https://www.law.cornell.edu/supremecourt/
text/410/113#writing-USSC_CR_0410_0113_ZO,
Retrieved: September 6, 2016.

518 Sir William Blackstone, *Commentaries on the Laws of
England in Four Books, Vol. 1* [1753] (Philadephia: J.B.
Lippincott, 1893), 97, http://files.libertyfund.org/
files/2140/Blackstone_1387-01_EBk_v6.0.pdf, Retrieved:
October 9, 2016.

519 Clifford Stevens, "The Rights of the Unborn from
Common Law to Constitutional Law," *Priests for Life –
Political Responsibility Center*, http://priestsforlife.org/
government/stevens3.htm, Retrieved: October 19, 2016.

520 C. Everett Koop, "Why Defend Partial Birth Abortion," *New York Times*, September 26, 1996, http://www.nytimes.com/1996/09/26/opinion/why-defend-partial-birth-abortion.html, Retrieved: October 20, 2016.

Conclusion

521 Mary Perry, "Bono: America is 'an idea'," *American Enterprise Institute*, July 6, 2014, http://www.aei.org/publication/bono-america-is-an-idea-that s-how-we-see-you-around-the-world-as-one-of-the-greatest -ideas-in-human-history, Retrieved: July 29, 2017.

522 John J. Dinan, *The Virginia State Constitution* (New York: Oxford University Press, 2011), 74.

523 *The U.S. Constitution: A Reader* (Hillsdale, MI: Hillsdale College Press, 2016), 617.

INDEX

CPSIA information can be obtained
at www.ICGtesting.com
Printed in the USA
LVHW020950130219
607389LV00001BB/1